REFLECTIONS ON LEADERSHIP

How Robert K. Greenleaf's Theory of Servant-Leadership Influenced Today's Top Management Thinkers

REFLECTIONS ON LEADERSHIP

How Robert K. Greenleaf's Theory of Servant-Leadership Influenced Today's Top Management Thinkers

Contributors Include:

Robert K. Greenleaf • M. Scott Peck

Peter Senge • Ann McGee-Cooper

Sheila Murray Bethel • Walter Kiechel III

Plus Twenty-One Additional Essays and Articles on Servant-Leadership by Authors, Executives, Consultants, and Journalists

Plus a Newly-Discovered Essay by Robert K. Greenleaf

And a Foreword by Max DePree

Edited by Larry C. Spears, Executive Director
The Greenleaf Center for Servant-Leadership

John Wiley & Sons, Inc.

New York • Chichester • Brisbane • Toronto • Singapore

Published by John Wiley & Sons, Inc.

Library of Congress Cataloging-in-Publication Data:

Reflections on leadership : how Robert K. Greenleaf's theory of
Servant-leadership influenced today's top management thinkers /
edited by Larry Spears.
p. cm.
Includes bibliographical references and index.
ISBN 0-471-03686-2
1. Leadership. 2. Organizational effectiveness. 3. Greenleaf,
Robert K. Servant-leadership. I. Spears, Larry, 1955–
HD57.7.R44 1995
303.3'4—dc20 94-40297

Printed in the United States of America

10 9 8 7 6 5 4

Contents

Foreword ix
Max DePree

Acknowledgments xi

Preface xiii

Introduction: Servant-Leadership and the Greenleaf Legacy 1
Larry Spears

Part One Robert K. Greenleaf: Grandfather of New Paradigm Thinking

1 **Life's Choices and Markers** 17
Robert K. Greenleaf

2 **Reflections from Experience** 22
Robert K. Greenleaf

3 **Robert K. Greenleaf and Business Ethics: There Is No Code** 37
Anne T. Fraker

4 **Claiming Servant-Leadership as Your Heritage** 49
Carl Rieser

5 **Tracing the Vision and Impact of Robert K. Greenleaf** 61
Joseph J. DiStefano

6 **The Strategic Toughness of Servant-Leadership** 79
Dennis L. Tarr

Part Two The Emerging Model of Servant-Leadership

7 **Servant-Leadership Training and Discipline in Authentic Community** 87
M. Scott Peck

8 **The Search for Spirit in the Workplace** 99
Chris Lee and Ron Zemke

9 **Servant-Leadership: Is There Really Time for It?** 113
Ann McGee-Cooper with Duane Trammell

10 **The Leader as Servant** 121
Walter Kiechel III

11 **Some Executives Are Trying to Make Companies Heed a Higher Authority** 126
Edward Iwata

12 **First Among Equals: A Corporate Executive's Vision and the Reemerging Philosophy of Trustees as Servant-Leaders** 129
Deborah Brody

Part Three Growing as Servant-Leaders/Managers

13 **Servant-Leadership and Corporate Risk Taking: When Risk Taking Makes a Difference** 135
Sheila Murray Bethel

14 **Becoming a Servant-Leader: The Personal Development Path** 149
Isabel O. Lopez

15 **Managing Toward the Millennium** 161
James E. Hennessy, John Killian, and Suki Robins

16 **Team-Building and Servant-Leadership** 169
Philip Chamberlain

17 **Power and Passion: Finding Personal Purpose** 179
Juana Bordas

18 **The New Leadership** 194
Michael Kelley

19 Servant-Leadership: A Pathway to the Emerging Territory 198
Richard W. Smith

Part Four Greenleaf's Legacy

20 Robert Greenleaf's Legacy: A New Foundation for Twenty-first Century Institutions 217
Peter M. Senge

21 Chaos, Complexity, and Servant-Leadership 241
Jeff McCollum

22 Pyramids, Circles, and Gardens: Stories of Implementing Servant-Leadership 257
Don M. Frick

23 Creating a Culture of Servant-Leadership: A Real Life Story 282
Tina Rasmussen

24 Servant-Leadership and the Future 298
Robert A. Vanourek

25 Meditations on Servant-Leadership 308
James B. Tatum

Afterword: Reflections on Robert K. Greenleaf 313
Newcomb Greenleaf

Notes 321

Permissions and Copyrights 327

Recommended Reading 331

Contributors 334

Index 343

Foreword

In a changing society, in our transition to a knowledge-based economy and facing the need to compete globally, one needs to ask: Is servant-leadership pertinent? Is it essential to our task? I believe it is. And I believe there is a building momentum for enlightened leadership in the for-profit world, the non-profit sector, and in many areas of government today. In a number of areas, it has the marks of a movement.

Good books that deal with the beliefs and convictions that nurture this movement are not easy to find. This is one. *Reflections on Leadership* is a worthy and worthwhile gift to all those who attach high value both to their responsibilities and to the people with whom they work. It is a book for people who feel the responsibility to lead in the areas of society beyond the commitments of their specific job.

The essays herein build effectively on the principles of good leadership—leadership that relies primarily on building competence in relationships with people who, together with the leader, produce the required results and conditions. Together, they continually reach for both personal and organizational potential.

These essays teach us that servant-leadership is not a skilled response to ratios and policies. Its fidelity lies in an enticing and workable vision, in beliefs about persons, in enabling values, in actions taken on reflection—all rooted in what can be learned from research, from experience, and from worthy mentors.

This book illustrates beautifully how servant-leadership has at its heart a working sense of moral purpose. To be a servant-leader is a deeper and better way to lead, but it is never easy. Sailing without wind, it isn't. Problems of ambiguity, discomfort, and contrary opinion seem natural to servant-leaders; they help us achieve better results.

Servant-leadership is never permissive. It always sets high standards of being and doing. It is an idea and a process that follows a path of study, reflection, practice, and evaluation. It is the one setting in which the mystery of potential can be adequately plumbed.

We know that leadership is a serious meddling in other peoples' lives. This book never trivializes that fact. It makes clear that crucial to good practice in leadership is the understanding that what we intend to be determines what we are able to do. *Reflections on Leadership* is a book Bob Greenleaf could endorse.

Max DePree

Acknowledgments

I am particularly indebted to several of my colleagues at the Greenleaf Center—Don Frick, Richard Smith, and Geneva Loudd, for their encouragement and able assistance on various aspects of this book. I also wish to express my appreciation to my other colleagues at the Center: Anne Fraker, Michele Lawrence, Marcia Newman, Jim Robinson, and Kelly Tobe for their support. My own journey in servant-leadership has also been enriched through my partnership with the following past-and-present Greenleaf Center Trustees: Bill Bottum, Linda Chezem, Diane Cory, Joyce DeShano SSJ, Joe DiStefano, Harley Flack, Newcomb Greenleaf, Carole Hamm, Jack Lowe, Jr., Jeff McCollum, Andy Morikawa, Jim Morris, Paul Olson, Bob Payton, Sr. Joel Read, and most especially Jim Tatum.

I am most grateful to two institutions—the W.K. Kellogg Foundation (especially Larraine Matusak, John Burkhardt, and Stephanie Clohessey) and Lilly Endowment Inc. (particularly Craig Dykstra) for their unwavering support of servant-leadership and The Greenleaf Center.

My special thanks go to Ruth Mills, my editor at John Wiley & Sons, and to Janice Borzendowski, Johanna Zucaro, Nancy Land, and Kim Nir for their editorial assistance. I am also grateful to Karl Weber and Neal Maillet for initially suggesting that I do this book.

I also want to thank my family and friends for their love and encouragement along the way, especially my wife, Beth Lafferty, and my sons, James and Matthew.

Finally, I wish to express my deepest appreciation to the many women and men everywhere who are striving to become servant-leaders. Your efforts at building spirit in the workplace truly inspires others to servant-leadership.

Acknowledgments

Preface

This collection of 27 essays brings together into one volume some of the most recent and significant pieces on servant-leadership and the growing influence of Robert K. Greenleaf's legacy.

These essays were written by some of the leading thinkers and practitioners of servant-leadership.

Part One, Robert K. Greenleaf—Grandfather of New Paradigm Thinking, begins with two essays written by Robert Greenleaf. *Life's Choices and Markers* recounts five significant influences in Greenleaf's life which led him to focus on servant-leadership. *Reflections from Experience* marks the first appearance of this previously unpublished essay from the Greenleaf Archives, and the first new essay by Greenleaf to appear since 1987. It is but one of several dozen previously unpublished essays, written by Greenleaf over a 50-year period, which the Greenleaf Center plans to publish over the next few years. The third essay in Part One, RKGC archivist Anne Fraker's, *Robert Greenleaf and Business Ethics: There Is No Code,* also draws upon some of the rich, unpublished materials contained in the Greenleaf Archives. Business Writer Carl Rieser's essay, *Claiming Servant-Leadership as Your Heritage,* is an adaptation of a talk given to a meeting of AT&T employees in 1987. *Tracing the Vision and Impact of Robert K. Greenleaf* was written by a former student and friend of Robert Greenleaf's for nearly 30 years, Joe DiStefano. Educator and consultant Dennis Tarr has contributed *The Strategic Toughness of Servant-Leadership.*

Part Two, The Emerging Model of Servant-Leadership, begins with an edited talk given at the Greenleaf Center's 1993 servant-leadership conference by M. Scott Peck, the noted author of *The Road Less Traveled* and *A World Waiting to be Born.* Peck's address is titled *Servant-Leadership Training and Discipline in Authentic Community. The Search for Spirit in the Workplace,* by Ron Zemke and Chris Lee, originally appeared in *Training* magazine and superbly traces back to Greenleaf much of the current emphasis on the emerging model of business management and leadership. Ann McGee-Cooper and Duane Trammell, coauthors of the best-selling *You Don't Have to Go Home from Work Exhausted!*, have contributed *Servant-Leadership: Is There Really Time for It? The Leader as Servant*, by Walter Kiechel III, originally appeared in *Fortune* magazine. Edward Iwata's *Some Executives Are Trying to Make Companies Heed a Higher Authority* first appeared as a nationally syndicated newspaper article from *The Orange County Register* in California. Deborah Brody's *First Among Equals* was published in *Foundation News*.

Part Three, Growing as Servant-Leaders/Managers, starts with *Servant-Leadership and Corporate Risk Taking: When Risk Taking Makes a Difference,* an original essay by Sheila Murray Bethel, business consultant and author of *Making a Difference*. Isabel Lopez has written *Becoming a Servant-Leader: The Personal Development Path* for this book. *Managing Toward the Millenium* by James Hennessy, John Killian, and Suki Robins originally appeared as a chapter in the book of the same title. Indiana University professor Phil Chamberlain has contributed *Team-Building and Servant-Leadership*. Juana Bordas, of the Center for Creative Leadership, has written *Passion and Power: Finding Personal Purpose. The New Leadership,* written by newspaper reporter Michael Kelley, originally appeared as a nationally syndicated newspaper article, via *The Commercial Appeal* in Nashville. Richard W. Smith, of the Greenleaf Center's staff, closes out this section with *Servant-Leadership: A Pathway to the Emerging Territory*.

Part Four, Greenleaf's Legacy commences with *Robert Greenleaf's Legacy: A New Foundation for 21st Century Institutions,* by Peter M. Senge, author of the best-selling book *The Fifth Discipline*. This essay is an adaptation of Peter's 1992 keynote address at the Greenleaf Center's annual servant-leadership conference. *Chaos, Complexity and Servant-Leadership,* by RKGC Trustee Jeff McCollum, shows the powerful relationship between servant-leadership and some of the leadership lessons emerging from the newer sciences. Don Frick, of the Greenleaf Center's staff, takes a look at the experiences of several institutions in their corporate practice of servant-leadership in *Pyramids, Circles, and Gardens: Stories of Implementing Servant-Leadership*. Tina Rasmussen, Management Development Manager at the Nestlé Beverage Company, has written *Creating a Culture of Servant-Leadership: A Real Life Story. Servant-Leadership and the Future* by Robert

Vanourek, President and CEO of Recognition International Inc., in Dallas, provides encouraging insights into the circular nature of institutional structures. Missouri businessman and former RKGC Chairman Jim Tatum has contributed *Meditations on Servant-Leadership*. Newcomb Greenleaf, Robert Greenleaf's son, closes this collection with a personal remembrance of his father in an Afterword titled, *Reflections on Robert K. Greenleaf*.

As you read these essays, I invite you to reflect upon the deep meaning and growing significance of servant-leadership. If you are intrigued, inspired, or moved by what you are about to discover, I encourage you to contact me for more information concerning the wide array of servant-leadership programs and resources at:

The Greenleaf Center for Servant-Leadership
921 E. 86th St., Suite 200
Indianapolis, IN 46240
(317) 259-1241 (phone)
(317) 259-0560 (fax)

—Larry Spears
January, 1995

Introduction

Servant-Leadership and The Greenleaf Legacy

Larry Spears

> Caring for persons, the more able and the less able serving each other, is the rock upon which a good society is built.
>
> Robert K. Greenleaf

Societal change may be either *revolutionary* or *evolutionary* in nature. Generally, revolutionary change is something that is achieved in a short span of time and is often political in nature. Evolutionary change usually occurs over a long period of time and often involves personal growth and change by individuals. One can reasonably argue that evolutionary change is more likely to last than is revolutionary change. Servant-leadership, now in its third decade as a specific leadership and management approach, is clearly in the category of organic, personal, evolutionary change. This book brings together, for the first time, an overview of the growing influence this unique concept of servant-leadership is having upon people and their workplace.

As we near the end of the twentieth century, we are beginning to see that traditional autocratic and hierarchical modes of leadership are slowly yielding to a newer model—one that attempts to simultaneously enhance the personal growth of workers and improve the quality and caring of our many institutions through a combination of teamwork and community, personal involvement in decision making, and ethical and caring behavior. This emerging approach to leadership and service is called *servant-leadership.*

The words servant and leader are usually thought of as opposites. When opposites are brought together in a creative and meaningful way, a paradox emerges. Here, the words servant and leader have been brought together to create the paradoxical idea of servant-leadership. Its seeds have been planted, and have begun to sprout in many institutions, as well as in the hearts of individuals who long to improve the human condition. Servant-leadership is providing a framework within which many individuals are helping to improve the way in which we treat those who do the work within our many institutions. Servant-leadership truly offers hope and guidance for a new era in human development.

> *Despite all the buzz about modern leadership techniques, no one knows better than Greenleaf what really matters.*
>
> *Working Woman* magazine

The term servant-leadership was first coined in a 1970 essay by Robert K. Greenleaf (1904–1990) entitled, *The Servant as Leader.* Greenleaf, who was born in Terre Haute, Indiana, spent most of his organizational life in the field of management research, development, and education at AT&T. Following a 40-year career at AT&T, Greenleaf enjoyed a second career that lasted 25 years. During that time he served as an influential consultant to a number of major institutions, including Ohio University, MIT, Ford Foundation, R.K. Mellon Foundation, the Mead Corporation, the American Foundation for Management Research, and Lilly Endowment, Inc. In 1964 Greenleaf founded the Center for Applied Ethics. The Center, which was renamed the Robert K. Greenleaf Center in 1985, is now headquartered in Indianapolis, Indiana.

A lifelong student of how things get done in organizations, Greenleaf distilled his observations in a series of essays and books on the theme of "The Servant as Leader." His objective was to stimulate thought and action for building a better, more caring society.

The Servant-as-Leader Idea

The idea of the servant-as-leader came partly out of Greenleaf's half-century of experience in working to shape large institutions. However, the event that crystallized Greenleaf's thinking came in the 1960s, when he read Herman Hesse's short novel, *Journey to the East,* an account of a mythical journey by a group of people on a spiritual quest. The central figure of the story is Leo, who accompanies the party as the servant and who sustains them with his caring spirit. All goes well with the journey until one day Leo disappears. The group quickly falls into disarray, and the journey is abandoned; the group cannot manage without Leo. After many years of searching, the narrator of the story stumbles upon Leo and is taken into the religious order that sponsored the original journey. There, he discovers that Leo, whom he had known as a servant, was in fact the head and guiding spirit of the order—a great and noble leader.

Greenleaf concluded that the central meaning of this story is that great leaders must first serve others, and that this simple fact is central to his or her greatness. True leadership emerges from those whose primary motivation is a desire to help others.

In 1970, at the age of 66, Greenleaf published *The Servant as Leader,* the first of a dozen essays and books on servant-leadership. Since that time, more than 500,000 copies of his books and essays have been sold worldwide. Slowly but surely, Greenleaf's servant-leadership writings have made a deep, lasting impression on leaders, educators, and many others who are concerned with issues of leadership, management, service, and personal growth.

What Is Servant-Leadership?

In all of these works, Greenleaf discusses the need for a new kind of leadership model, a model that puts serving others—including employees, customers, and community—as the number one priority. Servant-leadership emphasizes increased service to others, a holistic approach to work, a sense of community, and shared decision-making power.

Who Is a Servant-Leader?

Who *is* a servant-leader? Greenleaf said that a servant-leader is one who is a servant first. In *The Servant as Leader* he wrote: "It begins with the natural feeling that one wants to serve, to serve first. Then conscious choice brings one to aspire to lead. The difference manifests itself in the care taken by the servant—first to make sure that other people's highest-priority needs are being served. The best test is: Do those served grow as persons; do they, while being served, become healthier, wiser, freer, more autonomous, more likely themselves to become servants?"

It is important to stress that servant-leadership is *not* a "quick-fix" approach. Nor is it something that can be quickly instilled within an institution. At its core, servant-leadership is a long-term, transformational approach to life and work, in essence, a way of being that has the potential to create positive change throughout our society.

Ten Characteristics of the Servant-Leader

> *Servant leadership deals with the reality of power in everyday life—its legitimacy, the ethical restraints upon it and the beneficial results that can be attained through the appropriate use of power.*
>
> *The New York Times*

After some years of carefully considering Greenleaf's original writings, I have identified the following 10 critical characteristics of the servant-leader:

1. *Listening:* Traditionally, leaders have been valued for their communication and decision-making skills. Servant-leaders must reinforce these important skills by making a deep commitment to listening intently to others. Servant-leaders seek to identify and clarify the will of a group. They seek to listen receptively to what is being said (and not being said!). Listening also encompasses getting in touch with one's own inner voice, and seeking to understand what one's body, spirit, and mind are communicating.

Listening, coupled with regular periods of reflection, are essential to the growth of the servant-leader.

2. *Empathy:* Servant-leaders strive to understand and empathize with others. People need to be accepted and recognized for their special and unique spirits. One must assume the good intentions of co-workers and not reject them as people, even when forced to reject their behavior or performance. The most successful servant-leaders are those who have become skilled empathetic listeners. It is interesting to note that Robert Greenleaf developed a course in receptive listening in the 1950s for the Wainwright House in Rye, New York. This course continues to be offered to the present day.
3. *Healing:* Learning to heal is a powerful force for transformation and integration. One of the great strengths of servant-leadership is the potential for healing one's self and others. Many people have broken spirits and have suffered from a variety of emotional hurts. Although this is a part of being human, servant-leaders recognize that they have an opportunity to help make whole those with whom they come in contact. In *The Servant as Leader* Greenleaf writes: "There is something subtle communicated to one who is being served and led if, implicit in the compact between servant-leader and led, is the understanding that the search for wholeness is something they share."
4. *Awareness:* General awareness, and especially self-awareness, strengthens the servant-leader. Making a commitment to foster awareness can be scary—one never knows what one may discover! Awareness also aids in understanding issues involving ethics and values. It enables one to view most situations from a more integrated position. As Greenleaf observed: "Awareness is not a giver of solace—it is just the opposite. It is a disturber and an awakener. Able leaders are usually sharply awake and reasonably disturbed. They are not seekers after solace. They have their own inner serenity."
5. *Persuasion:* Another characteristic of servant-leaders is a reliance upon persuasion, rather than positional authority, in making decisions within an organization. Servant-leaders seek to convince others, rather than coerce compliance. This particular element offers one of the clearest distinctions between the traditional authoritarian model and that of servant-leadership. The servant-

leader is effective at building consensus within groups. This emphasis on persuasion over coercion probably has its roots within the beliefs of The Religious Society of Friends (Quakers), the denomination with which Robert Greenleaf himself was most closely allied.

6. *Conceptualization:* Servant-leaders seek to nurture their abilities to "dream great dreams." The ability to look at a problem (or an organization) from a conceptualizing perspective means that one must think beyond day-to-day realities. For many managers this is a characteristic that requires discipline and practice. Traditional managers are consumed by the need to achieve short-term operational goals. A manager who wishes to be a servant-leader must stretch his or her thinking to encompass broader-based conceptual thinking. Within organizations, conceptualization is, by its very nature, the proper role of boards of trustees or directors. Unfortunately, if the board or the trustees become involved in day-to-day operations (something that should always be discouraged), they may fail to fulfill their visionary function. The most effective CEOs and managers probably need to develop both conceptual and operational perspectives, and staffs must be mostly operational. Servant-leaders must seek a delicate balance between conceptualization and day-to-day focus.

7. *Foresight:* The ability to foresee the likely outcome of a situation is hard to define, but easy to identify. One knows it when one sees it. Foresight is a characteristic that enables servant-leaders to understand the lessons from the past, the realities of the present, and the likely consequence of a decision for the future. It is deeply rooted within the intuitive mind. Thus, foresight is the one servant-leader characteristic with which one may be born. All other characteristics can be consciously developed. There hasn't been a great deal written on foresight, and it remains a largely unexplored area in leadership studies. Nevertheless, it deserves careful attention.

8. *Stewardship:* Peter Block (author of *Stewardship* and *The Empowered Manager*) has defined stewardship as "holding something in trust for another." Robert Greenleaf's view of all institutions was one in which CEOs, staffs, directors, and trustees all played significant

roles in holding their institutions in trust for the greater good of society. Servant-leadership, like stewardship, assumes first and foremost a commitment to serving the needs of others. It also emphasizes the use of openness and persuasion, rather than control.

9. *Commitment to the growth of people:* Servant-leaders believe that people have an intrinsic value beyond their tangible contributions as workers. As such, servant-leaders are deeply committed to the personal, professional, and spiritual growth of each and every individual within the institution. In practice, this can mean making available funds for personal and professional development, taking a personal interest in employees' ideas and suggestions, encouraging worker involvement in decision making, actively assisting laid-off workers to find other employment, and so on.
10. *Building community:* Servant-leaders are aware that the shift from local communities to large institutions as the primary shaper of human lives has changed our perceptions and caused a certain sense of loss. Thus, servant-leaders seek to identify a means for building community among those who work within a given institution. Servant-leadership suggests that true community can be created among those who work in businesses and other institutions. Greenleaf said: "All that is needed to rebuild community as a viable life form for large numbers of people is for enough servant-leaders to show the way, not by mass movements, but by each servant-leader demonstrating his [or her] own unlimited liability for a quite specific community-related group."

The preceding 10 characteristics of servant-leadership are by no means exhaustive. However, these characteristics communicate the power and promise this concept offers to those who are open to its invitation and challenge.

Tracing the Growing Impact of Servant-Leadership

Servant leadership has emerged as one of the dominant philosophies being discussed in the world today.

Indianapolis Business Journal

There are a half-dozen major areas in which servant-leadership principles are being applied in significant ways. Servant-leadership crosses all boundaries and is being applied by a wide variety of people working with for-profit businesses, not-for-profit corporations, churches, universities, and foundations.

Servant-Leadership as an Institutional Model

The first area has to do with servant-leadership as an institutional philosophy and model. In recent years, a number of institutions have jettisoned their old, "top-down" hierarchical models and replaced them with a servant-leader approach. Servant-leadership advocates a group-oriented approach to analysis and decision making as a means of strengthening institutions and improving society. It also emphasizes the power of persuasion and seeking consensus. Some people have likened this approach to turning the hierarchical pyramid upside down. Servant-leadership holds that profit is not the primary purpose of a business; instead it is to create a positive impact on its employees and community.

Many individuals within institutions have adopted servant-leadership as a guiding philosophy. An increasing number of companies have adopted servant-leadership as part of their corporate philosophy or as a foundation for their mission statement. Among these are the Sisters of St. Joseph's Health System (Ann Arbor, Michigan), TDIndustries (Dallas, Texas), Herman Miller Company (Zeeland, Michigan), and Schmidt Associates Architects, Inc. (Indianapolis, Indiana). Some institutions have taken this a step further and have actually reorganized their corporate structures along the *primus inter pares,* or first among equals model of servant-leadership. Examples of these institutions include Schneider Engineering Company (Indianapolis, Indiana), Townsend & Bottum Family of Companies (Ann Arbor, Michigan), and the Housing Facilities Dept., University of Michigan (Ann Arbor, Michigan).

TDIndustries, one of the earliest practitioners of servant-leadership in a corporate setting, is a Dallas-based heating and plumbing contracting firm. Recently, it was profiled in Robert Levering and Milton Moskowitz's book, *The 100 Best Companies to Work for in America.* In their profile of TDIndustries, the authors discuss the longtime influence that servant-leadership has had upon the company.

TDI's founder, Jack Lowe, Sr. stumbled upon *The Servant as Leader* essay in the early 1970s and began to distribute copies of it to his employees. The employees were invited to read through the essay, and then to gather in small groups to discuss its meaning. The belief that managers should serve their employees became an important value for TDIndustries.

Now, more than 20 years later, Jack Lowe, Jr. continues to use servant-leadership as the guiding philosophy for TDI. Levering and Moskowitz note: "Even today, any TDPartner who supervises at least one person must go through training in servant-leadership." In addition, all new employees receive a copy of *The Servant as Leader* essay.

Some businesses have begun to view servant-leadership as an important framework which is helpful (and in fact, necessary) for ensuring the long-term effects of related management and leadership approaches such as continuous quality improvement. Several of the authors represented in this book suggest that institutions which want to create meaningful change may be best served in starting with servant-leadership as the foundational understanding and then building upon it through any number of related approaches.

Servant-leadership has influenced many noted writers, thinkers, and leaders, including several of the authors represented in this book. Max DePree, Chairman of the Herman Miller Company and author of *Leadership is an Art* and *Leadership Jazz* has said, "The servanthood of leadership needs to be felt, understood, believed, and practiced." And Peter Senge, author of *The Fifth Discipline*, has said that he tells people "not to bother reading any other book about leadership until you first read Robert Greenleaf's book, *Servant-Leadership*. I believe it is the most singular and useful statement on leadership I've come across." In recent years, a growing number of leaders and readers have "rediscovered" Robert Greenleaf's own writings through the writings of DePree, Senge, and others.

Education and Training of Not-for-Profit Trustees

A second major application of servant-leadership is its pivotal role as the theoretical and ethical basis for "trustee education." Greenleaf wrote extensively on servant-leadership as it applies to the roles of boards of directors and trustees. His essays on these applications are widely distributed among directors of for-profit and nonprofit organizations. In his essay, *Trustees as Servants,* Greenleaf urged trustees to ask themselves two central questions: "Whom do you serve?" and "For what purpose?"

Servant-leadership suggests that boards of trustees need to undergo a radical shift in how they approach their roles. Trustees who seek to act as servant-leaders can help to create institutions of great depth and quality. Over the past decade, two of America's largest grant-making foundations (Lilly Endowment, Inc. and the W.K. Kellogg Foundation) have sought to encourage the development of programs designed to educate and train not-for-profit boards of trustees to function as servant-leaders.

Community Leadership Programs

The third application of servant-leadership concerns its deepening role in community leadership organizations across the country. A growing number of such groups are using Greenleaf Center resources as part of their own education and training efforts. Some have been doing so for more than 15 years.

The National Association for Community Leadership (NACL) has adopted servant-leadership as a special focus. Recently, NACL named Robert Greenleaf as the posthumous recipient of its National Community Leadership Award. This award is given annually to honor an individual whose work has made a significant impact on the development of community leadership worldwide.

In *A World Waiting to be Born,* M. Scott Peck says the following about the importance of building true community: "In his work on servant-leadership, Greenleaf posited that the world will be saved if it can develop just three truly well-managed, large institutions—one in the private sector, one in the public sector, and one in the nonprofit sector. He believed—and I know—that such excellence in management will be achieved through an organizational culture of civility routinely utilizing the mode of community."

Service-Learning Programs

The fourth application involves servant-leadership and experiential education. During the past 20 years, experiential education programs of all sorts have sprung up in virtually every college and university, and even some secondary schools. Experiential education, or "learning by doing," is now a part of most students' educational experience.

Around 1980, a number of educators began to write about the link between servant-leadership and experiential learning under a new term called "service-learning." Service-learning has become a major focus for experiential education programs over the past few years.

The National Society for Experiential Education (NSEE) adopted service-learning as one of its major projects. NSEE also published a massive three-volume work, *Combining Service and Learning*, which brings together many articles and papers about service-learning.

Leadership Education

The fifth application of servant-leadership concerns its use in the many formal and informal education and training programs taking place through leadership and management courses in colleges and universities, and in corporate training programs. Also, a number of noted servant-leadership authors, including Peter Block, Ken Blanchard, Max DePree, and Peter Senge have acclaimed servant-leadership as a concept that is compatible with, and enhancing of, other leadership and management models such as total quality management, learning organizations, and community-building.

Dozens of management and leadership consultants now utilize servant-leadership materials as part of their corporate education and training programs. These consultants and educators are touting the benefits of building a total quality management approach upon a servant-leadership foundation. Some companies that have included such materials are AT&T, the Mead Corporation, and Gulf Oil of Canada. Through internal training and education, such institutions are discovering that servant-leadership can truly improve the way in which business is developed and conducted, while still successfully turning a profit.

Personal Transformation

The sixth application of servant-leadership involves its use in programs relating to personal growth and transformation. Servant-leadership offers individuals a means to personal growth—spiritually, professionally, emotionally, and intellectually. It has ties to the ideas of

M. Scott Peck (*The Road Less Traveled*), Parker Palmer (*The Active Life*), Ann McGee-Cooper (*You Don't Have to Go Home from Work Exhausted!*), and others who have written on expanding human potential.

A particular strength of servant-leadership is that it encourages everyone to actively seek opportunities to both serve and lead others, thereby setting up the potential for raising the quality of life throughout society. A number of individuals are working to integrate the servant-leader concept into various programs involving both men's and women's self-awareness groups and 12-step programs like Alcoholics Anonymous. There is also a fledgling examination underway of the servant-leader as a previously unidentified Jungian archetype. This particular exploration is discussed in a book titled *The King Within*, by Robert Moore and Douglas Gillette.

Servant-Leadership and Multiculturalism

The word servant prompts an immediate negative connotation for people who have been oppressed, such as women and people of color. Some may find it difficult to accept the positive usage of the word servant. However, those who are willing to dig a little deeper come to understand the inherent spiritual nature of what is intended by the pairing of the words servant and leader. The startling paradox of the term servant-leadership serves to prompt new insights.

Women leaders and authors are now writing and speaking about servant-leadership as a twenty-first century leadership philosophy that is most appropriate for women to embrace. Patsy Sampson, President of Stephens College in Columbia, Missouri, is one such person. In an essay on women and servant-leadership ("The Leader as Servant"), she writes: "So-called (service-oriented) feminine characteristics are exactly those which are consonant with the very best qualities of servant-leadership."

In an article titled, "Pluralistic Reflections on Servant-Leadership," Juana Bordas, of the Center for Creative Leadership, has written: "Many women, minorities, and people of color have long traditions of servant-leadership in their cultures. Servant-leadership has very old roots in many of the indigenous cultures. Cultures that were holistic, cooperative, communal, intuitive, and spiritual. These cultures centered on being guardians of the future and respecting the ancestors who walked before."

A Growing Movement

Servant-leadership works like the consensus building that the Japanese are famous for. Yes, it takes a while on the front end; everyone's view is solicited, though everyone also understands that his [or her] view may not ultimately prevail. But once the consensus is forged, watch out: With everybody on board, your so-called implementation proceeds wham-bam.

Fortune magazine

Interest in the philosophy and practice of servant-leadership is at an all-time high. Dozens of articles on servant-leadership have appeared in various magazines, journals, and newspapers over the past few years. Many books on the general subject of leadership reference servant-leadership as an important model for now, and in the future.

The Greenleaf Center for Servant-Leadership is an international, not-for-profit, educational organization that seeks to encourage the understanding and practice of servant-leadership. The Center's mission is to fundamentally improve the caring and quality of all institutions through a new approach to leadership, structure, and decision making.

In recent years, the Greenleaf Center has experienced tremendous growth and expansion. Its programs include: the worldwide sales of more than 60 books, essays, and videotapes on servant-leadership; a membership program; workshops and seminars; the Greenleaf Archives Project; a Speakers Bureau; and an annual International Conference on Servant-Leadership. A number of notable Greenleaf Center members have spoken at annual conferences, including: Peter Block, Max DePree, Ann McGee-Cooper, M. Scott Peck, and Peter Senge. Each has spoken of the tremendous impact the servant-leader concept has played in the development of his or her own understanding of what it means to be a leader.

Paradox and Pathway

The Greenleaf Center's logo, shown here, is a variation on the geometrical figure called a mobius strip. A mobius strip is a one-sided surface that is constructed from a rectangle by holding one end fixed, rotating the opposite end through 180 degrees, and applying it to the first end, thereby giving the appearance of a two-sided figure. In visual terms, the mobius strip symbolizes the servant-leader concept—a merging of servanthood into leadership and back into servanthood again, in a fluid and continuous pattern. It also reflects the Greenleaf Center's own role as an institution seeking to both serve and lead others who are interested in leadership and service issues.

PART ONE

Robert K. Greenleaf: Grandfather of New Paradigm Thinking

1

Life's Choices and Markers

Robert K. Greenleaf

In the spring of 1984, Mr. Greenleaf was invited to give a commencement talk at Alverno College, a Catholic Women's College in Milwaukee. The text of this talk follows.

Five ideas have been significant markers in my past, ideas that guided choices in my work. The first is distilled from early experience with my father, to whom I was very close. He was a good, intelligent man with but a fifth grade education, and he had a life of limited opportunity. But he managed, by a prudent use of his life, to leave a little corner of the world a bit better than he found it. In the perspective of considerable experience, he stands tall as a true servant.

The first idea that influenced my life's work came in the last half of my senior year in college. I went to college with a clear vocational aim that I would become an astronomer, like a favorite uncle who encouraged me. I quickly concluded that, although I had the aptitude for science and mathematics that qualified, I did not have the temperament for an astronomer; I was not cut out for it. This conclusion did not bother me, and I laid aside the matter of vocation until after graduation. Then I assured myself I would look around and make a choice.

These were the euphoric boom years of the mid-1920s, and jobs were plentiful. One had choices.

That last term I elected a course in the sociology of labor problems. The professor was old (or so he seemed to me), and he was neither a great scholar nor an exciting teacher. But he had been around, and he was wise in the ways of man and institutions, and I was sensitive to that quality. One day, in the course of a rambling lecture, he made a comment in about these words: "We are becoming a nation of large institutions; everything is getting big—business, schools, governments. There has not been before a society like ours, and these big institutions are not serving us well. Now, you can do as I do and stand outside and criticize and bring pressure; but nothing constructive will happen until someone who is inside and has her or his hands on some of the levers of power and influence decides to change something. These big institutions rarely can be changed constructively from the outside. My advice to some of you is that you make your careers inside of one of these big institutions, stay with it, and become one of those who responds to suggestions that they change for the better."

My doors of perception must have been open a bit wider than usual that day because that message came through loud and clear. My career aim was settled by this advice. I would get inside the largest business that would hire me and stay there if I could. It would be a business rather than some other kind of institution because there were no professional hurdles, businesses seemed more malleable, and they may have been in greater need.

After graduation, I quickly established that AT&T was the largest, and I chose it for that reason alone. In a few weeks, I was digging postholes with a line construction crew near Youngstown, Ohio. I spent 38 years with the company, mostly in New York. I am not a manager by temperament, and I settled for staff work from which I might influence that vast company with ideas. Life there was not always easy or pleasant, and it needed much more help than I could give it. There were some dreary, depressing years, and a few dreadful ones that really tested my sustaining spirit. But I stayed with it; I cared intensely about the quality of the institution, and I kept a deep interest in the company's history and myth. I believe I accomplished what my old professor advised. But I did not wield enough influence to save the company from being broken up after I retired. I did try hard to save what was good about it.

Idea number three came when I was 25 and moved to New York and quickly became devoted to the writing of E.B. White in *The New Yorker* magazine. Mr. White, I soon learned, had two gifts that are seldom possessed by one person: the ability to see things whole, or more whole than most, and the language to tell us ordinary mortals what he saw. Much reflection was required for me to grasp the essential idea—seeing things whole. But when I got it, it was an impressive idea.

The fourth pivotal idea came when I was about 40, when I read an article by a great radio commentator of that day, Elmer Davis. The title of the article was, "The Uses of Old People." The gist of the article was that there are useful and necessary things to be done that are best done by old people, partly because old people have greater perspective of experience, but mostly because the things that need to be done do not fit into a career, or they are too risky for young or mid-career people. He advised that younger people should look forward to old age as presenting an opportunity to be prepared for, rather than as a time to be put out to pasture when one wears out. It was a persuasive argument and, again, my doors of perception were open a bit wider than usual and that message came through loud and clear: Begin now to prepare for what can best be done in old age.

The next 20 years were ones in which I was attentive to my work at AT&T, and I grew in it. Because of this preparation, I believe I was more effective in my last years there. But I had my eye on age 60 when I could exercise my first retirement option at AT&T. And the day after I hung up my sword there, I took off on radically different, more venturesome, and more exciting work. The years between ages 60 and 75 were, in some ways, my most productive and satisfying. I am grateful for my 38 years of disciplined organizational work in a huge institution. I needed that solid base of experience to be effective in my old age.

During my "retirement," I worked only on long-term consulting arrangements. Two of my clients in that period were universities during the years of student unrest and general confusion. I had close involvement with the radical students and I wondered much about the cause of this turmoil. In the course of foundation work I was also doing in that period, I visited a number of college and university campuses, and I always looked into the campus bookstores to see what students were reading, the avocational reading. Everywhere I saw stacks and stacks of books by the contemporary German novelist Hermann Hesse. I concluded that I might better understand the students of that period if I understood Hesse. So I devoted my reading time one winter to all of the books then in translation by Hesse. I read them in the order they were written, and I read a biography that told me what was going on in Hesse's life as each was written. Hesse, for much of his life, was a tortured man; in and out of mental illness, and much of the pain in his existence is reflected in what he wrote. Since the student unrest of that period appeared to me symptomatic of massive mental illness, their lives seemed to be resonating to the turmoil Hesse wrote about. This was not a useful learning.

But my search bore fruit in another way that proved very important to me. Near the end of Hesse's life, there was a turn to the relative serenity he achieved in his old age. The turning point is marked by a book titled, *Journey to the East,* which I found a hopeful book.

Journey to the East is an account of a mythical journey by a band of men on a search to the East, probably Hesse's own search. The central figure of the story is Leo who accompanies the party as the servant who does their menial chores, but who also sustains them with his spirit and his song. He is a person of extraordinary presence. All goes well with the journey until one day Leo disappears. Then the group falls into disarray, and the journey is abandoned. They cannot make it without the servant Leo. The narrator, one of the party, after some years of searching, finds Leo and is taken into the order that had sponsored the search. There, he discovers that Leo, whom he had first known as a servant, was in fact, the titular head of the order, its guiding spirit, a great and noble leader.

There has been much speculation on Hesse's life and work, some of it centering on this story which critics find most puzzling. But to me this story clearly says: The greatest leader (who may be a "little" person) is seen as servant first because that is what he is deep down inside. Leadership is bestowed on the person who is, by nature, a true servant. Leadership is something given or assumed, that could be taken away. Leo's servant nature was the real person, not bestowed, not assumed, and not to be taken away. Leo was servant first.

In my private musing, it pleases me to think that Hesse, through the means whereby he created this story, recovered his sanity and moved into a serene old age. The idea of the servant as leader that I got from reading *Journey to the East* started me to writing a series of essays on this theme dealing with the nature of leadership, the structure of institutions, trusteeship, seminaries, and religious leading in general. It has been for me a truly pivotal idea. And it kept me busy for the past 15 years.

The student attitudes of the 1960s seemed to me to stem from a lack of hope, a lack of belief by those young people that they could live productively in the world of institutions as they then were (and still are). This was a devastating prospect for those young people to live without hope in a highly structured but imperfect society.

When I started to write on the servant-leader theme, I was trying to communicate a basis for hope—not just to students, but to everybody. I did not believe that I could communicate this directly in writing to students. But I did try to give a basis for hope to teachers, trustees, churches, and administrators in general, with the intent that their combined influence might give a greater basis for hope than is now generally available to young people, and make for a better society. Particularly, I wanted to persuade teachers to find ways to serve students as I was served by my old professor who suggested that I take on the career task of becoming a leaven in a ponderous bureaucracy.

As I review my experience, it has been important that I be open to ideas, all of the time—and there have been many important ones. I have named five that now seem to me to have been important in giving a sense of direction to my work. First, the servant model of my father. Then the advice of Professor Oscar Helming when I was 21: Get into a big institution and stay there and help shape its character. At age 25, I encountered the writing of E.B. White and was alerted to the importance of seeing things whole. At age 40, Elmer Davis advised me to start preparing for a useful old age. At 65, Herman Hesse gave me the idea of the servant as leader that has occupied me ever since. It seems to me, in retrospect, that responding to each of these ideas when it was offered was the ticket of admission for receiving the next one.

The ideas I chose to follow did not make a design for becoming either rich or famous or for wielding a world-shaping influence. I doubt that I had it in me to achieve either of these anyway. These ideas did make an interesting and rewarding life and I am glad that I chose to respond to them. The pivotal ideas that have guided me in my work may not be the ideas that you choose to guide you in your work. But I am sure that you will choose, either consciously or by default. And to make good choices I have found it helpful to be open to ideas, to be expectant, to be hopeful. But this is risky; you just might get a great idea.

2

Reflections from Experience

Robert K. Greenleaf

I watched and participated in one major institution—AT&T—for almost 60 years, from the euphoric boom years of the mid-1920s, through the depression, the war, and the post-war expansion, to the break-up of the company on January 1, 1984. After retiring from active service there in 1964 I continued to receive the management bulletins, and I have a greater feeling for what goes on there than I have for any other place. My retirement experience has brought me in close contact with the work of trustees and directors that I never had in my staff work at AT&T. During this "retirement" period, I also had wide experience with other institutions, including large and small businesses, management consulting firms, foundations, churches, universities, and professional associations, in the United States, Europe, and the Third World. These reflections are a blend of these two quite different chapters of my experience.

The title I held in my last years at AT&T was Director of Management Research. I am not sure that anybody (including my bosses) knew what that meant, except as they defined it as "whatever I was doing." After I retired, I no longer had a label—and everybody needs a label. Since I had no recognized professional credentials, I invented a label: student of organization, how things get done. Organization, how things get done, has been my preoccupation since I was 22 years old, joined AT&T, and began looking critically at every institution that I encountered. (Of course, I looked closer and more extensively at AT&T because I spent 35 years in its corporate office.)

I use the word student advisedly. I doubt (and I rather hope) that the subject of how things get done will ever be fully understood. Certain knowledge could bode ill for the world. Where would we be today, for example, if Adolf Hitler had really known how to bring off what he set out to do? Furthermore, life is more interesting if a bit of mystery shrouds this subject, and, if we are honest, it keeps the best of us a little humble if we each accept the student rather than the expert role. Most of what I have learned about how things get done has come from intense watching and listening, not from reading or formal study. Whether it was the corner drug store or a vast business, or a church, or a university, I have had a sustained interest in what makes any institution go—or why they don't seem to go. In my later years at AT&T, I worked with a staff of professionals who engaged in formal studies. The field work on some of these studies was done by teams of active managers who gathered the data and worked out the interpretations of it. I was a member of a little club whose members did similar work in other large industries. We met a couple of times a year to exchange experiences.

Early in assembling the team of professionals to do this work at AT&T (the first of its kind in our business), the head of my department told me bluntly that he didn't like the idea of social scientists messing around in our business. I responded, "Well, just tell me to get rid of them and out they will go." He gave me a hard look and said, "As long as you have the job I'm not going to tell you how to run it." (He didn't say how long I might have the job.) In retrospect, this man was the most satisfactory of my many bosses. He was tough, but he was also clear and fair and absolutely dependable, and he never meddled in how I did my work. Once the direction was set, he let me do it my way. Ultimately, he came to like to talk to the psychologists and sociologists on my staff. He liked to hear their reports directly.

When I announced at AT&T that I was electing the earliest retirement option at age 60, I was immediately called in by the company's president. "What do you want to do this for?" he asked. "Aren't you happy here?" "I am very happy here," I replied. "But there are some things I now want to do that I can't do as long as I am on the payroll." "I don't understand," he said. "I have never known anybody, in this business or anywhere else, who, throughout his whole career did exactly what he wanted to do and nothing else more than you have. Where will you ever find anybody else who is willing to pay you for doing this?" "I don't know," I replied. "But I want to try."

I couldn't always do what I wanted to do, as some of the ensuing discussion will attest, but I believe that if that company president were alive today he would agree that the last 20 years have proven that I made the right decision to retire from AT&T at age 60.

Readers should bear in mind that these are reflections on my own experience, and not definitive essays on the subjects discussed. They are offered with the hope that others with different experiences will put their reflections beside mine to get a broader perspective about what goes on in American institutions.

How can I remember so much in detail? Because so much of my life has been work with institutions, and I made a point of remembering significant events, and I am continually reflecting on my experience and extracting new meaning from it. I try to keep it all fresh no matter how long ago it happened.

Power

I once asked the chief executive of a large company what was the primary motivation that kept him at his job. "The opportunity to wield power," was his prompt reply. "The money and the prestige would not be sufficient reward for carrying such a heavy burden."

The same question to the chairman of the board of directors of a large trade association brought a different reply. "The prestige of the office." He did not wield much power, and he did not choose to use much of the power of leadership that his position gave him.

In the late 1930s John L. Lewis, the president of the miner's union, had just put together the CIO—an assembly of industrial rather than craft unions. Violent labor controversy was at fever heat, and Lewis was regarded as an ogre in conservative circles. It was a tumultuous period. At the peak of this period, I attended a small gathering at the home of a friend who was entertaining the head of a large British company that was noted for its good labor relations. In the course of a discussion about how this company worked with its union, someone asked the visitor how it would work out if John L. Lewis represented his union. The visitor pondered the question.

Then he replied, "The answer to that question is that Lewis would not represent our employees. I know a little about the kind of people who operate mines in the United States, and nobody but a union leader like John L. Lewis could be effective in dealing with them. I have a theory that the employer determines the type of leader who will represent his employees. If the employer is rough and tough, the union, if it is to be effective, will produce a rough and tough leader (like Lewis). The typical worker is not mean by nature, but if the employer sets up conditions so that the worker has to be mean to exert his [or her] influence, he [or she] will be mean."

I watched the process unfold at close range at AT&T as the company moved from a few unions to full unionization. In those years, there was much acrimony and violence, and the unions produced a John L. Lewis-type of leader—a rough, tough guy. When the managers of the company ultimately came to accept the legitimacy of the power of their organized employees and dealt with them as equals, the unions came to be headed by more statesman-like people. The British industrialist's theory was confirmed.

Ralph Waldo Emerson's journal describes a particular "power" incident. One day he and his son were trying to get a balky calf into the barn. One was in front pulling on a halter, and the other was pushing from behind. The calf had its legs splayed, and for all practical purposes was immovable. A servant girl watched with some amusement from the kitchen window. When the Emersons gave up, she came out, stuck her finger in the calf's mouth, and walked into the barn with it. Emerson went to his study and recorded the event in his journal with the concluding comment, "I like people who can do things." I would add to this comment: There are ways to do most things without the overt use of power; valuable energy and time are often wasted trying to do them with such power. As I have noted elsewhere, coercive power is useful to stop something or destroy something, but not much constructive can be done with it. Latent coercive power in the hands of government seems to be a stabilizing element in society, but the use of it, even the visible threat of its use, too often is destructive. Persuasion is the better tactic.

I have used a little power. I say a little because I have not held a high executive position in which the incumbent controls important sanctions. Mostly, I have relied on influence and persuasion, some of which might have been seen as power. But I have had a good deal of power used on me. Since I have lived the life of an organization man and a bureaucrat, I know a good deal about what it is like to defer to power and to be pushed around by power.

Many years ago I saw a movie that stayed with me. It was a story of the transformation of a thoroughly henpecked husband. The early part of the film shows life in the home in which the big burly husband is cowed by a domineering, power-wielding wife. The husband, who worked as a laborer with a road construction crew, was greeted with a shower of pots and pans when he came home from from work each evening.

One day, the husband was relieved of his pick and shovel and given the flag to direct traffic. For the first time, he experienced the wielding of power. He raised the flag and the cars stopped. He motioned them forward and they came. And as the day wore on, there is a remarkable visual transformation. The flag comes to be handled with verve and authority. The husband abandoned his stoop, stood erect, and seemed to grow taller. His forlorn "hang dog" look gave way to an expression of serene confidence.

That day, he walked away from the job with an assured stride. When he arrived home and was greeted with the usual shower of pots and pans, he threw pots back at his wife. Power is matched with power. But the henpecked husband is gone.

This old movie seems to illustrate the problem of labor relations in some industries more than 50 years after the passage of the National Labor Relations Act and its confirmation by the courts. There are still some power wielders in high places who can't accept working with organized workers who have equal power. The nonviolent equivalent of throwing pots back at the thrower may be needed to bring them around.

The process took a number of years at AT&T. Even now, not every business has a union, and not all employees seem to want one. The employer's power is used in such a benign way that employees apparently feel no need for a countervailing power. "They that have power to hurt and will do none," wrote Shakespeare in the opening line of his 94th sonnet.

The most obvious consequence of the use of power on the power wielder seems to be arrogance. I have watched many people move into power-wielding spots or move up in the hierarchy and assume greater power. Arrogance does not always show; most successful executives have mastered an appropriate persona. But, almost universally, they fail the acid test of the genuineness of the facade. They cannot take kidding from a subordinate—at least not the kind of friendly kidding that is common among equals. And this is a loss of humanness. It introduces a stiffness into relationships within a hierarchy.

There is a justification for this. If one person holds power over another, it is a good idea to keep a little distance. A superficial friendliness makes life easier and facilitates the work, providing the subordinate stays in his or her place. This was what, in simpler times, we used to call "good human relations." In examining the consequences of the wielding of power, I believe that, unequivocally, we must label one of the consequences as arrogance, whether it is the blatant obnoxious kind or the kind that is smoothed over with a human relations veneer. As long as we accept the principle of hierarchy, some of this arrogance probably is inevitable.

My first job with AT&T in 1926 was with a line construction crew in Youngstown, Ohio. The crew consisted of a half-dozen men with a foreman and a truck. The foreman was a man with a farm upbringing and an eighth-grade education. But he was a man with a lot of native wisdom, and he was a good boss. I kept in touch with him until he died.

One day, when we were leaning on our shovels for a breather, he gave this opinion, although I can't recall what brought it on. "You know," he said, "if a fellow is an SOB, if this is what he really is deep down inside, he had just better go ahead and be one. If he tries to be something else, he will wind up being both an SOB and a hypocrite, and that's worse." That incident, which took place nearly 60 years ago, is as clear as if it were yesterday. Part of the reason for my clear memory is that I once had a boss who was exactly that—a real SOB with a nice smooth human relations veneer. And it *was* worse. Those of us who worked for him had to make our peace with him as a boss, but it would have been easier if he had just gone ahead and been what he was. He was treacherous, and for the two years I worked for him I learned to keep my back to the wall. The point of this reference is that, in the context of power in a hierarchy, good human relations is treating a symptom. The problem is the hierarchy!

An interesting anecdote survives from this experience. One evening, my wife came into the office at 5:00 PM to meet me for a dinner and theater date. While we were talking at my desk, this boss walked in about some business. He was introduced to my wife, and we shared about one minute of pleasant social conversation before he said good night and left. I looked across the desk at my wife, who was gripping the arms of her chair so hard her knuckles were white. "What's the matter with you?" was my startled question. "Is *that* man your boss?" she asked in a hoarse whisper. "I wouldn't trust him as far as I could throw this desk!" Unless I talked in my sleep she didn't know anything about this situation because I never took my job problems home. Yet in those few minutes when he was at his most affable, she had the complete measure of him. Feminine intuition? Perhaps. Or, perhaps, because she is an artist, she is accustomed to seeing things that less aware people may miss.

Later, when this fellow moved on to be president of a subsidiary (he was an able manager) I was alone with the president of AT&T when he made a laudatory remark about him. "Did you ever talk to anyone who has worked for that fellow?" I asked. He replied, "No, I don't believe I have." "Well," I said, "I have worked for him. Let me tell you what it was like." And I gave him a couple of examples of his treachery. The president stared stony-faced out the window for a long time. Then he turned to me and said softly, "We never knew."

A line from Shakespeare floated through my mind: "Uneasy lies the head that wears a crown." I have a tender feeling for intelligent, sensitive people (like this president) who get into important power-wielding spots. The usual hierarchical structure is a design to destroy such people. The hierarchy is a design for tough people.

The organization chart of the best-managed business I know about looks like a typical hierarchical structure. The one important difference does not show on the chart. All of the thousands of people on the payroll actually work for the personnel department. The people who do the work are loaned to the various divisions by the personnel department. They are not assigned to a particular manager. If you don't like their work, or if they don't like you, either of you can ask the personnel department for a change. The result is not an idyllic situation. There is an occasional failure, and somebody gets fired. But the company has taken a giant step toward mitigating the negative consequences of power in a hierarchy. They have simply taken a practical step to get their ablest people in charge of a critical problem. The SOB boss I described earlier would not have lasted long in that company—or he would have been reformed.

It is difficult to get people to work well just by paying them, and it seems sensible to accept that not every able manager is skilled at holding the power of an employer over people. Logic suggests that the person who is best at it be given the responsibility for dealing with employees as people, as their real boss. The responsibility of other managers should be limited to the technical direction of the work.

The idea of hierarchy has been around at least since the time of Moses and is deep in the culture. It probably will be around awhile longer. Ultimately, though, it will have to go. Lip service has been given for a long time to the idea that people are the most important asset in some companies. But only recently have companies begun to question the traditional organizational assumptions that do not favor people giving their best effort.

"Power tends to corrupt and absolute power corrupts absolutely," said Lord Acton. Later in the letter from which this much-quoted (but often misquoted) sentence was taken, there is another, rarely quoted sentence that seems even more powerful, "There is no worse heresy than that the office sanctifies the holder of it."

Lord Acton was professor of history at Cambridge University and an active and vocal Catholic layman. The thoughts quoted here were written in the course of his vigorous opposition to the assumption of papal infallibility in 1870. Rumor has it that Acton came close to excommunication because of his views.

Acton was not the first to give voice to the idea that power corrupts. One hundred years earlier William Pitt, addressing the House of Lords, said, "Unlimited power is apt to corrupt the minds of those who possess it." Let us speculate about what these two statements may be saying to us.

What is the corruption that both Acton and Pitt are referring to? Pitt was referring to the abuse of power by the Crown in dealing with the colonies. Acton probably had in mind the gross abuses of power by the church, like the Inquisition. He had a passionate concern for freedom and he wrote extensively about power in that context. Acton did not say *all* power corrupts, the way he is frequently quoted. He said "power *tends* to corrupt." It was only absolute power that he condemned as corrupting absolutely. This leaves open the possibility that some power can be used without corrupting. I would like to explore some of the more subtle uses of power that are quite extensive and in which the corrupting effect may be very damaging but where there is the possibility—and the hope—of the power wielder being protected against that corruption.

Personality distortion seems to be a common corruption that results from wielding power. This distortion can range from barely discernable to the mean and pathological. As examples, I would put Abraham Lincoln and Pope John XXIII at the top end of this scale (barely discernable) and Senator Joseph McCarthy and Adolf Hitler at the bottom.

My own experience has shown that one of the common corruptions is impairment of the imagination. So many (not all) power-wielding people seem devoid of ideas. This is partly what staff people in a hierarchy are for: to supply ideas to managers who may not have much imagination. Consider this old movie about a young man who is a clerk in the office of a coffee company. He enters a slogan contest of a rival coffee company and wins a $25,000 prize. The head of his coffee company says sharply: "You work for us. If you have ideas like this why don't you give them to us?" To which the young man replies, "I've been trying for years and nobody will listen." Later, Mr. Big stands and looks out the window as he soliloquizes, "After all, how do I know an idea unless somebody else recognizes it?"

Managers may be pardoned for lacking imagination required to produce ideas—their role may preclude this. But they certainly should be faulted for not having the discrimination to know a good idea when they see one. That, after all, is what managing is about.

Power's effect on one's imagination came out sharply in the years that I ghostwrote speeches for people in important places. Usually, these were bright people who generally had good judgment, made decisions that were fair and sound, knew the difference between good and bad ideas, could write, and were not lazy. Even so, most of them could not write a speech because they could not produce the appropriate ideas. I don't recall anyone ever asking me to write a speech using specific ideas. Producing the ideas, along with writing the speech, was my job. All I got from them was a description of the occasion. Some of these people were great performers who could deliver a ghost-written speech with style and conviction. But they could not produce the ideas or write the speech.

Once, and only once, in a tense emergency, I wrote a short speech for a chief executive who delivered it on the radio without having read it in advance. But he came across as the able manager that he was, with the flavor that he had carefully thought out what he was saying.

I was once challenged by a thoughtful person, "Isn't ghostwriting unethical?" to which I responded, "Maybe so, but with the institutions of our society structured the way they are, I see it as unavoidable."

This is a small observation, but I did enough ghostwriting for enough different power wielders in different settings to have quite a firm feeling that holding power impairs the imagination in many otherwise able power wielders.

Abraham Lincoln

How, then, do we account for the exceptional writing gifts of Abraham Lincoln, who did not have a ghostwriter? One reason might be that the presidency was his first major power-holding role, but, more important, he seemed to have a deep interior life. E.B. White has made the comment that ghost-written speeches are rarely great speeches. If Abraham Lincoln had used a ghostwriter, White says, the Gettysburg address would have begun,"Eighty-seven years ago." The style of even the most gifted ghostwriter does not equal the style of a great writer delivering his or her own stuff.

Pope John XXIII

Pope John XXIII was another exception. I don't know about his writing ability, but he certainly had imagination. However, his biography reveals a very nonstandard temperament for a high-ranking hierarchical executive. He was very bright and a linguist. After he had advanced a few steps in the hierarchy, he was apparently branded as a radical and spent many years as nuncio in Turkey, where there are not many Catholics. His big break came at the end of the war when de Gaulle returned to France and banished that nuncio, who had been a collaborator. Undoubtedly, finding someone who could serve as nuncio to France, a very important post, and who would be acceptable to de Gaulle presented a problem to the Vatican. The Vatican apparently realized that this would take someone like John, whom they had long kept in exile.

John really distinguished himself in Paris during the post-war years. This was where he established himself as a great leader. The Vatican probably could not have made a better choice for that tough spot. When he was made Pope at age 80, he may have been regarded as a caretaker until a longer-term person could be chosen. But his four years as Pope were among the greatest in Catholic history.

One of John's first acts as Pope was to go to the room where the dossiers on church executives were kept and demand to see his own file. Normally, this request would not be granted, but he was the Pope. In his file he discovered that an early judgment made regarding him was as "a radical." He took a pen and wrote beside this remark, "I am not a radical."

My speculation is that John had a lively, rebellious spirit which, through his deep interior life, he kept alive during his long years of "exile." When he became Pope, this spirit enabled him to hold power and resist the corruption of his imagination and determination.

Theodore N. Vail

During my 38 years at AT&T I made a close study of the company's history, not only from the archive, but from talks with older staff members who had been active during the great building years—1907 to 1920—when Theodore N. Vail was the chief executive.

Vail, who served as CEO between the ages of 62 and 75, had great imagination. He wrote his own speeches, annual reports, and articles that bristled with ideas. While he was a tough and sometimes authoritarian executive, clearly he was a reflective man. He was very creative in his earlier career, and in his active presidency he withdrew for long periods to his farm in Vermont. Chief executives today seem not to be reflective people, and they rarely produce important ideas. If anything, they seem to be over-committed people as they work their way up the hierarchy to the top job. Vail did not do this. He was installed there by J.P. Morgan (the elder) who took control of the company in 1907. (Vail had been the first general manager of the first telephone company in 1878. But he became disaffected with the conservative Boston owners who only wanted to exploit their patents for profit. He left in 1887, and for the next 20 years he was an economic adventurer around the world. Morgan knew him during this period.)

Walter S. Gifford

Vail's successor after a brief interval was a "figure" man who had few ideas, and he presided over the business for 23 dull years. But, he had the reputation for having ideas because, shortly after becoming president, he installed an able public relations man, Arthur Page, who was a good writer. Early in Gifford's tenure, Page wrote a speech for him stating the company policy (and probably suggested that the speech be given and engineered the invitation). It was delivered to a meeting of the National Association of Public Utility Commissioners. This one speech made Gifford famous and, after 60 years, there are still references to it in textbooks on business policy. I once asked Page where the ideas came from that went into that speech. His prompt rely was, "I found every single idea in Vail's papers."

Chester I. Barnard

In my AT&T experience there was one fascinating man with whom I had only limited personal contact. Chester I. Barnard was a genius who left Harvard without a degree because he refused to take a required elementary course in a subject in which he had already passed advanced courses with high marks. (Later, after he was famous, Harvard gave him the degree.) He entered AT&T in 1909 as a foreign language translator and, under Vail's tutelage, he quickly moved up. In the early 1920s he became vice-president for operations of Bell Telephone Company of Pennsylvania, in which post he inaugurated humanities training for his young managers (probably the first ever of this kind of manager education) at the University of Pennsylvania. In 1927, he became president of the newly formed New Jersey Bell Telco. He retired from that position at age 60 to become president of the Rockefeller Foundation, of which he had been a trustee.

During his long tenure at New Jersey Telco, he wrote several widely acclaimed books on the executive role, lectured extensively at Harvard Business School, and served with distinction on important commissions. He seemed to have great imagination.

He held the usual power of a chief executive in New Jersey Telco, but he did not use it. He delegated it to a heavy-handed manager who ran the company competently for him. He did little other than attend to the public functions of his job, such as presiding at board meetings, for which he would be briefed like a trial lawyer getting ready to try a case that other lawyers had worked up. A consequence of this neglect of his job was that when he retired he left a thoroughly beaten down company whose top management had to be supplied from the rest of the Bell System for the next 20 years.

An academic friend of mine met Barnard at a meeting and commented to him that it must be interesting to write his books about executives from his own experience of being one. Barnard replied that his writing and his experience as an executive were two wholly separate worlds. To me, this meant that Barnard kept his creative imagination alive by really not using the power that he nominally held, but by delegating it to a good, tough manager. At Rockefeller Foundation, I am told, he performed brilliantly for five years as its chief executive. A close observer noted a comment by Barnard that, for the first time in his life, he felt at home in his job.

I have often wondered why the managers at AT&T would let Barnard—probably the best mind in the business—sit across the river for 20 odd years in a job he didn't want to do. Why didn't they bring him to the AT&T staff, where his kind of mind might have evolved policies that could have saved the business in 1984? Perhaps the answer is that the top staff at AT&T were managers and power users who were not sufficiently reflective and did not have the imagination that such a decision would have required.

An interesting anecdote survives from the early 1930s. An Italian scholar named Pareto wrote a couple of ponderous tomes called *General Sociology*. At a conference, Barnard was talking with the head of my AT&T department about ideas he got from Pareto's books that were applicable to our business. My boss, a competent manager but with a streak of vanity, pretended that he knew about such things. In a few days he received a five-page, single-spaced letter from Barnard really pinning him down about some of Pareto's ideas. In due course, this letter was passed down to me with my boss's request, "Will somebody please write an answer to this letter?" For the next few months, I held up my boss's end of this correspondence. I don't recall how it terminated, but Barnard was a lively correspondent.

Barnard, it seems to me, kept his imagination alive for many years by using *it* and *not using* the administrative power he held. But by holding a manager's job and not managing, the company suffered.

Concluding Observation on Power

I have noted people such as Abraham Lincoln and Pope John XXIII who held great power and did not seem to suffer the common corruptions of power. I believe that this was because their own deep spiritual resources were strong, but, most of what is written here is drawn from my own experience. Others drawing on their own experiences may reach different conclusions.

If some of the serious corruptions of holding and using power are arrogance, impairment of one's imagination, or personality distortion, then perhaps the first step in protecting oneself from those impairments is to sustain a sharp awareness of the danger. One of the characteristics of hazardous occupations is a constant awareness of the danger, by everybody involved. It is not an obsession that makes them sick; rather it is a sustained alertness, a readiness to react and deal promptly with an emergency.

I do not sense this awareness among foundation staff and their administrators. I do not sense it in business, church, or university hierarchies. In the case of research laboratories, where so much of their success depends on creativity, there is more sensitivity to the need to nourish the imagination and watch for influences that might stifle it. But even they do not seem disposed to be experimental about how this is done. I have not found research directors to be experimental about their own work. Curious?

So, awareness of the danger of arrogance, personality distortion, and the corruption of imagination by holding and using power is suggested as the first step. While obvious, it is not necessarily easy. People are sometimes more comfortable when they are not aware of demanding things. The next step, beyond awareness, may be much more difficult, and perhaps, even harder to accept.

The reference to Abraham Lincoln and Pope John XXIII suggest that part of the defense against these losses as a result of holding and using power may be the cultivation of a deep inner spiritual life. One's active role in the outer world may be the less important part of the essential person even when the role in the outer world is of staggering proportions—as it was with these two men. And I doubt if we can ever account for how they got their inner spiritual resources. Nor can we assure any person who doesn't have it that there is a way to get it. Lincoln and John provide examples, but they do not offer models.

If I were coming of age today and had the perspective I now have, and if I realized that I did not possess these substantial inner resources, I would make a determined effort to get them. I don't know how I would go about it, but I would try. One might begin by looking at the available literature, such as *The Limits of Language*, edited by Walker Gibson; *The Psychology of Invention in the Mathematical Field*, by Hadamard; *On Knowing*, by Jerome Bruner; *The Nature of the Judicial Process*, by Benjamin Cardozo; and *Human Potentiality*, by Gardner Murphy.

3

Robert K. Greenleaf and Business Ethics: There Is No Code

Anne T. Fraker

The subject of ethics, what is morally right, is one that everybody should be concerned with every day of his [or her] life.[1]

Ethics in business (or anywhere else) starts with a person, an individual person. . . . Even if the tradition of high ethical practice is long established in a business, unless individuals continue to inject new life into it and adapt it to new conditions, it is likely to deteriorate.[2]

Robert K. Greenleaf

Robert K. Greenleaf: Background

If one were to ask for a Robert K. Greenleaf code of ethics, the response would be negative, as he believed there is no code. He felt that codes outlining rights and wrongs were not very useful as they differed "among individuals, among families and neighborhoods, among cultures, religions, vocational groups, and they change with the passage of time."[3]

Greenleaf had no formal training in the academic field of ethics; rather, he developed a sense of ethics from his own Judeo-Christian upbringing and later Quaker affiliation, his experiences in the workplace and other organizations, his searching and seeking, his meditation, and his concern that the traditional institutions that formed the foundations for people's behaviors were no longer stable sources for values. It was up to the individual to exert a great deal of effort in developing ethical behavior. But he felt businesses could play an important role in making the world better and in assisting individuals to develop ethical behavior. In several writings, including a speech he wrote for a business school dean, Greenleaf said that he believed business had this role because it is the "most persistent, insistent force that keeps the world tied together and gives it hope for a better future. . . ."[4]

To understand Robert K. Greenleaf's approach to the subject of ethics in business, one must know something of his personal life and his career. Like many aspects of Greenleaf's life which seem deceptively simple, his concerns about ethics in business also were deceptively simple. But on further examination, one finds something so complex that deep contemplation and searching are required. It is impossible to separate Greenleaf's concept of servant-leadership practice from ethical practices in business; they are inextricably linked in his eyes. In an unpublished, undated essay, "The Ethic of Strength," Greenleaf stated that ethics are norms gleaned from years of experience, but that there was a much larger problem—people simply did not care enough to serve.

Father and Son

In a December 3, 1926 letter, written by George Greenleaf to his son "Rob" when Robert Greenleaf was teaching math to Ohio Bell workers after hours, George supported and counseled his son: "I am especially pleased to learn that you have been helping the boys who never had a chance. Whatever you do for one of the least of these my brethren, you do for me, and if you still think you owe me something just continue to pay in that kind of coin." Further advice came in a November 13, 1928 letter urging Rob to appreciate the opportunities he had to "broaden your own mind while helping others and at the same time improve the service of your employers."[5]

These letters were only part of a lifetime influence George Greenleaf had on his son's aspirations for his own career and for a better society. Robert Greenleaf says of his father that he "was an ethical man with deeply felt concerns on which he acted responsibly. He left a profound influence on me that grows with the years."[6]

George Greenleaf was a union man, a machinist, who was also active in civic affairs. George said that he valued his union, his political activity, and the church—in that order—in terms of their ability to accomplish the best for society. In some ways the elder Greenleaf's hierarchy of organizational usefulness paralleled that of the larger society of the times. The early 1900s were a time of pragmatism in approaching social problems; people had a strong belief in the efficacy of political solutions to all problems. Little Rob went with his father to many union rallies and community meetings; these activities remained in Robert's memory all of his life as examples of ways in which his father was trying to make his hometown a better place to live and work. Robert also accompanied his father on "troubleshooting" consultations where George was asked to locate difficulties in machine operations. Even such a mechanical operation taught Robert a life lesson—the importance of seeing things whole.

Other Influences

Robert's years in elementary and high school were times of increased fervor for social justice across the United States. Accompanying this trend was a generally increased social conscience. Muckrakers and other social reformers were quite active. This was also a time when businesspeople were interested in more efficient enterprises. An answer to this wish came in the form of Frederick Taylor's book, *The Principles of Scientific Management*, in which he offered formulas for quantifying everything in the workplace to make it run more efficiently.

Robert Greenleaf's childhood experiences with his father's community, work, and labor activities, coupled with his own early work experiences, shaped his views on work and workers throughout his long career at AT&T and during his years as a consultant. During one period between college terms, Robert worked at a construction company in his hometown of Terre Haute, Indiana. Even though the majority of the workers were vastly different from him in behavior and thought, Greenleaf developed an affinity for these "routine" workers. And at the end of his tenure, he felt that he left something behind. The contrast between Greenleaf's view of "sophisticated" workers and "routine" workers puzzled him. He felt that the "routine" workers had more integrity, "precious humor and grace."[7] He questioned whether the more sophisticated had lost something—especially humor.

Greenleaf and AT&T

Robert Greenleaf carried his father's lessons and his own observations with him as he launched his own career in the giant American Telephone and Telegraph Company and became in his words a "kept revolutionary." Throughout his career at AT&T, which began at Ohio Bell in 1926, Greenleaf studied its history, observed its daily operations, and reflected on ways he might be able to make AT&T a better institution. Some of this interest came about, in part, as a response to Greenleaf's sociology professor's suggestion that institutions were becoming dominant in our society and, if we were to have a good society, changes must be made within these institutions. "I was concerned, among other things, with its values, with its history and myth, and intimately with its top leadership."[8] He says that throughout his involvement with folks at AT&T and in various other sectors of society, he found common threads: "A need, a searching that will permit a person to achieve a measure of serenity in an open, tradition-poor society."[9]

In addition to his published writings, which document the principles guiding Greenleaf throughout his AT&T career and beyond as he contemplated his concerns, there are many unpublished manuscripts in the Robert K. Greenleaf archives at Andover Newton Theological School. In writings dating from the early 1970s, Greenleaf stated his primary thesis: "Caring for persons, the more able and the less able serving each other, is the rock upon which a good society is built. Whereas, until recently, caring was largely person to person, now most of it is mediated through institutions—often large, complex, powerful, impersonal; not always competent; sometimes corrupt. If a better society is to be built, one that is more just and more loving, one that provides greater creative opportunity for its people, then the most open course is to *raise both the capacity to serve and the very performance as servant* of existing major institutions by new regenerative forces operating within them. [Emphasis added.]"[10]

Greenleaf's Codeless Code of Ethics

In the middle of Greenleaf's career at AT&T as head of the Management Development Section, he and his staff were involved with studies of management development programs throughout the Bell System. On March 8, 1955, Greenleaf presented a summary of the three phases of this project at a Hot Springs conference. Even though the word ethics does not appear in the summary of what the recommendations were for human resources, the points outlined are part of what Greenleaf saw as ethical behavior in business. A key point was the desire for a management philosophy that stimulated good performance by all employees by enhancing conditions favorable to individual responsibility, participation, and a sense of belonging. The way in which the studies were implemented reflected Greenleaf's philosophy in that he and his staff worked with the various companies under the AT&T umbrella, rather than writing and pronouncing from on high.

The first Greenleaf quote that appears at the beginning of this chapter comes from writing he did in the late 1950s, following his teaching of an executive seminar on business and managerial ethics at the Massachusetts Institute of Technology. Greenleaf carried out this teaching activity simultaneously with his work at AT&T, so he was integrating the practical with the theoretical—a part of the process of seeing things whole. Rather than outlining a standard code of ethics, something Greenleaf viewed as too simplistic, he presented traits managers should possess in order to approach ethical behavior. He did this because he saw the Judeo-Christian ethic that dominates our culture as being continually enlarged by new knowledge and by cross-cultural ideas. Any step-by-step codes were useless.

Greenleaf's suggestions are not the typical step-by-step processes to which most businesspeople are accustomed. His guiding points were integrally related to his view that one should be a "seeker" throughout one's life. He distinguished two types of seekers: those who "seek to find" and those who "seek to seek."[11] For Greenleaf, a seeker should follow the latter course—be joyful in searching and opening new vistas; hope to grow. A seeker must not have a goal, but be consumed with the search. If the seeker fails to follow this course he or she will not be "free, spontaneous, limitless."[12] So, too, should managers "develop the point of view and habit of research" and "become interested in the search for the sake of the search; not because the objects of the search are expected to add up to something. The search is the thing. . . . Only then is something likely to happen."[13]

In the teaching-related draft documents on managerial ethics, Greenleaf elaborates on five concerns a manager should develop in the "search." A manager should have a concern for responsibility in which a person is disposed "to think, speak, and act as if he [or she] is personally accountable to all who may be affected by his thoughts, words, and deeds."[14] Once again, there are no tests or lists one consults in pursuing responsible behavior. Awareness, openness, freedom from self-righteousness, sensitivity to others' needs and aspirations, and acceptance of compromise are some of Greenleaf's guidelines to managers pursuing ethical behavior. These points continue to reflect Greenleaf's view of life and work and the notion of servant-leadership.

Strength

The traits Greenleaf outlined in unpublished documents from his teaching experience and personal reflections on business ethics are difficult to grasp. One of the most important traits an ethical manager should have is "strength," which Greenleaf defined as "the ability to see enough choices of aims, to choose the right aim and to pursue that aim responsibly over a long period of time."[15] Consistent with Greenleaf's holistic view of life, he believed that making the right choices must include individual judgments tested by one's own frame of reference for life's meaning and by traditional ethical and moral values. This strength is not something one acquires through traditional corporate ladder climbing; rather, it is something that is given and, according to Greenleaf, it can be whimsical in its comings and goings. So, what is a manager to do?

Openness to Knowledge

A second concern a manager should have is openness to knowledge. Greenleaf noted three keys to openness to knowledge (which he distinguishes from a quest for knowledge). One should respect, seek, and "take reference from the available formal knowledge"; cultivate one's "own resources of intuitive knowledge"; and contribute what one "can to the general pool of management knowledge."[16]

Foresight

Two other concerns Greenleaf outlined are even more abstract than the first two and, hence, more difficult to grasp and implement. A manager, said Greenleaf, "must see future events that will involve him [or her] before other people see them" (foresight).[17] According to Greenleaf, "serious ethical compromises are often attributable to yesterday's failure to foresee today and take the right actions yesterday. This is really a failure of leadership. . . . Leadership thus degenerates into command, the power to issue orders. And the result may be ethically bad choices because the leeway within which to initiate action has been narrowed and only bad choices remain."[18] This thought is echoed in Greenleaf's later writing, *The Servant as Leader* in which he stated that "foresight is the central ethic of leadership."[19]

Entheos

The fourth concern for a manager focuses on the need for the sustaining power of enthusiasm (entheos). Even though the words are related, they differ subtlely in meaning with Greenleaf preferring entheos—"The essence, the power actuating one who is inspired."[20] According to Greenleaf, "entheos is an imperative if the ethical obligation to develop strength is accepted—if it is accepted as a prime concern over the adult life span."[21]

Again, one sees Greenleaf's link between the spiritual and the "rational" workday world by his examination of this fourth concern. In essence, it appears that Greenleaf saw entheos as the foundation upon which the other concerns were built which, in turn, combined to develop strength in a person. Greenleaf believed that entheos is a sustaining force, a support for "venturesome, risk-taking action," a prod to the conscience keeping one open to knowledge, an influence on keeping the future in the present, and a link between one's religious beliefs and one's workday actions.[22] In the unpublished book draft, Greenleaf offers "invalid" and "valid" tests to measure the growth of entheos. Greenleaf's invalid tests run contrary to commonly accepted valid tests of success propagated by our dominant cultural influences. These invalid tests of the growth of entheos are: "status and material success, social success, family success and busyness."[23] Greenleaf's valid tests of the growth of entheos are "concurrent satisfaction and dissatisfaction with the status quo" and a "concurrent feeling of broadening responsibilities and centering down."[24] Ultimately, there is a "growing sense of purpose, an overriding purpose, in all that is undertaken."[25] This purpose should not be an obsession; rather, it should quietly enrich all of one's thought.[26] To sustain oneself in the quest for "strength," Greenleaf recommended that a person should seek a confidant with whom to share problems encountered in the quest and with whom to develop a firm bond.

Sense of Purpose; Ability to Laugh

A fifth concern for those seeking to be ethical managers is to develop a sense of purpose and an ability to laugh. Fulfilling a sense of purpose is very serious—one must have contact with "ultimate purpose" if one is to be trusted. To serve as a balance to this serious aspect of seeking ethical behavior, Greenleaf recommended that one must be able to laugh, to have fun. "If I had the chance to rub Aladdin's lamp, one rub, one wish, I would wish for a world in which people laugh more. One can cultivate purpose to the point of having a glimpse of the ultimate and still remain connected with people and events, *if* one has humor, if one can laugh with all people at all stages of their journeys." Greenleaf reiterated that "purpose and laughter are the twins that must not separate. Each is empty without the other. Together they are the impregnable fortress of strength . . ."[27]

The theme of strength recurs in Greenleaf's essay, "The Ethic of Strength." The overarching concern prompting Greenleaf to write this essay was the discussion of business ethics that grew out of the question of what kind of industrial society "will serve us best" and his seeing a major problem in the young people not caring enough to serve and "not to hurt."[28] Greenleaf abandoned the use of the word ethics for what he felt was the more important need for "emerging adults" to "learn to grow in *strength*," the strength referred to in "A View of Managerial Ethics" and the unpublished book draft. Rather than concentrate as much on the individual as he did in the 1959 essay, Greenleaf considered, in this essay, the ways young adults might be imbued with strength. He suggests how this might happen through institutions—namely, colleges and universities, and businesses.

A major roadblock to achieving any of this in a corporation lies in the chief executive officer who might be arrogant and a power wielder. However, Greenleaf believed that "building strength in a business comes naturally when the top leader accepts that the process is best started in oneself."[29] Ultimately, the nurturing of strength in a person requires individual commitment by the student and teacher, and some form of education. The hoped-for outcome is "that a much larger than usual number of strong leaders will emerge who are determined to exert a continuous ethics-raising influence wherever they are, and throughout their careers."[30]

Robert K. Greenleaf, the Ghostwriter

Robert Greenleaf wrote not only for his own purposes, but also as a ghostwriter for other people from the business and education sectors. In the collection of unpublished Greenleaf essays, there are some manuscripts that appear to have been written by Greenleaf for presentation by leaders in education. Even in these documents, the familiar Greenleaf themes appear.

In a manuscript that seems to be a speech given by a business school dean, Greenleaf defined an ethical person as one who has no codes or rules and may or may not be religious, but who has courage. Greenleaf, through this speaker, viewed ethics as "the way you are." Any big "to-do" about being ethical or instituting ethical behavior should be seen with suspicion because there is no basis for trust. The individual ethical man or woman may not have chosen to be that way. However, one can make other choices that contribute to ethical behavior. Greenleaf says one may choose to be competent and industrious, to develop foresight, resiliency, insight, wisdom, and imaginative responses to all with which he [or she] deals.[31]

Reflecting the familiar theme that people come first, Greenleaf emphasized that the concern is for a person who can be an effective manager doing his or her "creative responsible best."[32] But, how can ethical managers, who will guide businesses in making a better world, be cultivated? Institutions—in this specific instance, schools of business—can play important roles in fostering that development. Greenleaf said that the ethics of education require that any school "concern itself importantly with the ethical development of its students."[33] Different schools have different approaches to this process, but each has the same obligation to fulfill. Again, the familiar themes of individual strength and institutions that inculcate ethical behavior are stressed.

The Chief Executive Officer

The themes developed about ethics in business in Greenleaf's writings in the later years of his career at AT&T, and in his early publications are echoed in a piece he was commissioned to write for the Business Roundtable in December 1978. This piece entitled "An Observer's View of The Chief Executive Officer's Role: Some Aspects of What It Might Be," was submitted to the Roundtable for its consideration. Greenleaf apparently presented ideas in his paper that made the reviewers uncomfortable, and he did not hear from the group's members after the first draft was submitted. Just as with all of Greenleaf's writings, this piece presents ideas that run counter to the traditionally accepted hierarchical modes of thinking about organizations, especially businesses and, perhaps, represent a threat to some leaders. Just the language Greenleaf utilized in this paper and his other writings probably would be alien to many organizational leaders even today.

Greenleaf's definition of a successful organization is integral to his whole view of people's roles and behavior in them. He said that the most productive organization is one where "there is the largest amount of voluntary action; people do the right things, things that optimize total effectiveness, at the right times—because they understand what ought to be done, they believe these are the right things to do, and they take the necessary actions without being instructed."[34] (This definition of a successful organization was hinted at in the 1955 document detailing the AT&T management objectives study which is mentioned earlier in this chapter.) The strength exhibited by the employees will, in turn, build an organization of strength (the term strength as used here is based on Greenleaf's own definition indicated elsewhere in this chapter).[35]

The first thing a CEO must do to build such a strong, successful organization is to internalize the belief that "people are first." If the CEO does put people first and the organization does operate productively, he or she must be willing to accept a change in roles from that of chief to one of *primus inter pares,* first among equals. The CEO must also acquire the ability to use and deal with power in such a way as to implement it "affirmatively to serve." CEOs should also fulfill the role of facilitating and fostering the leadership capabilities of others, rather than feeling threatened by potential developments. According to Greenleaf, it is important that a CEO not only internalize the new attitude toward people and the organization, but also that he or she reflect that change in language usage.[36]

This piece was written when the theme of corporate social responsibility was popular. This issue, which was not a faddish cause for Greenleaf, does not elude his attention in the Roundtable paper.

However, he did not "preach" at great length about social responsibility. Consistent with his overall emphasis on people first, and the invaluable role of strong leadership, Greenleaf suggested that the key to corporate social responsibility is the chief executive officer's own views of social obligations. Once again, people are the key.

Greenleaf also gave some attention to institutions themselves. As in other writings, he discussed the importance of nourishing potential ethical leaders through study. He also saw employers as being responsible for providing young people with opportunities to learn. Because of the importance Greenleaf placed on the role of institutions in fostering ethical behavior, he proposed his idea of the need for a "theology of institutions" to assist these organizations as they attempt to provide foundations for nurturing the development of people and their ethical actions.[37]

Conclusion

This short examination of some of Robert K. Greenleaf's writings reveals the complexity of his thought on the topic of ethics in business. As noted earlier, nothing is ever simple when trying to understand and implement Greenleaf's ideas. One important key to understanding his view of ethical business behavior is his emphasis on living a holistic life, where all facets are integrated into a healthy whole. In a sense, developing ethical behavior is one positive outcome of a person's quest to become a healthy, whole person.

Certain words and phrases repeatedly appear in Greenleaf's writings, words that are not easily defined and, perhaps, are alien to some in the business world. Defining these words within the context of one's own life becomes part of the searching/seeking process which he deemed so important to one's ongoing personal development. One's own development and the nurturing of others are important first steps in creating an ethical organization and a positive supportive network.

An individual striving to be ethical in business practices must be trusting, accepting, open to new ideas, resilient, wise, insightful (have foresight), imaginative, positive, and possess humor and the ability to laugh. Business leaders working to attain these levels of behavior would, Greenleaf hoped, infuse their organizations with their positive behavior. If the individuals are more caring and serving, the organization also will become more caring and serving. But Greenleaf threw an obstacle in the paths of those individuals and organizations attempting to develop ethical behavior. In the published essay, *Servant, Retrospect and Prospect,* he debunks another of the great American business myths. He asserts that "if we are to move toward a more caring, serving society than we now have, competition must be muted, if not eliminated. Serving and competing are antithetical."[38]

It all begins with the individual leader putting people first. It requires revisions in thinking about organizations, leadership, competition and cooperation, communication, and relating to others. But this quest for ethical business behavior, individually and corporately, will ultimately result in making the world a little better place in which to live and to work.

4

Claiming Servant-Leadership as Your Heritage

Carl Rieser

I have been told that sign language has the uncanny ability to cut through to the real meaning of a word, and I believe it. In sign language, the sign for servant is this: hands out in front with palms up and moving back and forth between the signer and the signee. In this case, the sign takes us back to powerful implications that servant seems to have had four millennia ago—long before the word was reduced to mean a servile household drudge, or slavery, as the Victorians used to call the downstairs maid, poor soul.

This simple gesture says some very powerful things about trusting, being open, offering help, caring, and being willing to be vulnerable. It has a strong sense of mutuality; it connects us.

The gesture evokes what I call the servant within, who is there to help and to serve both you and me. Not just you *or* me. Us. I have come to see this archetypal servant within as the key to my relationship with myself, with other humans, and perhaps with creation. I have even made this gesture a part of my own daily devotional life because it catches this thought so beautifully.

"Nurturer of the human spirit." This is Greenleaf's own epithet for the idea of the servant. I am struck with how well it describes the way in which, traveling my own path, I have come to feel. I have been deeply immersed in reflecting, reporting, and writing on servant-leadership. I have learned many fascinating things on my journey and am eager to share these with others. I also have much to learn.

A Bit about Robert K. Greenleaf

First, I want to talk about Robert K. Greenleaf, the author of *Servant-Leadership.* I want to tell you a little about the kind of man he is and how he got his luminous notion. I will touch briefly on the central core of his thinking, and, I will describe how his influence is spreading quietly but powerfully through our society, and offer some thoughts on why this is happening.

I met Bob Greenleaf in the course of some writing I was doing. Thereafter, I was never able to shake off the impression he and his thinking made on me. He had just gone into what he described as his "second retirement" and was living at a Quaker retirement center near Philadelphia.

I found a man who clothed visionary views about the human spirit in the unadorned, straightforward speech of a Hoosier and a Quaker, touched with a droll sense of humor. He was gaunt, with a long, bony face, and a manner that was at once friendly and relaxed, yet alert and slightly remote. If you wish to get to know him, you still can do so through a series of videocassette interviews and talks produced several years ago. You can also read about him and his remarkable career in John Brooks's history of AT&T called *Telephone.* Greenleaf, who felt large corporations were the institutions of the future, went to work for AT&T just after leaving Carleton College in 1926. He began his basic education in the world of work digging postholes. Then he was an instructor in Bell's renowned foreman training course. A few years later he was in the New York headquarters and on his way to becoming Director of Management Research, an important post at AT&T because Greenleaf made it so.

This put him close to the center of power as advisor to a succession of CEOs. "I was an institution watcher," he said, but others have called him "the conscience of AT&T." One of the CEOs even called him AT&T's "kept revolutionary." "Bob didn't give a damn about status," says one man I know, who worked with Greenleaf as a consultant in those days. "If you asked him a question, he told it like it was." Peter F. Drucker says that "Bob is one of the few truly wise men I have met." Many regard him as a major prophetic figure in modern organization and human relations.

It was Greenleaf's conviction that the modern world has stifled the creativity of its leaders in the straitjacket of the rational and analytical. There has been serious neglect of the intuitive and spontaneous side of our nature. He managed to get elbow room at AT&T for these ideas by organizing the famous resident program in the humanities for Bell executives at Dartmouth and other universities. This became the model for many similar programs in corporations during the 1950s.

Then, in 1964, he took early retirement to begin his second career. "The day I hung up my sword at AT&T," he has said, "I took off on radically different, more venturesome, and more exciting work." He collaborated with John Gardner, who at that stage of his distinguished career was head of the Carnegie Corp. and talked about the "antileadership vaccine" that bedeviled the universities. He lectured and taught at MIT and the Harvard Business School. He consulted with top corporate, university, and foundation leaders here and abroad.

Then came the often-violent eruptions on American campuses in the late 1960s, which gave his work urgency and focus. Greenleaf found it a "searing experience" to watch "distinguished institutions show their fragility and crumble." He felt he was seeing a particularly painful and convulsive indication of the widespread loss of faith in institutions of all kinds, which were failing to respond to the needs of people.

Hermann Hesse's novel *Journey to the East* was then a best-seller on campuses, and Greenleaf read it for the clues it might yield on how to get through to students. He found there the parable of Leo, a charismatic leader who comes on at first as a humble guide, then turns out to be the person on whose strength all rely for guidance. There it suddenly was: the notion of the servant-leader.

Greenleaf spoke of the powerful leadership exerted by this somewhat mysterious Leo. He said that Leo was one who "ostensibly served only in menial ways but who, by the quality of his inner life that was manifest in his presence, lifted men up and made the journey possible."

This provided the touchstone, the catalytic element, that brought together the ideas he had been wrestling with over many years. These concerned the great themes of trust and caring in our society, and the roles of leaders and trustees in creating these conditions.

The following two quotations capture the central themes in his work. The first quotation:

> Caring for persons, the more able and the less able serving each other, is the rock upon which a good society is built. Whereas, until recently, caring was largely person to person, now most of it is mediated through institutions—often large, complex, powerful, impersonal; not always competent; sometimes corrupt.
>
> If a better society is to be built, one that is more just and more loving, one that provides greater creative opportunity for its people, then the most open course is to raise both the capacity to serve and the very performance, as servant, of existing institutions by new regenerative forces operating within them.

The second quotation:

> A servant-led society is one in which the majority of its institutions—churches, schools, businesses, philanthropies, government units—are led by servants.
>
> And who is a servant? What is a person like who, if in a leading or managing position, will make an institution servant-led? I prefer to identify such a servant in terms of the consequences of her or his influence on people.
>
> Will all (or almost all) of the people touched by that leader's influence grow as persons? Will they, while being served, become healthier, wiser, freer, more likely themselves to become servants? And what will be the effect on the least privileged in society; will that person benefit or, at least, not be further deprived?
>
> I judge the quality of any society by what the least privileged in it achieve.

It is very apparent that Greenleaf made few concessions to what he once called "that busybody, modern man." He tended to write in an aphoristic way. He was reflective, and a little thorny. He had a somewhat disconcerting habit of simply stopping when he had said his say. This follows from his own advice that the leader is not afraid of a little silence, but asks, "In saying what I have in mind, can I really improve on silence?"

I received a direct mailer from an outfit called Fast Track. It starts off by telling me this: "You can do it in the car. On a commuter train. On a plane. In a waiting room. At the office. In your study. Walking. Running. Bicycling. Anytime you have an extra minute." Do what? Listen to the best business books summarized on tape. It says here that I can put myself on the fast track by knowing more than the next person, without spending extra time studying. Not by cooperating with you, but by knowing more than you and presumably beating you out.

Against that kind of rhetoric, it has naturally taken time for the quiet but powerful idea of the servant-leader—who shares with others and works through them—to get around.

But the news is spreading. When I first met Bob Greenleaf, he had only a small band of admirers. Among the most ardent, incidentally, were Catholic sisters from various orders, who were experiencing a sense of liberation after Vatican II. Here and there, a few entrepreneurs and others were interested in his ideas, and he had staunch supporters among some people in academe and foundations. A lot of interest among knowledgeable people, but not much beyond that, or so it seemed.

When I next encountered him in 1986, I was pleasantly surprised to find that a quiet but powerful groundswell seemed to be developing. It was a little hard to identify, but, nevertheless, something important seemed to be happening. Many people were trying, each in his or her own way, to assimilate the servant-leader idea into their daily work and lives: An air conditioning distributor and a public utility in Dallas incorporating servant-leadership in their corporate cultures. A construction company and a retirement center in Ann Arbor trying out aspects of it. And a college, too, in Milwaukee.

Management consultants were promoting the idea, and one had a course on visioning. In Indianapolis, a minister was developing a whole community program based on peoples' willingness to become servant-leaders. In Arkansas, a young scholar was writing a thesis on leadership inspired by the Greenleaf model. In Maryland, a communications consultant joined with colleagues in a government agency to run their own servant-leadership seminar in the lunch hour. In

Atlanta, a retired Anglican bishop had set up an Institute of Servant-Leadership at Emory University. A couple hundred people from businesses, churches, and colleges went to it each year. In New England a top-ranking corporate executive had imported the concept into a large manufacturing company.

And so it went. But the interesting thing was that few of these servant-leaders were aware that there were any others out there doing the same thing.

Have Americans Lost Their Social "Glue"?

What accounts for this extraordinary interest in the quiet ideas of a Quaker philosopher? Fundamentally, I think that it is the realization that the central issue of American society generally in these last few years of the century is the rebuilding of trust—of people's trust in their bosses, in their unions, in their corporations, in their schools, in their government, in each other. And that is the key to the divisiveness, hostility, anger, and, yes, mean-spiritedness of our time: We have become afraid of each other.

To use Greenleaf's own phrase, we Americans have lost what he calls our social "glue." I detect a great difference in the kind of internal struggles we have waged in the past half-century. In the Depression, it was a class struggle, and the stakes were social and economic justice. In the sixties, it was people against institutions for racial and sex equality and sometime misguided personal autonomy. We have opened up our communities and institutions—not fully yet, but the change is great—and now we find that the conflict has shifted to within families, institutions, and communities. We feel that we live in a world of strangers—often including ourselves.

We see that our divisiveness has become a paycheck and pocketbook issue—and it is the Japanese who are teaching us this. We rightly locate a large part of the secret of Japanese business efficiency and success in their team-building, quality circles, consensual methods, and other humanistic practices, some of which, ironically enough, they originally borrowed from us.

These have been absorbed into the Japanese social system, based on mutuality and trust, that pervades their corporate structures. Japanese managers are trained from infancy in the virtues of teamwork and consensus.

I mentioned John Gardner earlier. In his latest paper on leadership, called "The Task of Motivating," he said: "Many things have contributed to the recent successes of the Japanese, but no one doubts that among the predisposing factors is their belief in Japan, their fervent loyalty to the collective identity at every level—family, work team, nation. They do have shared values and one of the highest is group loyalty." Gardner says, "Leaders must rehabilitate the idea of commitments beyond the self."

The Japanese corporations have now become our masters, and we the apprentices, in applying these cooperative and highly successful techniques in the abrasive, divisive, and even hostile American industrial environment. Cooperation works; it pays off.

In the end, we cannot do it their way, which is based on the tribal loyalties of an almost totally homogeneous people. The "glue" in our highly diverse society must be derived from something else, something that is native to our own soil and our own rich cultural and spiritual traditions.

The Servant Within

The most powerful thing Greenleaf does is to unlock the often-suppressed need inside us to serve others by evoking the figure of the servant. Servant is now a degraded term, but it once had potent meaning. The servant had a special place in society and a special relationship with the master in early Biblical history. The servant was not exactly family, nor was he or she a hired hand or—most assuredly—a slave. A servant under some circumstances could even inherit the master's property. In Leviticus, you will find the rights and duties of both parties spelled out. At the jubilee year, servants' contracts were considered to have been worked out and the servant was free. The master was enjoined to give them a start in the world and to treat them like a friend. Trust and mutuality are inherent in the relationship.

The servant image has embedded itself deeply in our psyches, and it is from this level that I draw my own image of the servant within. Servants appear in many different guises in myth, dreams, and literature as powerful archetypal images. Hermann Hesse's Leo is an example. And there is also the underlying religious image of the Suffering Servant.

On being introduced to Greenleaf's thinking, people often experience an inward change. Someone at a conference told me, "I feel more at peace. I am attempting more, but I'm willing to accept myself and the results." Another said, "The great power of the servant-leader idea is that it releases us by giving us permission to serve others." Thus, Greenleaf has introduced—maybe "smuggled" is the right word—a spiritual element into the managerial function.

Greenleaf says, "The servant views any problem in the world as *in here,* inside oneself, not *out there.* And if a flaw in the world is to be remedied, to the servant the process of change starts *in here,* in the servant, not *out there.*" To show what a wonderfully universal idea this is, Greenleaf traces this idea back to Confucius.

The self-fulfillment and self-realization movements never really made this link between self and others. Michael Ray and Michelle Myers, who teach the "Creativity in Business" course at Stanford, now say that true creativity in business isn't possible without spirituality. They also say, "If business has discovered the importance of intuition in this decade, we predict that it will next discover the importance of compassion." It is fair to point out that Greenleaf has already built this bridge.

Community-building efforts today are almost all built in some way on the notion that change always starts inside each of us. It so happens that many courses are modeled—or at least certain aspects of them are—on the program of the American Leadership Forum. This is the pioneering effort to apply wilderness experiences and other such learnings in attempting to build trust in potential community leaders across urban barriers. Here again we find the influence of Bob Greenleaf.

The program was begun by Joe Jaworski, the son of Judge Leon Jaworski, who won renown as the Watergate prosecutor. The younger Jaworski, in making his own commitment to devote himself to a public cause, was deeply inspired by Robert Greenleaf. He told me that he keeps going back for refreshment to his dog-eared, marked-up copy of Greenleaf's book *Servant-Leadership* and always finds something new and revealing. He has publicly paid his debt of gratitude to Greenleaf in speeches.

The city of Hartford, Connecticut, had the prototype Leadership Forum program. During a recent session, the participants wore T-shirts with "servant" printed on one side and "leader" on the other. Whether participants wore theirs to or fro depended on how they felt when they got up that morning. I think this amusing parable helps to drive home my earlier point about the mutuality of the servant relationship. We can be both servant and leader, and we serve each other no matter which we are.

Continuity and Follow-Through

There is another lesson to be learned. It has to do with continuity and follow-through. Certain intense and stimulating experiences are potent in opening us up to ourselves and to others, and in bringing about our personal growth. But intense as they are, these experiences tend to fade and vanish. And they will, unless, like Joe Jaworski, we keep going back to the fountain for refreshment.

We put a finger here on a source of modern corporate weariness and disillusion: the big morale build-up and letdown. It has been happening ever since the 1950s, with the T-groups and sensitivity training. Corporate people go to seminars and workshops, build up a head of steam and expectations, go back to work on Monday—and nothing is changed. And often, people realize that nothing is going to change. This creates skepticism, and rightly so.

Greenleaf made a distinction between what he called "people-building" and "people-using" institutions. He warned against the use of such devices as work enlargement, participation, and motivational management—which were then coming into vogue—as quick fixes. They can be used like aspirin, he said, for fast relief but, in the end, people see through this as manipulation. In the people-building institution, which practices the Greenleaf motto "people first," the work of building team spirit, consensus, participation, goes on continuously.

Ann McGee-Cooper, who has the longest experience of anyone I know as a trainer and consultant in servant leadership and business creativity said, "I'd go into seminars and see wonderful things happen. Flowers would sprout, and then, without tending, they would fall back into the old ways of being. It almost seems immoral to me to go in and get someone all excited about what they can do and then not provide a reasonable support system to help them grow."

Work for the Person as Much as the Person for the Work

Let us turn to another Greenleaf concept. An *AT&T Journal* containing a review of Greenleaf's book *Servant-Leadership* had this quotation from Greenleaf: "The new ethic, simply but completely stated, will be: The work exists for the person as much as the person exists for the work." There was also this quote: "The new ethic requires that growth of those who do the work is the primary aim." There is another Greenleaf quote I would like to add to these: "The business exists to provide meaningful work for the person as it exists to provide a product or a service to the customer." Those three brief statements—rather radical ones, when you think about it—express the heart of the servant-leader message.

There is a wonderful advantage in doing the truly meaningful kind of work Greenleaf mentions, such as producing "caring" products and services that give people with handicaps a more whole and satisfying life. Workers who do these kinds of things are in continuous touch with the people who need and buy their products. This simply *has* to make the work fulfilling and significant. Such a continuing, sensitive, and caring interplay with users is very important.

Such a discovery was made the hard way by the maintenance department at the Glacier Hills Retirement Center in Ann Arbor. The maintenance people always thought that their job was to repair the air conditioning, and they were very efficient, but the friction between them and the guests was considerable when they were on a service call. But when the center began practicing servant-leadership, then came the revelation: The mission was not to repair air conditioners but to make people comfortable and contented. As the head of the maintenance department said, "I had lost my servant's heart."

Incidentally, Greenleaf makes an interesting observation about profit and not-for-profit institutions. "The common assumption," he says, "seems to be that for-profit is tainted with self-serving, whereas not-for-profit is presumed selfless. In my experience, both are false." And he adds: "The opportunities to serve with distinction are the same." This thought may be useful in developing your own mission or vision statement as servant-leaders.

Attributes of Servant-Leaders

Let's look at some of the attributes of the servant-leader that Greenleaf identifies. We've already mentioned intuition. Greenleaf was way ahead of his time on this. He was preaching the idea when he taught at MIT and the Harvard Business School years ago. Greenleaf says the leader comes to rely on an intuitive *feel* for patterns through the ability to generalize on what has happened previously. That helps him or her to make better-than-average guesses about the future. Intuition is "knowing the unknowable and foreseeing the unforeseeable." This may seem a little far out in the context of doing daily work. But remember the importance that Greenleaf rightly places on the vision of what business is all about. Greenleaf called the "art of conceptualizing" the prime leadership talent. This means conveying that larger vision which can inspire people to act creatively on their own behalf. One of the great values of the vision or mission is that the leader can appeal to that in giving legitimacy to what he or she is asking others to do.

People, however, must be able to buy into the vision. They must identify with it. There is such a thing as a group vision, and there are techniques now for achieving this. I have been involved in a servant-leader visioning workshop, and found it an intensely absorbing experience.

Let's come a little closer to where we all live daily with another basic servant-leadership principle. The servant-leader, Greenleaf says, listens and understands, not with the purpose of pinning a problem on someone, but in order to find out from others what "*I* can do about *my* problem." Bennett Sims, who runs the Institute for Servant-Leadership, calls this "feeling for the other side."

Here is another one close to home: The servant-leader always empathizes and always accepts the person, but sometimes refuses to accept the person's effort or performance as good enough. "People grow taller when they are accepted for what they are," is Greenleaf's way of putting it. In other words, the servant-leader has too much respect for herself or himself and cares too much for others to let them perform at less than their best level. Again, Bennett Sims calls this "holding the other side to account," and emphasizes that each side must bear responsibility.

I also mentioned Ann McGee-Cooper, who has been helping TDIndustries in Dallas train servant-leaders for nearly 15 years. TDI is the pioneer in the art of applying servant-leadership. Ann likes to quote Greenleaf's remark, "Anyone could lead perfect people, if there were any." The real challenge, she says, "is to learn to develop the imperfect people who we all are." And she goes on to say this: "Pretty soon they get the message that their greatest value will be to teach others what they've learned about responsible workers. That's a hard message to get across, but that is the message. It is really servant-leadership: I enable and empower you through my love and patience and my firmness. I love you enough not to let you do less than your best. But I don't shame you into it: I invite you into it. One day you may be impatient and say, You're letting yourself and others down. The next day you may be gentle and say, How can I help you? I don't see the leader as some namby-pamby milk toast."

Here is further confirmation of that thought: "Some will judge the servant-leader weak. It will not be easy. But strength will come from the united, committed, voluntary action of those led. There is absolutely no tough decision that can't be implemented by such a group of united, committed, volunteers under a servant-leader." The preceding quote is from Robert Vanourek, former group vice-president of mailing systems at Pitney Bowes.

Conclusion

Let me go back a moment to your journey. A very interesting thing emerged in my talks with people that have experienced courses that are intended to awaken people's awareness of themselves and of other people. The sensitivities that people develop often work back into their private lives first, and they begin practicing new behavior there even before they start practicing it in their work settings. It is supposed to work the other way around, carrying our values out of our private lives into the world outside. This is a fascinating insight into the quiet power of the servant.

I guess this just proves that we humans are really all of a piece, and no matter how hard we try, it is very painful for us to split and compartmentalize our lives the way we have come to do in our modern world. In the end, I rather feel that this is what servant-leadership is all about: the search for wholeness in a broken world.

5

Tracing the Vision and Impact of Robert K. Greenleaf

Joseph J. DiStefano

This is an attempt to trace the evolution of Bob Greenleaf's ideas, and comment on their impact.[1] I first met Bob Greenleaf through "divine intervention," which is to say that Les Rollins arranged for me and a fellow Harvard Business School student to go to New York from Boston twice a month for a private seminar with Bob in 1963–64.[2] From that first set of meetings covering a stimulating eight months grew an ongoing relationship which I prize as much as any in my family . . . quite a statement for a Sicilian to make! Over the years I have benefitted from his ideas, experiences and exchanges.

There are two objectives to be accomplished here. First, I would like to suggest my understanding of the roots of his ideas. Second, I would like to outline some of the dynamics that underline their evolution.

Some Themes in Robert K. Greenleaf's Life

There are two sets of factors that are fundamental to understanding the roots of the ideas in Bob Greenleaf's writings. Bob identified five ideas that gave a sense of direction to his life, ideas, and writing. First, he noted that the servant theme was modelled by his father. Second, at 21 he heeded the advice of his sociology professor to join a big institution, stay in it, understand it, and help shape its character. Third, from age 25 and throughout his life he followed the writings of E. B. White from whom he gained the insight to "see things whole." At 40, he listened to the advice of radio commentator and author, Elmer Davis, to start preparing early for a useful old age. Then, at 65, he read the works of Hermann Hesse. Bob drew the servant-leader theme from Hesse's novel, *Journey to the East*. There is no need to elaborate on these themes, but it is important to note that these five ideas are background factors that should be kept in mind, in view of my perspectives on Bob's writings.

In my opinion, these five elements are not the only ones important to understanding the origins of Bob's writing and the evolution of the themes. As I have read and reread his work, talked to him about his life, coaxed him to write some short, unpublished autobiographical pieces, and enjoyed both responding to and resisting his mentoring, I have developed some observations about what has given rise to the powerful ideas about which he has written.

Readiness and Preparation

Readiness is the overarching element. Bob has evidenced a consistent readiness to experience life, to write about his experience, and to initiate actions that would enrich his experiences. His readiness to write on the great themes he has addressed is rooted in *preparation*. His preparation has been deliberate, though not always focused or directed toward a particular goal. Rather, his preparation has been characterized by eclecticism, which, in turn, has been driven by curiosity about ideas and about people, openness to others and to experience, and reflection on the knowledge and experience gained through his curiosity and openness.

To underscore his eclecticism, let me cite a few of the many dimensions of the man. His father, who Bob has noted only had an elementary school education, gave him a deep appreciation for the richness of poetry in capturing and illuminating man's condition. From his uncle, he gained a lifelong interest in astronomy. Unlike the majority of his head office colleagues, he took advantage of the resources of the Bell Labs to keep up to date on advances in physics by periodically visiting, questioning, and experiencing the myriad explorations being conducted there.

His eclecticism manifested itself in the company he kept, as well. He sought out professors of literature, ethics, theology, business, communications, psychology, history, semantics, and so on and kept up a lively interaction with them throughout his life. His friends included physicians, futurists, activists, industrialists, labor organizers, clergymen and -women, leaders of voluntary agencies and organizations, university presidents, students—people of every stripe and station.[3]

The range of authors he read matched the variety of people he met, and equally reveal the curiosity and openness that fired his eclecticism. In my first few meetings with him in 1963–64 his "assignments" included Hesse's *Siddhartha,* Kesey's *One Flew Over the Cuckoo's Nest,* Hadamard's *On the Psychology of Invention in the Mathematical Field,* Cardozo's *On the Nature of the Judicial Process,* Van der Post's *Journey to the Interior,* White's *Lives in Progress,* and essays by E. B. White, poems by Frost, and others that I can't retrieve from my memory. What I did not recognize at the time, although I now retrospectively "see whole," is the common thread of preparation in all of these works. His curiosity led him to determine which books were being read by young people at that time; his openness led him to read them; his reflection led him to his writing.

Patience, Faith, and Humility

Another element that is key to understanding much of his writing, especially his suggestions for implementing his ideas, is *patience.* Bob's patience is reinforced in *faith,* faith in the efficacy of serving and in processes. Among the processes in which Bob's faith is expressed both implicitly and explicitly in his writing are seeking, listening, exercising power benignly (versus coercively), persuading, consensus decision making, meditating, and acting from where one is. Even this partial list suggests the importance of Quaker values in shaping Bob's orientation.

Other characteristics of Bob implicit in his work are a sense of *awe* and a genuine *humility.* These are evidenced by his acceptance of mystery and his comfort with ambiguity.

Finally, I would suggest that Bob's pattern has been to produce a *synthesis* from his eclectic preparation; the synthesis is drawn from patience, faith, and humility. I would argue that his seeing things whole is a result of his work, not just a gift from E. B. White. In fact the cycle of hard work, followed by reflective withdrawal, yielding an integrated insight is a theme of many of the books that were noted earlier. In my view, it is a pattern paralleled in Bob's life and writing and is fundamental to understanding the roots of his work.

These processes and characteristics evidenced throughout his life enabled him to be ready to write. That readiness did not magically appear, but was a result of those experiences and preparation which he both sought and accepted. The implications of these observations of the underlying elements in his work for those of us who would apply his ideas are important, I believe, for I suspect that successful application of his ideas requires many of these same processes and characteristics, which in my experience rarely occur in a single individual or circumstance. However, they are to be striven for, not to emulate Bob Greenleaf or to re-create his vision, but to develop further the ideas and to apply them creatively and effectively where we happen to be. In Bob's case, 60 years of repetition of these patterns did make him ready to write.

The list of essays Bob published can be grouped into three categories: those about servant leadership, including the three "core" essays, "The Servant as Leader," "The Institution as Servant," and "Trustees as Servants"; those with a focus on seminaries; and those explicitly autobiographical (the latter also introducing the theme of nurturing the human spirit). We now turn our attention to the evolution of these ideas with the initial examination of the first three essays.

Development and Evolution of Three Themes

The motivation to write on the servant theme actually was rooted in Bob's participation in a seminar that failed. He had gone to an experimental college in Prescott, Arizona to spend a week working with the students at the request of the president, Ronald Nairn. For reasons Bob never understood, the faculty had undermined the seminars, and Bob left the campus early. As he and his wife, Esther drove to San Francisco, they talked through the experience, and Bob decided to do some writing as an alternative way to influence students in the country to take on more responsibility. He had no master plan to produce a series of essays. He simply decided to put down on paper, in a succinct way, some ideas to deal with what he saw as an urgent need for more leadership.

The focus on servant-leadership was derived from a different experience, however. Previous work with foundations and universities had brought him onto many campuses. He took advantage of these opportunities to visit the bookstores on these campuses to see what students across the country were reading.[4] He noticed everywhere the large number of Hesse novels on display. Because of their clear popularity, he made it a project to read them all, in the order in which Hesse had written them. Furthermore, he simultaneously read a biography of Hesse so he would know what was going on in his life as he had written the novels. Now *that's* preparation! Keep in mind that this was before he had decided to write. As noted earlier, it was in Hesse's *Journey to the East* that he discovered the servant-leader idea, which he subsequently used as the title of his first essay.

When "The Servant as Leader" was finished, he sent about 200 copies out to people he thought would be interested in its theme. From this modest initial distribution, the sales of that essay alone have totalled more than 200,000 copies—literally to all parts of the world. The biggest purchases were made by various orders of Roman Catholic sisters. Bob speculated that this was because they have the closest familiarity with the servant idea from their own commitment to serving. My observation (as one of the 200 who received the essay) was that there was an enormous, unmet need for treating the leadership theme in a way that was accessible to a wide variety of people. Approaches to leadership by studying great world leaders, either admirable or despicable, left readers unsatisfied because even the best of the subjects were hopelessly beyond their ability to emulate. On the other hand, academic studies of leadership were conceptually interesting, but difficult, if not impossible, to put into practice in everyday life. It seemed to me that "The Servant as Leader" not only presented ideas that could be applied by most people, but especially appealed to people inside large organizations who wanted to serve better themselves and wanted to be better led by those in authority.

Following publication of the first essay, Bob had frequent interaction with its readers and with people who had used it with others with whom they had worked. The feedback and discussion of reactions to the ideas, together with his own thinking about the other major determinants of a high-quality society, led him to the recognition that there were two interlocking phenomena: People serving and institutions serving.

Bob then turned his attention to understanding what might make institutions serve more effectively. He started with consideration of his own experiences in AT&T. He had learned to understand and work with and through that colossus. Listen to his words from an interview I videotaped: "It took a lot of Machiavellian strategy to maneuver within it and to make any contribution to it. But I was comfortable in that relationship and I realized that a lot of people were not. A lot of people were really ground down by it." The implication for him was to address the realities of organizational structure and processes that led to this result for so many people. Bob saw it important to do so because he believed that the quality of modern society was much more dependent on large organizations which mediated the caring for individuals formerly done on a one-to-one basis. The implications for us who either work in large organizations or work with people who do, is that we need to help those in, or headed into, big institutions to find their appropriate modes for contributing to their improved performance. Bob's writing in his first two essays helps us to do that.

The core ideas in the second essay, "The Institution as Servant, viz., primus inter pares" (first among equals) and the mediating of caring by large institutions, were derived from his reflecting on his own knowledge and experience. That such reflection produced such innovative ideas is a testimony to the importance of preparation. In the years before he started to write, he had become a diligent student of the many different kinds of organizations including businesses, churches, universities, and foundations. Most of the organizations he studied or worked with were very big. Among them were Philips, Royal Dutch Shell, and Unilever, all of which employed some elements of the *primus inter pares* idea, although Philips was the only one that actually used the term as such.

It is interesting to contrast the reactions of readers to the two essays. "The Servant as Leader" enjoyed an incredible popularity and distribution—incredible in the sense of the consequences of word of mouth advertising. A brief example from my own experience will suffice to illustrate how the "multiplier effect" of word of mouth has occurred. I used the essay for some programs at The Niagara Institute.[5] The program director with whom I worked, a talented man named

Ray Rouse, was taken with the ideas and started distributing the essay on other programs at the Institute. They had already used more than 3,000 copies of Bob's essays. Through this distribution the Liberal Party[6] in Ontario became aware of the servant-leader idea and has publicized it in an editorial in their official magazine, *de Novo*. From this citation, even more essays have been purchased and distributed.

One reason people embraced the ideas in "The Servant as Leader" is, as noted earlier, the extraordinary thirst for leadership that remains unquenched. For example, in my field of organizational behavior, there is a renewal of interest in leadership studies and a burgeoning literature on the topic. When I introduce leadership issues with educators, students, and managers from all kinds of different organizations, the response is more similar across these diverse audiences than for any other issue I raise. Why? Because we haven't adequately dealt with the needs of people for leadership development. We have neither given enough attention to the topic, nor have we done it sufficiently skillfully or personally. In formal contexts we are too preoccupied with narrow issues. For example, in my own field we tend to focus on managerial techniques, specialties, and functions. We miss opportunities at an institutional level to tie leadership implications and themes into our work, our disciplines, our curriculum, our organizations on a formal, systematic and organized basis. In informal contexts we are similarly neglectful. We are too busy, for example, to pick out those with unusual capacity for leadership and give them individual nurturing. I expect that you and your organizations are not significantly different from my own experience. And while I am glad that Bob Greenleaf's ideas are helping to fill the gap of our omissions, we can do a lot more where we are.

Quite a different response to "The Institution as Servant" has emerged, even though I believe, with Greenleaf, that there is as great a need to improve our organizational structures and practices as there is to behave as individual servant-leaders. This essay has met major resistance among nearly all to whom I've introduced it. Bob and others have reported similar reactions. My view is that there are two major reasons for these negative responses. First, the ideas require a paradigm shift—to think in *primus inter pares* terms, rather than in terms of pyramidal structures and processes. The resistance is more than that of not wanting to reorganize our thinking; the shift runs counter to a deeply felt, strongly held value in North America that stresses individualism over the lateral relations implicit in the *primus inter pares* concept.[7] (Bob was influenced by the group-oriented aspects of the Asian and European countries he visited.)

The second reason for resistance to "The Institution as Servant" is that the ideas contradict the hierarchical structures that provide power and status to people. This, too, is linked to a set of culturally conditioned values. One indication of how strong this conditioning is (and an indication of its "hidden" nature as a cultural variable) is the vehemence and unreasoning nature of the reactions, especially in contrast to the calm, rational engaging of the ideas from "The Servant as Leader." One head of a major U.S. company, for example, distributes the first essay to each new managerial recruit with a strong endorsement of its concepts. Yet he shouts when I inquire about the ideas in "The Institution as Servant," "You *can't run* an organization that way!!"

Bob acknowledged this phenomenon and noted that societies cannot be run without recognizing the elements of power-striving and status-seeking. In my view, the key is the temperament of those in positions of authority to be servant-leaders, regardless of whether their labels are "chief" or "primus." And, as I will later suggest in discussing "Trustees as Servants," if the servant-leader orientation is matched by strong self-confidence, then the person is more likely to accept the idea of being *primus inter pares* and even to embrace the idea as more likely to produce better results than the organizing principles more traditionally used.

Bob, himself, was sanguine about the resistance to his second essay. In response to my queries about this, he replied, "Well, I suspect if the essay has accomplished anything (and I have no way of judging what it did accomplish), it has helped to smoke out into the open an issue that I think we sort of swept under the rug, and that is: 'What do we really value and what qualities are important to nurture in people who may evolve as strong people in leadership positions?'"

Having "smoked out" the issue, I think we need to follow up on it. Minimally, we need to do two things to foster the *primus inter pares* idea. First, we need to elaborate on Bob's rationale for its relevance. For example, the increased complexity of tasks, the increased specialization to cope with the increased complexity, and the increased knowledge within specializations all require integrative and cooperative behaviors which are implicit in the *primus inter pares* concept. Second, we need to develop skills to deliver the necessary cooperation and integration in a culture that tends to neglect the development of abilities in lateral relations in favor of individual prowess.

Starting with the premise that the quality of caring for individuals is the mark of the quality of a society, Bob wrote his first two essays in an attempt to improve individual performance and to reconstruct the organizations within which individuals work and through which they exercise much of their caring. From that base, he seemed to search for even more fundamental causes for our shortfall from what is needed, especially given the significant resources we have available to use. Although it is a homely analogy, he seems to be "peeling an onion," successively examining reasons why we aren't doing as good a job as we can and looking for opportunities for improvement. He starts with individuals, moves to institutions and, then, in his third essay, turns his attention to the trustees of our institutions.

"Trustees as Servants" emerged partly as a result of the resistance of organizational leaders to "The Institution as Servant" and partly because of Bob's view that trustees and directors were also falling short of what was desirable. One way to influence the thinking of executives was to have trustees, particularly the chair of trustees, take a more active role. In order for that to happen, it was necessary to understand how a more effective role might be defined, and to develop reasons for assuming it. Just as he did with his first two essays, Bob drew on his experience, especially on that within AT&T, and on his preparation and reflection based on work with other organizations.

In particular, he took seriously the legal basis of the corporation to be "managed by a board of directors or trustees" and looked at AT&T's history in that light. He noted that major changes took place during the period of 1907 to 1920 when it was transformed into a major company. He attributed that change to Theodore Vail, who during that period emerged not only as an effective leader of the organization, but also as a major business statesman.[8] But the reason for Vail's success, Bob asserts, was primarily because of J. P. Morgan's (the elder) mentoring. Bob believes that Morgan's reputation as a robber baron has prevented business historians from seeing how important and effective his guidance of Vail was. As an owner/trustee, Morgan's influence on his CEO's development stands in marked contrast to today's more prevalent model of executives managing their boards. In Bob's view, Morgan was key to Vail's statesman-like ability to work with government and his leading AT&T into its premier position as a covenantal company, a preeminence Bob would argue it subsequently lost because of its lack of statesman-like leaders, because

Table 5.1
Evolution of Three Core Essays

THE SERVANT AS LEADER	Written to stimulate young people to take on more responsibility.
Reactions from readers and interactions with them lead to:	
THE INSTITUTION AS SERVANT	Written as a parallel to "The Servant as Leader" in order to raise the level of performance of organizations.
Resistance from executives to these ideas and the conviction that trustees, too, needed to conceptualize their role in order to serve society better and to raise the level of performance of organizations and their leaders led to:	
TRUSTEES AS SERVANTS	Written to urge directors to accept a more active role, but one distinct from managers.
Recognition that it was necessary to further develop and foster this trustee role and to provide training for those who would accept it led to a series of essays on the servant-leader theme in seminaries.	

of its lack of servant-trustees of Morgan's orientation, conviction, and skill.

Table 5.1 provides a recap of the evolution of the first three servant-leader essays. Although the summary contained there is oversimplified, it suggests the main elements that I believe drove the development of the "core essays" in the form they took.

Seminaries' (Potentially) Pivotal Role

From these first three essays, Bob moved to a focus on seminaries. The explanation that I see for this transition is, of course, subject to legitimate questioning on *post facto* rationalizing. It is also in sharp contrast to Bob's own view that the development of the essays was a result of his intuitive processes, of seeking and seeing and reflecting, and then writing about the results of these processes.[9] Nevertheless, I offer the following perspective on how the seminary theme emerged.

Most business directors to whom "Trustees as Servants" is largely, if not primarily, addressed are themselves managers. They are therefore unlikely to be nurturers of the executives who report to the boards they are on. They are too much "doers" themselves, too identified with and sympathetic to the doer orientation. Indeed, because of this, they are likely to expect, even demand, doer behavior from the executives they oversee, a demand that the executives are already predisposed to meet. So it is highly unlikely that such trustees will see the importance of developing executive statesmen or respond to the urging in Bob's essay to do so.

Part of the reason I advance this view is because of my experience that boards of nonprofit organizations are more receptive to the ideas in "Trustees as Servants." On such boards the trustees generally are lay volunteers, individual professionals who do not work in large organizations, such as housewives, and so forth. These people are less conditioned to think and behave like executives. But Bob is not so sure that these people are *really* more receptive to his ideas. He warns that their interest may be based more on "intellectual titillation" than on a desire to implement. He noted their proclivity more to talk about than to act on the ideas.

Let me cite two examples from my own experience, which may shed further light on the evolution of Bob's writing from the first essays to the seminary theme. The first example comes from my being a trustee of Rensselaer Polytechnic Institute for more than 23 years. During that period I worked with seven different CEOs. Only one (George Low) structured his relationship with the board so the board managed him and his team. He did so without the guidance or insistence of the board chair to operate this way. My observation is that his behavior was a function of his belief system and his psychological make-up. First, he firmly believed that this type of Board-CEO relation was best, that it was the legally correct way, *and* that it was more likely to produce excellent results, primarily because of the collective wisdom of the board members and their greater objectivity. Second, he was able to act on his beliefs because he was psychologically strong; he was both self-confident and self-critical. His self-concept was secure enough so he could accept the scrutiny and advice of his board members.

My second example is Lloyd Barber of the University of Regina. He attempted to apply the ideas of both "The Institution as Servant" and "Trustees as Servants." In the initial structuring of his top team, he broke with conventional wisdom and had a single vice-president (integrating the usual, dual vice-presidencies of academic and administrative roles) and operated with a tight group of senior people with very close relations with an active board. Later he reported the erosion of these operating modalities and attempted to rejuvenate the ideas and the activities. Talking to him provides further evidence of the twin requirements listed above, *viz.*, strong belief in the ideas coupled with a healthy psyche.

And this produces a major paradox for me, a much greater paradox than the juxtaposition of servant-leader concepts: that is, that only the strongest will act to be guided and nurtured and managed by trustee-servant boards. I think the few who do so are motivated by a very deep caring *for* the institutions they are leading.

The implications for me are to:

- Help develop the trustee role (an activity parallel to that of management development) and
- nurture the caring for institutions, not just for individuals.

How does all this lead Bob Greenleaf to writing about seminaries? His conclusion from these perspectives is that directorships ought to be rooted in a sense of concern and responsibility. (His view has certainly been corroborated by my own observations of executives who have applied the ideas.) The question, then, of getting trustee-servants is basically theological. Yet, most trustees don't feel responsibility and do not *want* to feel it. Unlike Morgan who cared deeply about the quality of the institutions he controlled, most directors are in the positions for the honor, the prestige, the dollars, and/or to be "in the know" with only superficial involvement (I have never heard a director refer to his or her responsibility as a "job"). Even though director liability may be starting to make people more careful, it hasn't seemed to alter their basic notion of the role. And directors who see their functions as serious responsibilities and act that way are sometimes stymied. Arthur Goldberg resigned from the TWA board and explained his act publicly in a letter to *The New York Times* by noting that the executives refused to provide him with the information he believed essential to carrying out his duties.

This example points out the need both for developing a theory of trustee role, and setting up facilities for training trustees, especially chairpersons, for filling it. I argued with Bob and others that the universities should accomplish these functions and that business schools, in particular, should take on the tasks. Bob disagreed and said, "No, it is not realistic to expect them to do it. They should do well what they are now doing; it is a big enough task and there are other organizations better suited to doing the job of developing trustees." This may be true, but I believe that, as a minimum, people in higher education should be conditioning people to the differences between managers and trustee/directors so that the roles are not confused by the very people who are most likely to be assuming them. Also, more should be done in universities to encourage the ablest to embrace the trustee-servant and servant-leader modes of behaving.

Bob Greenleaf's concern was for selecting the type of institution that might best shape:

1. The trustee-servant idea (he does *not* see his formulation as a fully developed one).
2. Values regarding the quality of institutions.
3. How to identify and develop new sources of potential trustees beyond the usual pool of managerial people.

Using these criteria, he concluded that seminaries and, in turn, churches would likely be the best institutions to take on these three tasks. It was this conclusion that led him to write a series of essays applying his ideas to the seminaries.

There were several influences on his thinking about seminaries, most of which preceded his choice to focus on them as potential instruments of change (a fact that again illustrates the themes of readiness and preparation noted earlier). Several experiences with professors of ethics, especially his long friendship with Abraham Heschel, got him into seminaries and exposed him to their possibilities. Most of these people he had sought out in connection with his personal interests and his professional responsibilities for management research and development. Finally, Bob's consulting experience with churches and clergy provided him with first-hand exposure to seminaries.

From these and other experiences Bob concluded that seminaries are pivotal institutions; but similar to his evaluations of the performance of other institutions he had examined, he also concluded that most fall far short of achieving their potential, given their current mode and mission. Notwithstanding this shortfall, he saw seminaries as the base of prophetic thinking that guides and stimulates churches, and he saw churches as the most important institutions for nurturing the spirit of people and preparing some of them for the critical roles in society, including trusteeships.

Bob used as evidence of the potential for churches to be such positive forces the examples of The Church of the Saviour in Washington, D.C. and Westminster Presbyterian Church in Indianapolis.[10] But he also noted that both of these churches were led into such activities by their pastors, both of whom were personally oriented to such a mission, not from their exposure to such ideas in their seminary experiences.

To summarize the logic:

1. Some seminaries (a few are all that is necessary) will develop a theology of institutions and a theory of trusteeship.
2. They will set up laboratories called Institutes of Chairing to accomplish the development of the theory and to provide the necessary training.
3. This will support churches and give them prophetic vision.
4. The churches will develop more caring people
5. These people will become servant-leaders and servant-trustees.

Bob identifies the current constraint preventing seminaries from adopting this vision as the Biblical tradition of caring for individuals by individuals. The foundation of the seminaries is rooted in this tradition; therefore, their theology is a theology of individuals. The need is to enlarge this theology in keeping with the modern reality of large institutions mediating so much of the caring for individuals. I believe this insight to be one of Bob Greenleaf's major contributions to thinking on these issues.

For my part, I see a parallel between the resistance of seminaries to adopting this role and the resistance of managers in accepting the ideas in "The Institution as Servant." Both have their comfortable *modus operandi* threatened; both would be required to unlearn old habits and acquire new concepts and skills. So I remain highly skeptical not only of the likelihood of seminaries assuming the role and doing it sufficiently well to make a difference, but also of the eventual impact of such an effort, the "trickle-down theology" theory.

For all of Bob's conviction and persuasiveness, he still understood the difficulty of overcoming the inertia of the *status quo*. While he remained committed to the ideas of "starting where you are" and "one person acting one at a time," he was also savvy to the importance of help during a startup phase. He urged that one or two foundations stimulate one or two seminaries, which would be unlikely to assume the new mission without an infusion of both ideas and money.

It is important to note that project ideas rarely come from the beneficiaries of the work. Usually, they result from a "pull" strategy launched by the foundations, not requests by people or institutions who wanted to do the work. It is also worth noting that if foundations only see their roles as donors, as institutions who entertain proposals and fund those they like, then they are unlikely to see the possibilities for influencing change. Consequently, there would be little likelihood that seminaries would change; whereas that possibility would sharply increase if a foundation planted the idea and nourished it. The irony may be that the foundations, too, need better trustees who might shape more of those institutions to take on initiator roles. Foundation boards, too, need very strong and able people to take on trustee-servant responsibilities. Their large financial resources make them no more immune to that need than any institution in any society in human history.

This last observation gives rise to the question of how to nurture the spirit of people with the potential to take responsibility for leadership. Before examining this theme, I have attempted in Figure 5.1 to represent the "nesting" of the themes developed so far. This is one way of conceptualizing the logic of the evolution of Bob's ideas.

Nurturing the Human Spirit

The question of how to nurture the spirit of able people is the capstone idea that emerged at the end of Bob's career. Clearly, Bob's understanding of Morgan's influence on Vail and the loss of AT&T covenental spirit much later in the company's history was very important in his seeing the need for nurturing, even among very strong and experienced people. His 1934 trip to Europe, part of which was focused on understanding cooperatives, which he had seen in New York City as important institutions during the Depression, also gave him an early appreciation of spirit in nurturing others.

Another critical factor was the early influence of Gerald Heard, a remarkably broad thinker, who steered Bob toward reading biographies

Figure 5.1
The "Nesting" of the themes.

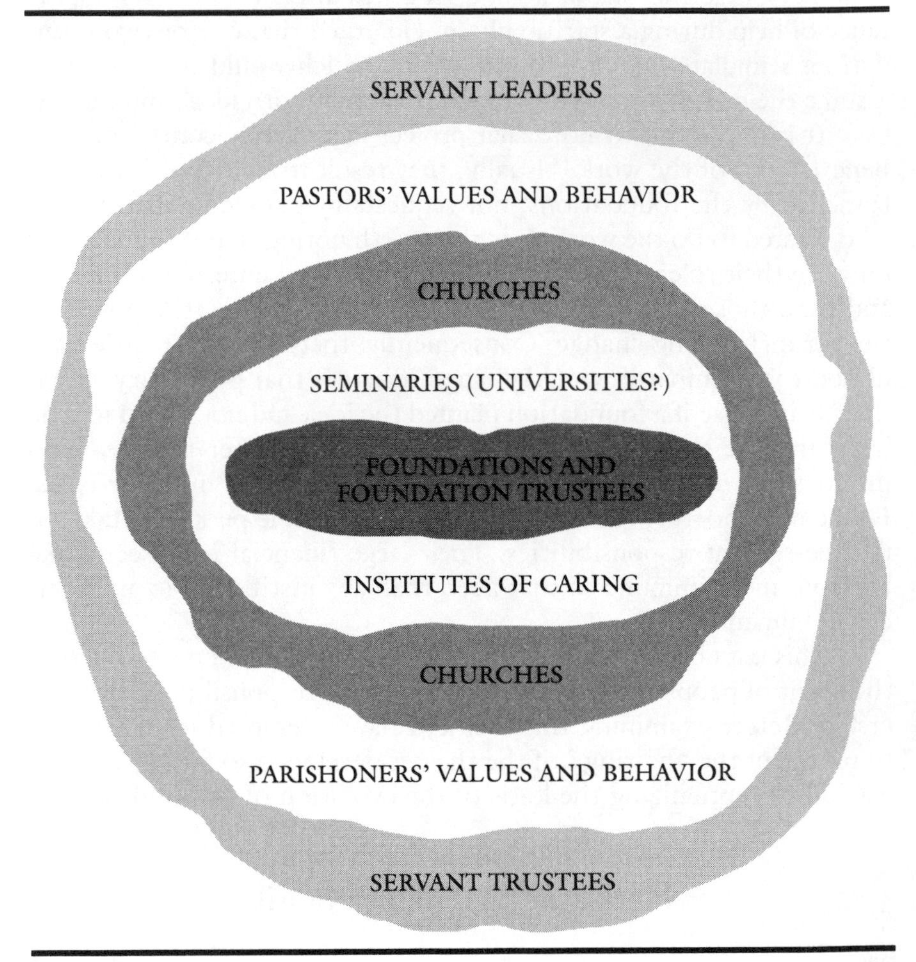

of great world figures. This, too, shaped the theme of nurturing the spirit, because so many great leaders credited their own effectiveness to their being nurtured by others. One example Bob wrote about was Pope John XXIII, who throughout his life was sustained by a great spirit. If he hadn't had such sustenance, he would likely have been ground down by 20 years of exile in Bulgaria and Turkey. Yet, after World War II, he was called on by Pope Pius XII to be the papal representative in Paris because he was the only bishop the Pope believed was capable of dealing with Charles de Gaulle.

How did this come about? By John's being *ready,* by his being *prepared.* He had been a great student of history, and had developed a keen patience rooted in his genuine humility. These qualities had been nurtured by three mentors who Pope John XXIII identified on his death bed as having been critical influences on his development. All, he said, loved him, believed in him, and helped him develop.

Another important element worth noting is receptiveness to nurturing. I have seen many senior people leading very large organizations who need nurturing and who show clear signs of *wanting* nurturing, but who resist or deny it when it is offered. Part of the determinant of such a reaction, of course, is how the nurturing is done. The indirect, subtle influence of the nurturer is so crucial. But another key factor is whether the nurturing of senior people is seen as "normal" or as "unusual." If it were legitimized as part of the formal responsibilities of one or two trustees, it would be easier for executives to accept without loss of face or status.

This leads back to how to prepare people for this delicate role of nurturing the spirit of potential leaders. The central element of the human spirit is essentially theological, and Bob saw it as a mystery. But how to address its development is not. I hope that Bob's urging of foundations and seminaries to take up this challenge will be grasped and developed in the coming years.

Let me conclude with a personal anecdote. My story goes back well over a decade to an infamous gathering, since hallowed with the special label of "The Brown County Meeting." Constantine Simonides, Paul Olson, Les Rollins, Lloyd Barber, and several others were gathered in Indianapolis to discuss Bob's manuscript of *Teacher as Servant,* then entitled *Jefferson House.* We were called together to think about how the ideas in the book might be advanced. It was a most unusual collection of people: a psychiatrist from Woods Hole, a physicist from MIT, a Seventh Day Adventist from Pennsylvania, a laid back California futurist, a president of a major corporation, a foundation executive, the head of an order of nuns—just a typical gathering of Bob's friends!

Because even a casual glance at the list made clear that there were no common threads for attending other than our association with Bob, we started the meeting by going around the table and describing how we knew Bob and why we had assembled there. I explained how I had met Bob, noted the frequent and enriching interactions I had had with him, and then said that I was there because I was a masochist. That *did* require some explanation, even with the wide assortment of idiosyncratic people who were there. I elaborated by noting that every time I had seen Bob, we would talk about a number of ideas; I would ask him two or three questions; he would neatly turn them around on me with Rogerian skill, and I would go away traumatized by the prospects of wrestling with them, knowing full well that our next conversation would inevitably start by his "innocently" asking what I had thought about the questions in the interim. Then I would go back to see him and the cycle would be repeated all over again. "If that isn't masochism," I exclaimed, "I don't know what is!" After appropriate chuckles and some nods reflecting similar experiences, others related their stories.

The next morning I joined the group at breakfast at a big table in the dining room. Bob and his wife Esther had been the most recent additions to the group, and I sat down in the chair next to Bob. Without a word he slipped his hand into the side pocket of my jacket and deposited the paper "tag line" from the top of a Salada tea bag which had magically appeared in his teacup a few minutes before. It read, "The pearl caused the oyster great pain." Now *that's* impact.

6

The Strategic Toughness of Servant-Leadership

Dennis L. Tarr

To most of us, the concept of servant-leadership falls into the category of one of those "impossible things." It is not a popular idea. At this time, when the need for dynamic leadership is apparent in so many areas of our society, the concept of servant-leadership does not seem to be appropriate. In fact, most people dismiss the idea as one of weakness because it doesn't fit in with our mood of assertiveness, of looking out for number one, or our desire for real power and influence. Yet to truly understand the servant as leader is to unlock a secret source of energy, of legitimate power, and of the kind of toughness needed to be an effective leader today. Furthermore, such an understanding is at the very heart of any enterprise; it is something we often forget, and its principles are directly applicable to those who wish to lead in many different professions.

What is meant by the term servant-leadership? Who are the servant-leaders? Can these two roles, seemingly contradictory, be combined in one real person and still function? In his exhaustive study of leadership, the *Handbook of Leadership: A Survey of Theory and Research,* Ralph M. Stogdill suggests that leadership is not popularity, not power, not showmanship, and not wisdom in long-range planning, although some leaders possess those skills. In its barest form, leadership is simply getting something done with the help of others. And that is the essence of Robert Greenleaf's work, *Servant Leadership.* Inspired by Albert Camus and other writers, Robert Greenleaf wrote in his book that each of us must confront the exacting terms of our own existence, and, like Sisyphus, "accept our rock and find our happiness in dealing with it." He quotes Camus's final paragraph of his last published lecture, entitled "Create Dangerously," as summing up his concern for the servant as leader:

> One may long, as I do, for a gentler flame, a respite, a pause for musing. But perhaps there is no other peace for the artist than what he finds in the heat of combat. "Every wall is a door," Emerson correctly said. Let us not look for the door, and the way out, anywhere but in the wall against which we are living. Instead, let us seek the respite where it is—in the very thick of battle. For in my opinion, and this is where I shall close, it *is* there. Great ideas, it has been said, come into the world as gently as doves. Perhaps, then, if we listen attentively, we shall hear, amid the uproar of empires and nations, a faint flutter of wings, the gentle stirring of life and hope. Some will say that this hope lies in a nation, others, in a man. I believe rather that it is awakened, revived, nourished by millions of solitary individuals whose deeds and works every day negate frontiers and the crudest implications of history. As a result, there shines forth fleetingly the ever-threatened truth that each and every person, on the foundations of his or her own sufferings and joys, builds for them all.

To be a servant-leader, Greenleaf suggests the person is a servant first. "It begins with the natural feeling that one wants to serve, to serve first. Then conscious choice brings one to aspire to lead." That person is sharply different from one who is leader first, perhaps because of the need to assist an unusual power drive or to acquire material possessions. The leader-first and the servant-first are different types. The difference is illustrated in the care taken by the servant-first to make sure that other people's highest priority needs are being served. Greenleaf suggests the difficult test to administer is: "Do those served grow as persons? Do they, while being served, become healthier, wiser, freer, more autonomous, more likely themselves to become servants?"

He acknowledges that as one sets out to serve another person, one can seldom know that the result will be as hoped. "This is part of the human dilemma; one cannot know for sure. One must, after some study and experience, hypothesize—but leave the hypothesis under a shadow of doubt . . ." He firmly believes that it is the natural servant, the person who is "servant-first," who is ". . . more likely to persevere and refine a particular hypothesis on what serves another's highest priority needs than is the person who is leader-first and who later serves out of promptings of conscience or in conformity with normative expectations."

Greenleaf, whose long experience in research and management in the private, corporate sector led him later to teach at Harvard and Dartmouth, applies the concept of servant-leadership to a variety of practical settings including nonprofit institutions, universities, boards of trustees, foundations and churches, as well as to business and the corporate world.

The servant-leader is a listener, is task-oriented, has a strategic sense, is eager to understand, to empathize and to collaborate, but does not escape becoming the target of many challenges and tests. Among the difficulties are the following:

1. Being empathetic presents a challenge. It is not easy to walk the second or third mile in someone else's shoes. None of us "likes" to do it. It's much easier to walk away from a problem or unpleasant task. In fact, it takes an exceedingly tough person to be a true listener, to be a person who can empathize with another.
2. To be empathetic and mutually collaborative requires the servant-leader, as the giver, to share something of himself or herself. To be open to another human being involves a risk and a vulnerability, but it brings with it great rewards.
3. The third difficulty has to do with the collaborative process itself. There are many problems inherent in any collaborative effort—just ask anyone who is married. Different goals, different beliefs and values, and different methodologies, to name just a few, are problems as persons attempt to work together. It takes perseverance and strength to be a servant-leader.

Why should one be a servant-leader? What practical application does the concept hold? Let me suggest several reasons:

1. *It works:* Not a small part of the set of recommendations or conclusions that Thomas J. Peters and Robert H. Waterman, Jr. reach in their best-selling work, *In Search of Excellence,* has to do with servant-leadership. Their "lessons from America's best-run companies" underscore the role of servant-leadership, including how to develop a caring attitude toward your employees and how such an attitude pays off, and how "hands on" management can encourage the team spirit that leads to increased productivity with commensurate rewards all around. A simple summary of their research is that excellent companies *really are* close to their customers—attempting to satisfy their needs and anticipating their wants. In fact, they subtitle a section on "service obsession." "Other companies talk about it; the excellent companies do it."
2. *It reinforces the nature of one's profession and calls upon its more noble instincts:* One of the great strengths of educators is their ability to be the bridge between the academy and the "real world," between inquiry and delivery, between the mountain and the people. The profession is primarily a service profession. In our desire and valiant efforts to be recognized and accepted as first-class citizens within the university, we often forget that our primary function is in the role of a servant, to bring people together, to collaborate, to cosponsor, to break down walls—real and imagined—to assist in the learning process. If we perform that task with quality and integrity, the questions of power and influence will take care of themselves.
3. *It is action-oriented:* To be a servant-leader is to be action-oriented. Someone rightly said, "If you want to be a servant, you'll never run out of things to do." There is always another piece of luggage to carry, another meeting to arrange, another article to write, another seminar to teach, another workshop to schedule. The agenda is full of tasks to be done because the needs of the adult learner in our rapidly changing environment are so wide and so urgent. But the actions needed go beyond the narrow day-to-day facilitating and brokering. They have to do with the larger agenda of the organization, the community, the region, and the nation. They have to do with the whole learning system in our society. They have to do with being in the right place at the right time, of having that strategic sense to make the connections between business and the university, to develop the kind of partnerships needed with government

and the media, and others, if the organization is to be an active participant in providing educational services to the adult in the emerging learning society.

For example, the goal of continuing education is not to increase the size of a particular school, division, or staff, or the development of a "discipline" such as continuing or adult education. It is much more important than any or all of those achievements. It is to infuse into the attitudinal structure of the essence of the college, the university, and of higher education itself, a commitment to serving the lifelong learning needs of society. And a key to bringing that about is to understand the strength and power of servant-leadership. There is much to be done, indeed.

4. *Servant leadership is a commitment to the celebration of people and their potential:* After all is said and done, one of the reasons so many of us stay in the profession of continuing education is the fundamental belief that what we are about is the celebration of people and their potential. While most of us are committed to tilting the university where we are employed in the direction of making a solid commitment to providing educational opportunities to persons throughout their lives, which is no small objective, we need to rediscover the kind of toughness which is required to help bring that about through servant-leadership.

In the August 1984, issue of *INC. Magazine,* Tom Peters reflected on the things he learned since he published, with Robert H. Waterman, Jr., their popular book on excellence. One of the items he listed is that there are only three distinctive "areas of competence" in successful companies:

1. They have superior customer service.
2. They have an internal entrepreneurship.
3. The successful company or university or continuing education program has a "bone-deep" belief in the dignity, worth, and creative potential in *every* person in the organization.

It is precisely that kind of contagious spirit that the servant-leader brings to his or her chosen profession. And it is precisely that kind of spirit that ultimately will never lose.

PART TWO

The Emerging Model of Servant-Leadership

7

Servant-Leadership Training and Discipline in Authentic Community*

M. Scott Peck

Servant leadership is more than a concept. As far as I'm concerned, it is a fact. I would simply define it by saying that any great leader, by which I also mean an ethical leader of any group, will see herself or himself primarily as a servant of that group and will act accordingly. I'm talking not only about servant-leadership but also about authentic community. And right away that implies that there is such a thing as "unauthentic" community.

Words have a way of being distorted over time and cultures. One such word is "community." We tend to refer to Morristown, New Jersey, as a community or to the Third Presbyterian Church of Morristown as a community, when the fact of the matter is that Morristown is nothing but a geographical aggregate of people who

*(Based on a talk at The Greenleaf Center's 1993 Servant Leadership conference.)

have a certain tax base and a few social services in common, but precious little else that relates them together as human beings. And, sight unseen, I can pretty much tell you that the Third Presbyterian Church is not likely to be much of a community. I can say that because, when I go around lecturing, I ask people not to ask me questions during the break. Invariably, though, somebody will come up and ask me a question. When I respond by saying that I don't want to be disturbed, they'll say, "Yes, but I can't ask about this in the group because some of the members of my church are here." There are a few exceptions, but I am talking about the norm, the normal level of intimacy and vulnerability and community that exists in the places we'd most hope to find it, like our churches. People sitting in the same pew together, but not able to talk to each other about the things that are most important because they hide themselves behind their masks of composure. This is what I call unauthentic community.

Then what is "authentic" community? Unfortunately, there are some words, all of which have something to do with God—like love and prayer—that have never been adequately defined over the centuries, and one of those is community. It is too big for any adequate definition, but there are a couple of things that I can say about it. For the last few years, my wife Lily and I have been involved with the Foundation for Community Encouragement (FCE). Those of us at FCE use the word community not just to apply to a geographical aggregate of people, but to one that has made a specific commitment to each other, to learn how to communicate with each other at an ever more deep and authentic level. For us, community has to do with a commitment to communicate authentically.

There are many other possible definitions. For instance, a community may be any group that deals with its own issues. That may seem rather bland to you, but I can assure you that most business corporations, families, and other groups do not deal adequately with their own issues. A community may also be any group that deals with its own shadow, or a group where everyone feels safe and free to offer their gifts of leadership. By definition, everyone who is working in a true community is struggling, learning to know something about how to be servant leaders. Consider these six points:

1. There are technologies for community building, peace-making, and consensual decision-making. There is a technology for the training of servant-leaders. All of these are the same. Community building,

consensual decision-making, training of servant leaders, peacemaking—it's all the same business when you get down to the details. Just as we have developed a technology over the last 60 years to blow ourselves off the face of the earth, we have very quietly and unbeknownst to most people developed a technology of peacemaking. This technology has come from many quarters. Parts of it come from Alcoholics Anonymous and the 12-step programs. Other pieces come from Christian Monastism, the Quakers, the old sensitivity group movement, the Tavistock model, and management consulting—including, very definitively, from Robert K. Greenleaf. When FCE started, we thought that we were just teaching people how to build community. It gradually dawned on us that we were also teaching servant-leadership. So there's also a technology of servant-leadership training.

2. This technology is analogous to software. Software, as you know, is what one feeds into the hardware to teach it to operate. This technology is a system of rules that are fed experientially into human beings to teach them how to operate effectively and healthily in groups. And a system of rules can also be defined as a discipline. A discipline is a collection of interrelated rules. Disciplines can be taught, to a certain extent. So this technology, this discipline, can compose what might be called a pedagogy, a system of teaching.

3. There's nothing magical about this technology. One of the reasons I hesitate to use the word technology is because, to people like me, technology is something magical. But there is nothing magical about this technology. These rules are not different than the rules of love, except that we don't know much about the rules of love—particularly in groups. These very complex and paradoxical rules need to be specified, but, they are rules of love and they are the rules of how to be a servant-leader. Being a servant leader is not a simple business. It is a very complicated business.

4. Technology works. I like the technology analogy, because we have technology that works. Suppose you could take five Anglos, 15 Boers, and 35 blacks and put them in the same room and get them to agree to learn this technology. Within the course of three or four days, they would come out of that room not only caring deeply about each other, but able to work together with profound efficiency and effectiveness. Of course, the first problem is getting

them in that same room to learn this. If you can do that, the technology would work.

5. This technology, which includes the technology of servant-leadership training, can be learned only by doing, and be sustained only by practice. Some old fogies like me had well-developed lifestyles by the time computers came along, and we never took the time to learn how to use them. Hence, we remain forever computer-illiterate. You can't learn about computers by listening to somebody talk about them or by reading a book about them. You've go to *do* computers. And so it is, with the technology of servant-leadership: You cannot really learn about servant leadership by hearing about it, you've got to do it. You've got to practice to learn it, and you've got to practice to sustain it.

   I could give you several examples of major businesses that have used servant-leadership training, or community building, at times of terrible crisis and have worked themselves out of the crisis. Practicing servant-leadership and community building had absolutely enormous benefits for them. Then they threw it away. Why? Because, as soon as the crisis passed, they said, "Why exert ourselves?" The problem is not how to build community or teach servant-leadership in the first place, but to get organizations to continue to use it and imbed it into their culture.

6. There is currently enormous resistance worldwide to learning this technology and practicing it. It may interest you to know that as far as I can ascertain, the resistance is greater in the United States than any place else.

Four Stages of Community Building

Since you've got to *do* this to learn it, I'm going to describe what happens at FCE's community building workshops. The same dynamics go on whether we are working with an organization or business or some other organization of people who know each other, who have a past and a future together.

The groups go through four stages. We did not invent these stages, they have been described by management consultants for years, but we have names for them that I think are more descriptive than others. We call these four stages pseudocommunity, chaos, emptiness, and true community.

Pseudocommunity

When you gather a group of people together, the first thing they do whether they are strangers in a public workshop or people in the business is pretend that they are already a community. The basic pretense is that we are all the same, that we all have the same dislike of Ronald Reagan and the same belief in Jesus Christ. This pretense is maintained by manners, a set of unwritten rules that everybody knows. For instance, you should do your very best not to say anything that offends, antagonizes, alienates, or upsets anybody else. If someone else says something that offends, antagonizes, alienates, or upsets you, you should pretend that absolutely nothing has happened and that it hasn't bothered you in the least. If a disagreement starts to surface, you should change the subject. These are rules that any good hostess knows, right? It makes for a very smooth-functioning dinner party, but it has nothing to do with reality or authentic communication.

One of the ways in which this pretense is maintained is by speaking in generalizations: "One does this." "People feel that." And so on. Our leaders teach that it is easier and quicker to achieve a sense of community if people speak personally and use "I, my" statements.

Chaos

When individual differences are not only allowed but encouraged to surface, the group will evolve into chaos. Chaos can be very painful and unpleasant, but is one step closer to reality than pseudocommunity.

In a pseudocommunity, the basic premise is to pretend that there are no differences. In chaos, the basic premise is to try to eliminate the differences by converting or healing people out of them. It works something like this: Somebody says, "The reason I came to this workshop was because I have this little problem and I thought I might get a solution here." This statement says nothing that reveals too much about the speaker, but at least it's an admission of a problem. A second person, in trying to take care of the speaker or fix the problem, will say, "I had that problem once and I did this. I went out running (or something) and that took care of it." The first person might then say, "I tried that, and it didn't work for me." Then a third person might say, "Well, I acknowledged Jesus to be my Lord and Savior, and that took care of that problem and every other problem in my life." But the first person might respond, "I'm sorry, but that 'Jesus, Lord, and Savior' bit just doesn't really grab me. It's not where I'm at, at the moment." Still another person will add, "As a matter of fact, it makes me want to puke." A fifth person might rebut, "But it's true!" And they're off.

There's a term therapists use; it's "resistance," which refers to people who don't like to or want to be healed or converted, so they resist. After a while, the healers try harder, and the converters try harder, until their victims finally get their backs up against the wall and turn around and try to heal the healers and convert the converters. It's absolutely glorious chaos. After a while, therapists say, "We don't seem to be doing very well at achieving community." Somebody else says, "No, it's because of this." Somebody else says, "No, it's because of that." And, they're at it again. Generally, people would rather fight than switch. It's easier.

After a while, it's time to take a long break. It's time to think about where we are going wrong—because we obviously are doing something very wrong. If you're into prayer, it's time to pray; if you're not, it's time to be quiet and reflective.

Emptiness

After the break, the group usually will begin to move from chaos into the third stage—emptiness. People are absolutely terrified of emptiness. They sit there and think, "If we're not here to heal and fix each other and convert, what on earth are we doing here and what is all this about and what's he going to talk next about, and maybe it will be me . . ."

The most common strategy people use to avoid the discomfort of emptiness is to form themselves into organizations and subcommittees to debate the meaning of emptiness and derive at a definition of true community. But, as we point out to them, an organization in and of itself is never community. And the only way—with or without organization—out of chaos to community is into and through emptiness. In this crucial stage of emptiness, the group will slowly and effortfully begin to empty itself of everything that stands between its members and community. Many of these things that need to be emptied are just human universals, prejudices that we all have, prejudices against fat people, old people, young people and so on. Or expectations that we have about what a workshop is going to be like. People also form instant likes and dislikes. We are often so busy trying to make something or someone conform to our expectations that we are not even able to experience the thing or the person. We need to empty ourselves of our need to heal and fix and convert, which is usually terribly selfish. This is part of the technology that came from AA. It is also something that Greenleaf talked about in terms of the arrogance of helping.

I talked about emptiness in *The Road Less Traveled,* where I referred to it in terms of "bracketing." We don't have to totally eliminate theology or ideology, but we have to bracket it, to set it aside so we can listen. For instance, how many of us are so busy preparing our reply to what somebody is saying that we aren't able to hear that person? It's universal. Another thing that is really a bugaboo for leaders is the need to control. These are universals.

There also are particulars. Somebody might come back from the end of the break and say, "Well, I realized during the silence that I have to empty myself of my anger at my mother. I am so angry at her that I haven't even been able to hear anything that's been going on for three weeks now." This can be very painful. It has to do with giving up and sacrifice. A man who came to one of the early workshops was an older man with a hard, somewhat depressed face. I liked him immediately. Although I didn't know it at the time, he was quite a famous man, and, like many famous men, a workaholic, in his late sixties. About three hours into the workshop, as we had begun to talk about emptiness, this man suddenly punched his chest and said, "Oh my God, I'm scared. It feels like I'm dying. I'm terrified." People started gathering around, thinking that he was having a heart attack. He said, "This business about emptiness, I mean I don't have to do anything? All my life I've done things. You mean I don't have to do anything?" And his wife said, "No, Harry, you don't." This is a very scary realization. And not only for individuals, but for groups as a whole. Somebody, speaking for the group will say, "This isn't what I expected. This is like dying." Afterward they will refer to it as "that bad period." The most difficult part of being a leader is to sometimes sit helplessly by, without being able to speed up the process, watching a group in its death throes. But die it does.

True Community

There is a particular moment when death comes, and it is magical. There will be a silence, and it will come in on a spirit of peace that literally pervades the room. It is palpable. Then somebody will start talking at a level far more deep and authentic than anyone had previously touched. Then there will be another silence. Another person starts talking about himself or herself at that same deep level, often without mentioning the first. But the feeling one gets is not that the first has been ignored but that the second person goes up and lays himself or herself on the altar next to the first person. There will be another silence. And then a third person will start talking in that same deep authentic level, or will make a remark that is more pithy and pointed, and appropriate than anything that has been said thus far. In short order, community will have been born. A great deal of grief and joy will be expressed. And a great deal of healing and converting will begin to occur when people have learned how to stop trying to heal and convert. Community will have been born.

I mentioned silence. One of the things that characterizes a true community is silence. Once a group gets into true community, half as many words are spoken, and two to three times as much is said. As a famous opera singer once told me, "You know Scotty, more than half of Beethoven is silence." You can't have music without silence.

Community Building as Servant-Leadership

This process of building community constitutes a pedagogy of servant-leadership in many more ways than I can possibly detail here. I've talked about how it teaches emptiness. This is the most crucial thing. It teaches people how to empty themselves, how to really listen. How to change. How to give up expectations. It teaches an increased consciousness. Consciousness of themselves, consciousness of other people, increased awareness of interpersonal differences, and, above all, consciousness of the group. FCE teaches consciousness of the group, becoming aware of the group that you're in. It is something about which most people have very little understanding. How is this board operating? How is this organization operating that I'm a part of?

It has now become a standard part of this technology that, toward the beginning of a workshop, our leaders will tell people that building community has to do with communication. Among the innumerable sins of communication two of the greatest are: speaking when you're not moved, and not speaking when you are moved. The latter, of course, is a form of disobedience. Think of the complex technology there—monitoring what's in you and the spiritual aspects of this. What these community-building experiences do is give people a basic course on building not only community, but on becoming servant-leaders.

Advanced Education of Servant-Leaders

Robert Greenleaf was a great prophet. He was prophetic in realizing that we need to identify, nurture, and train servant-leaders in our society. How pregnant his works were. Yet he really offered us very little as to how to identify, nurture, and train servant-leaders. FCE has had the experience of identifying and training leaders to lead people, and to teach servant-leadership. We've worked with leaders to update their training, and monitored them. I'm going to run through some things that we have learned thus far in this business.

1. Servant-leaders are both born and made. This simply confirms something that Greenleaf repeatedly suggested: You can, to a certain degree, teach servant-leadership, but you can't totally make a servant leader. It's a sad reality. FCE selects its leaders based on certain criteria. One is a sense of humor. I think a servant-leader has to have a sense of humor, and I defy you to try to take someone who has no sense of humor and teach him or her to have a sense of humor.
2. Substantial identification, advanced training, and nurturance of servant-leaders can probably only be done in the context of a complex organization with either a primary or a major secondary mission of training and nurturing servant-leaders. For FCE, it is a secondary mission. Our major mission is to teach community, but we must train the trainers and teach the teachers.
3. The desire to be a servant-leader is not the same as having a calling to be a servant-leader. Simply because someone wants to be one doesn't mean that he or she will be one, or could be one, or could be a good one. This confirms something that Greenleaf suggested and what monastic experience teaches: that just because someone wants to be a monk or nun doesn't necessarily mean that God is calling that person to be a monk or nun. Sometimes it is necessary to make absolutely brutal decisions and say, "I'm sorry, but we don't think that you have a calling, despite your desire." So, there has to be selection. Selection can only be done in an organizational setting. It should never be done by an individual. I don't think it possibly could be. It needs to be done by a board of senior servant-leaders within the organization.
4. The selection process must be done experientially and intuitively. We have criteria for our leaders, but after we go through them and

ask whether this candidate for a leader meets this criteria, then we throw out the criteria and make our final judgment intuitively. Our leaders have agreed that this is the only way it can be made. It also has to be made experientially, and that means having experience with the person. You cannot do it with some kind of test they have filled out, or by looking at them. You must work with them in this community-building process or some other work setting. We are not the only organization to have discovered this. The Peace Corps used to have elaborate psychological and psychiatric testing for new members. On the basis of that testing and examination, they rejected about 60 percent of applicants. The remaining 40 percent were trained and sent overseas. They had an absolutely atrocious attrition rate, drop-out rate, and psychiatric casualty rate. Clearly, it wasn't working. They learned something from the military, revised the system, and now have no psychiatric or psychological examination for candidates. They admit everyone who meets the other qualifications for training. They don't weed out people until the end of a six-week or two-month training period, after they have had the experience of seeing the candidates in action and evaluating how they handle the training. It has to be done experientially.

5. Effective servant-leaders don't always stay effective. Consequently, there has to be ongoing monitoring. One of our single greatest FCE leaders, for instance—an absolute genius who designed much of our training—had to be put on an extended leave of absence because of a mixture of drug and psychological problems. He went from being a genius to being destructive. What happens to servant leaders when they get tired? I don't know whether I'm a servant-leader, but I am getting tired. You know, T.S. Eliot once said, "Middle age is when they keep asking you to do more and more, and you're not yet decrepit enough to turn them down." I am about to declare myself decrepit. So, servant-leaders can go over the hill or around the bend. They need to be monitored. This is one of the reasons we always send our leaders out in pairs. It is one means of checking up on each other.

6. Although there has to be a rigid selection process, I support liberal selection criteria. After we have selected leaders; done their initial training; and decided to keep them on, we divide them into primary leaders, secondary leaders, interns, and those who still

need more training before we send them in as interns. We are very glad we have done this over the years. A number of the people we have held back for more training, have grown astonishingly over the years. Many have moved up, and some have moved down, whereas some of the primary leaders became secondary leaders or were deselected. Be liberal, because most of the people in this work grow.

7. The training must be experiential in a variety of ways. That means experiential in an organizational setting, in role-playing, and in didactic training. The best experiential training is not only in workshops and role-playing, but in working in organizations, where one must actually function as a servant-leader.

8. Training needs to be ongoing because servant-leadership and community leadership, whether you are aware of it, is a frontier. It is going to be the job of servant-leaders to continually push the frontier to learn how to do it better. This is never going to be a static art.

9. The training itself should be nurturing. If it isn't, there is something wrong with the trainers or trainees or the organization and its norms, in selecting, training, and nurturing servant-leaders. The same thing is true in organizational life. If organizational life does not nurture servant-leaders, then something is wrong—particularly if the organization includes the training of servant-leaders as part of its mission.

10. Expectations of nurturance can tend to be excessive. An organization's obligation to be nurturing must be finite. This is what Greenleaf was referring to when he talked about unlimited liability. It is an area—about the only area I can think of—that I take any issue with him. A corporation's obligation to be nurturing needs to be as limited and specific as possible. Otherwise, people are going to get confused and expect the organization to be "Mommy and Daddy," and give them more than the organization can give.

11. One of the major changes we've made in FCE over the years is ceasing to use the word community as a noun; we use it as a verb. Community is something you do. It is a mode in which we operate. For instance, the board of FCE is not a community; it is a board of a business organization that chooses to operate in a

community mode for most of the time when it meets. So we refer to community as a way of operating, rather than a thing.

12. Last, the training of servant-leaders is an inherently spiritual business that is inseparable from selection and deselection. When you select and deselect people, you are already training people for what you want and what you expect of them. The process must be taught both by example and through the organizational culture. You cannot teach spirituality, except by example through culture. For example, at FCE the one value that takes precedence over all of our other values is integrity, which I suggest is a spiritual value. People bring integrity with them. It's one of the ways in which servant-leaders are born. We teach that integrity is submission, submission to the group, to the needs of the group, and not to the desires of the group. Occasionally, leaders need to "die for the group," on an emotional level.

The last sentence of FCE's mission statement, a strange sentence to be in any organization's mission statement reads, "As we seek to encourage others, so we remember our reliance upon a spirit both within and beyond ourselves." While I think there is no question that being a servant-leader is, in the long run, more educational and growth-producing for the leader himself or herself than any other style of leadership, I think the burdens of servant-leadership sometimes are overlooked. Among other things, I think that the genuine servant-leader is going to bear far more pain than a person who is not a servant-leader. I know men and women who can fire people without a qualm; a servant-leader cannot do this. It will be necessary, no matter how hard you work at community and how good a servant-leader you are, from time to time to fire people. And, for the servant-leader, it's going to hurt like hell. After a while, one of the things that tires people is the pain.

There is something about this work of servant-leadership and community building that is inherently ethical. An unethical mission is simply not compatible with community. Otherwise, there are virtually no limitations. Organizational structure and community, rather than being incompatible, *are* potentially synergistic.

8

The Search for Spirit in the Workplace

Chris Lee and Ron Zemke

Even during the summer, cold, soul-numbing winds hold a wintry grip on the corporate landscape. The litany should be familiar by now. The *Fortune 500,* the largest manufacturers in the country, have eliminated some four million jobs since 1982. Former icons of corporate stability—General Motors, Digital Equipment Co., IBM—are scrambling to survive by closing plants and slashing jobs. In the new global marketplace, there's no guarantee you'll have a job, a company, or a career next week.

The current symbol of success? General Electric and its CEO, Jack Welch. Welch, one of America's 10 toughest bosses (according to *Fortune*), has turned his company into "the world's most powerful corporation" (according to *Forbes*) by selling $11 billion worth of existing GE businesses, buying $26 billion of new businesses, cutting head count by 300,000 people, and doubling managerial span of control. As the ex-CEOs of General Motors, IBM, American Express, and Sunbeam-Oster found out, there are no executive exceptions to the order of the day: Get tough, get results, or get out.

Welcome to the 1990s. The wonderful world of work has become a place where effort can count for little and longevity for nothing. The only rock-solid thing to hang on to is the assurance that whatever you thought was true last week will have changed by Monday morning.

In an environment racked with stress, insecurity, tough decisions, and 60-hour weeks, you might expect a resurgence of a management model based on Machiavelli's Prince, Leona Helmsley, or some other Theory-X icon. Instead, there's a stirring in the opposite direction: A flood of management books, articles, and musings try to make sense of the current chaos by proposing a management model filled with heart—and soul.

Consider some of the best-selling business books of recent years: *Zapp! The Lightning of Empowerment, Leadership Is an Art, Managing from the Heart,* and *The Republic of Tea.* All of them envision a workplace where managers and workers alike share a deep sense of purpose and meaning. The spring catalog from Berrett-Koehler, a San Francisco-based business book publisher, featured Peter Block's new book, *Stewardship: Choosing Service Over Self-Interest,* and listed several new titles that share a distinctive flavor: *Reawakening the Spirit in Work: The Power of Dharmic Management; The Healing Manager: How to Build Quality Relationships and Productive Cultures at Work; The Fourth Wave: Business in the 21st Century; Leadership and the New Science: Learning about Organization from an Orderly Universe.*

All of these books can be said to spring from a particular school of thought. Its guiding spirit was a devout Quaker management researcher named Robert K. Greenleaf, whose gentle precepts and 25-year-old essay, "The Servant as Leader," give us a label for this loosely woven movement: servant-leadership.

According to Greenleaf's philosophy, leaders exist only to serve their followers. Indeed, they earn followers only by virtue of their selfless, Gandhiesque natures. Servant-leadership emphasizes service to others, a holistic approach to work, personal development, and shared decision-making— characteristics that place it squarely in the mainstream of conventional talk about empowerment, total quality, and participative management.

But it goes beyond that. Greenleaf's philosophy is unabashedly spiritual, yet it's finding a home in the secular world of the corporation. It seems to have tapped into a growing need to find comfort and meaning in the stressed-out, insecure workplace of the '90s.

Why This?

Though the servant-leader philosophy complements the movement toward more openness and participation and a less-directing management style, why has this particular approach earned such a warm reception? After all, we're basically talking about the ideal of the participative manager who respects the skills and abilities of employees and sees himself or herself as coach, mentor, and facilitator rather than as a taskmaster. That's not exactly new.

As early as 1943, Abraham Maslow advanced a theory of human motivation that held that work—along with play and myriad other activities—could allow people to fulfill fundamental needs. In the '50s, motivational theorist Douglas McGregor proposed what he called the "Theory Y" view of employees, in which he encouraged managers to view their people as responsible, ambitious, energetic, ingenious, and creative. This set of assumptions led to a management style that emphasized trust and respect. McGregor contrasted Theory Y with "Theory X" assumptions, or the "commonly held" set of beliefs that say workers by nature dislike hard work and are lazy, untrustworthy, and resistant to change.

A few years later, researcher Frederick Herzberg demonstrated that McGregor's theories were correct. Employees who were given positive feedback, increased responsibility, greater opportunity, challenging work, and recognition for their performance worked harder and accomplished more. They also were more satisfied with their jobs than employees managed under Theory-X assumptions.

From the 1950s to the present, the literature of work has been dominated by social scientists—Kurt Lewin, Robert Blake, Jane Mouton, Rensis Likert, William Ouchi, Tom Peters, and Robert Waterman, to name a few—who view employees as responsible and trustworthy. The human potential movement of the '70s was nothing if not a manifesto of individuality in the workplace, with different strokes for different folks as its acoustical theme song. Peter Drucker, today's premier management thinker, summed up this recurrent view when he suggested, only half in jest: "Management's job is to find out what it is doing that keeps people from doing a good job, and stop doing it."

But members of this new school of thought step beyond the assumption that employees are responsible and worthy of trust. In *Leadership Is an Art*, for example, Max DePree, chairman of Herman

Miller, the office-furniture manufacturer in Zeeland, MI, begins with the premise that participative management is the most effective contemporary practice. But he ends up in a place where leaders create covenantal relationships (bonds that fulfill deep needs and give work meaning) with employees and the purpose of the corporation is redemption, not profit. "We need to weigh the pragmatic in the clarifying light of the moral," writes DePree. "We must understand that reaching our potential is more important than reaching our goals."

In *New Traditions in Business*, a collection of essays, contributor Michael L. Ray writes: "The gateway from the old paradigm to the new is the individual, and changes in the individual come from the inside, from inner consciousness or spirit. People involved in business transformation have come to it out of their own personal transformation." Another contributor, Charles F. Kiefer, unequivocally states, "The essence of leadership stems from the leader's soul rather than from his or her behavior."

Why the sudden interest in an implicitly *spiritual* idea of the manager as steward, the leader as servant? There are two separate streams of explanation: business reasons and social reasons.

Heading the list of business reasons is an upheaval in organizational structure. The traditional middle-manager roles have changed, as have the people who fill those slots in organizations. Historically, middle managers performed two functions: They acted as information conduits and straw bosses. Over the past decade, the rise of information technology, employee participation and self-direction have eroded those roles. Senior management has at its fingertips the same data as does middle management—and at about the same time. Nor does the production of quality goods and services any longer depend much on direct, line-of-sight supervision by a manager.

The people who hold middle-management positions—those who remain after the rampant downsizing and flattening of the past few years—have changed as well. Who are they? *Fortune* calls them "nonmanager managers" and identifies them as—you guessed it—baby boomers who bring a new set of values to the workplace: "The 78 million Americans born between 1946 and 1964 tend to be an irreverent bunch. Many don't see the CEO as much of a hero. In fact, they often think the big guy gets in the way. They like to call themselves leaders, facilitators, sponsors—anything but managers." To this new breed, "boss" is a four-letter word.

More important, these nonmanagers don't want to be stuck in the "between" role of simply passing paper up and down the pyramid.

They want bigger goals: creating new business, solving major problems, setting challenging visions, and helping the people who do the work.

The boomer manager's desire to be first among teammates—instead of "the boss"—fits pretty well with the wants and needs of the formerly governed, equally independent doers. Geoffrey M. Bellman, author of *The Quest for Staff Leadership* and *Getting Things Done When You're Not in Charge,* sees the servant-leader/manager-steward concept as both a philosophy and a response to an implicit demand. "People don't want managers anymore," he says. "They want leaders. And the leaders they want aren't out of the old kind of paternalistic or autocratic molds." Many of today's workers want manager/leaders who add their own unique perspectives and skills to a self-directed, participative environment but don't dominate it, says Bellman. In other words, they want a manager who helps, not one who controls.

He sees people searching for their own leadership qualities as well as for leaders who can help them find that sense of independence in themselves. "They want leaders who can help them work better and lead their lives better. Servant-leadership and stewardship have to do with how I identify myself in that part of my life, that community called work."

In *Stewardship: Choosing Service Over Self-Interest,* Block defines stewardship as "the willingness to be accountable for the well-being of the larger organization by operating in service, rather than in control, of those around us. Stated simply, it is accountability without control or compliance." To him, the leader-as-servant movement is an exercise in "what-if": What if we really didn't need managers or leaders? What would that kind of workplace look like?

"Stewardship is an argument against leadership," he says. "Stewardship is less prescriptive. It has more to do with being accountable and being responsible for what's been created than it does with defining, prescribing and telling others what to do." The real issues, he says, are power, control, and choice. Stewardship is not a single guiding principle but part of a triumvirate that includes empowerment and partnership. "The principles of stewardship bring accountability while partnership balances responsibility."

Leadership is just a word for a manager playing the role of parent, Block contends, if it is exercised as a caretaking function—that is, if the leader takes responsibility for the well-being of others. In an organization of adults, that is demeaning. "The question, 'How would partners handle this?' and 'What policy or structure would we create if this were a partnership?' are the most useful questions I know in the search for the alternative to patriarchy."

Why Now?

The appeal of the spiritual side of the servant-leader concept becomes clear if you stand it against the backdrop of larger social trends. For one thing, talk of spirituality or religion is no longer taboo or automatically suspect. When the buttoned-down editorial page of *The Wall Street Journal* applauds mystic actress Shirley MacLaine for giving a speech castigating the members of the American Society of Newspaper Editors for their condescending attitude toward religion, *something* is going on. Paraphrasing MacLaine, the editorial said, "Contrary to received wisdom . . . spiritual and religious values and those of a free democratic society go hand in hand. . . . A pity Ms. MacLaine's remarks aren't posted in newsrooms around the country."

Time magazine, for one, seems to have taken MacLaine's suggestions to heart. It even featured a cover story, "The Church Search," that examined the baby-boom generation's quest for a spiritual home. It seems that midlife crises combined with economic insecurity are persuading some boomers to return to their childhood religions, some to turn to unconventional churches, and some to the various 12-step programs of the "recovery" movement.

With the 40-something generation searching for soul, self, and meaning wherever it can find them, the workplace is not out of bounds. Connecticut psychiatrist M. Scott Peck, author of *The Road Less Traveled* and *A World Waiting to be Born* sees no reason why a spiritual rebirth couldn't or shouldn't happen in the workplace as easily as in a church. It is, after all, where most people spend most of their time.

This yearning for a spiritual connection in the workplace doesn't surprise Stephen R. Covey, author of *The 7 Habits of Highly Effective People,* a book with an implicit spiritual base that was on *Publisher's Weekly's* top 10 best-selling nonfiction books for more than 120 weeks. "Something very, very profound is going on," Covey says. "It is a true metamorphosis inside our society. I haven't any question about it at all. People have had it with giving their whole lives to a business. I'm sensing a lot of imbalance, an awareness of a hollowness in people's lives."

Out of this, Covey sees a trend: People are determinedly seeking spiritual and moral anchors in their lives and in their work. He attributes it to a trio of factors, using the metaphor of a stream with three primary currents: "One is just the sheer pain of the global marketplace and the deterioration of our society. That has been a chronic thing, but it has become so acutely painful that [people] are really paying attention now. The second current is the awareness that there are no quick fixes; there is no instant way to deal with the pain. Finally, people are feeling a need for values and principles that don't change."

"Top managers today make more decisions in one month than their grandparents made in a lifetime," adds Kenneth Blanchard, coauthor of the one-minute manager book series and coauthor with Norman Vincent Peale of *The Power of Ethical Management.* "People can't know what's going on in a traditional sense," he says. "And when people become unsure, the spiritual becomes important again."

The servant-leadership model allows managers to share their "not knowingness," says Blanchard. It allows them to turn to the collective wisdom of the group—employees, customers, suppliers, all the stakeholders—to glean knowledge. But managers won't be able to do that without a spiritual awareness that allows them to "open up to their own vulnerabilities and become willing to listen."

Blanchard suggests that all managers would profit from taking to heart the first three steps of 12-step programs: Admit their vulnerability, acknowledge there is a higher power, and get their lives in line with it. "It will change their lives," he says. "I'm talking about this all the time now. No one's getting upset. People don't say, 'You're crazy.'"

Fuzzy Lines

Should any of this come as a surprise? For years, a multitude of experts has been urging managers to turn themselves into leaders: people who create inspiring visions for their organizations, who embody values that provide a higher purpose for the enterprise, and who operate according to ethical verities. We've hailed spirit as the foundation for business success; the next step to the spiritual isn't a giant one.

"There is a sacred aspect to good leadership training," muses Randall White, director of specialized client applications at the Center for Creative Leadership (CCL) in Greensboro, North Carolina. "We talk about the idea of becoming committed to being a better person, and treating others as you'd want to be treated. For years, we've been talking about flipping over the organizational pyramid and serving all the people." In leadership training, and in the most progressive organizations, he says, the emphasis has shifted from looking at knowledge, skills, and behaviors to examining values, attitudes, and beliefs.

Values-driven organizations create credos and lay down rules about how employees will interact in the interest of the community, White says. That spurs personal mission statements and a search for answers to questions like "Who am I?" "Who are we?" "Where are we going?"

At the same time, most American workers have lost the sense of security and identification with the company that gave meaning to their work lives. Now, they are searching for a connection—a commitment to something larger to replace that lost dependence on the corporation. White theorizes that building a bridge between the secular and sacred worlds may be a natural outgrowth of this search for meaning and identity. Given the flurry of downsizings during the past few years, he says, "it's little wonder people are turning to a higher order to find meaning."

Hyler Bracey, president of the Atlanta Consulting Group, is coauthor of *Managing from the Heart*, a book that suggests managers need more than competence and confidence; they also need to be caring. He, too, sees the spiritual component of servant-leadership as a natural progression in management thought and literature. In Bracey's view, Greenleaf was ahead of his time. Over the last 50 years, he says, "We've evolved from treating workers as machines to realizing that they have feelings, and we could get them to be more responsive if we acknowledged that."

The profound change Bracey sees occurring in the '90s is twofold: One factor is a growing preoccupation among individuals with the spiritual side of life. "They've begun to think, 'There must be a bigger purpose here than my BMW and my job.'" The second is the acceptance of the whole person in the workplace. "We used to pretend that people didn't show up at work with their sexuality—now it's okay to talk about sexual harassment. We used to check our feelings, health, sexuality, spirituality, and family problems at the door of the workplace. We've matured enough to get beyond that. The unspeakable is now acceptable."

Bracey predicts we'll soon see Bible study groups and other groups grappling with spiritual questions in the workplace. In fact, an informal group of people who work at CCL is already doing just that. "We're a collection of individuals fascinated by [spiritual questions]," says one of the members. "We do our own reading, writing, talking, and thinking about it."

The recent surge in interest in the servant-leader concept seems to be tapping a deeply felt need of both leaders and people in organizations, he says. People are looking to work to provide spiritual growth—if it doesn't, they feel it's not worth their time. "For leaders, when you start talking about values and mission—and from whence those things come—you quickly get beyond the rational and logical to what lies deepest inside the individual. Their highest and best ideas come from the spirit."

Tom Peters, longtime champion of corporate vision, values, and spirit, is alarmed to see the enthusiasm for workplace spirit turn into workplace spirituality. In a recent syndicated column, titled "Spiritual Talk Has No Place in Secular Corporation," he wholeheartedly endorsed Greenleaf's premise: "The leader, from shop supervisor to President Clinton to Boris Yeltsin, should serve his or her constituents." But he gets uneasy, he continued, when people start assigning deeper meanings to that service: "In tapping . . . the imagination and curiosity [we need from workers in the viciously competitive '90s], let's leave the Bible, the Koran, and facile talk of spiritual leaders at home."

Further, Peters said, "There's nothing I believe in more than the Bill of Rights. When you cross the line between the secular and the spiritual you're edging up on something that bugs me.

"At the highest level of abstraction, we've obviously reached a point where nonintuitive, linear, rational management has made a mess of American companies," says Peters. "Moving away from that is positive." But he senses danger in overdoing it in the opposite direction. "By getting overtly into the spiritual stuff, the pendulum is swinging too far," he says. He fears that a leap into spirituality could backfire and squash the empowerment movement before it reaches full flower.

Corporations have successfully and rightfully stepped into the role of certain social institutions in this country, he continues. But while he applauds the corporation taking on the role of the public schools by teaching literacy skills to employees, the idea of the corporation taking on the role of a religious institution "makes me want to puke."

There are places in the human psyche, Peters contends, where you simply don't want a business organization screwing around. And that, of course, brings us to. . . .

The Dark Side

Though Peters doesn't mention it, there's also the law. Organizations these days are finding themselves under attack for things like Christmas créches and celebrations that offend non-Christians, as well as for Halloween and Easter-Bunny paraphernalia that offend fundamentalist Christians. When employees put religious greetings on their voice mail, their companies can find themselves in hot water with customers.

Spirituality has proved an explosive issue for trainers in recent years. While so-called New Age trainers have insisted that training must involve the whole person—body, mind, and spirit—organizations that have tried to follow that advice have sometimes ended up in legal trouble.

In the late 1980s, Pacific Bell was called to task by the California Public Utilities Commission when consumer groups protested PacBell's spending several million dollars on training designed by consultant Charles Krone and based in part on the teachings of an Armenian mystic named Georges Gurdjieff.

During the same period, a few other cases grabbed national headlines. A car salesman in Tacoma, Washington, was fired for refusing to attend a spirituality-based training program; he then sued his company. In Albany, Georgia, William Gleaton, a human-resources manager for Firestone Tire, was fired after refusing to conduct a training program because he felt it was tainted by secular humanism. As more and more companies pledge to "value diversity," such sensitivities will surely grow.

Harry Levinson, head of the Levinson Institute, a Cambridge, Massachusetts, consulting organization, sees other, equally pragmatic problems in the servant-leadership model. "Bob Greenleaf was a very thoughtful man and a Quaker who tried to put Quaker 'theology' into managerial practice," he says. On the positive side, Levinson sees a philosophy that can enhance people's dignity and ability to work together. On the negative side, he thinks it ignores accountability and the underlying fundamental aggression of people in the workplace.

Compatibility with the company's culture and systems is another consideration, says Levinson. At Herman Miller, chairman DePree successfully practiced the art of leadership by following Greenleaf's precepts. However, Levinson cautions, if this philosophy doesn't fit the culture, it may run into trouble. Much of the emphasis placed on empowerment and participation doesn't take into account people's different conceptual abilities, he says. For example, the average worker on the plant floor is unlikely to have a lot to contribute to, say, a discussion of how a major corporation ought to cope with the global marketplace. "I'm in favor of making the most of people's talents, but I'm not in favor of naively giving power," he says. "A lot of this talk ignores levels of competence and conceptual capabilities. There's a sort of glibness to it that masks underlying psychological realities."

Managers have to take charge and be appropriately aggressive, he contends. "If managers make believe they aren't taking charge, they'll do it in clandestine fashion and contribute to a lack of trust among employees. Baby boomers and contemporary literature say it's not nice to be boss. But power is power no matter what you call it. There's no escape from accountability, but you don't read about accountability."

The servant-leader orientation is helpful for managers concerned with respecting the feelings of the people who work for them, Levinson says, but as a philosophy, he suspects it concerns book writers and publishers more than practicing managers. "Whenever you make a conscious effort to implement values that fundamentally respect human beings, it resounds with everybody. But when you get into spirituality, you run the risk of intruding into somebody else's spiritual orientation."

Despite these hazards, the enthusiasm remains. Peters' column on keeping spiritual talk out of the corporate world prompted a thoughtful response from William W. George, president and CEO of Medtronic Inc., the biomedical company based in Fridley, Minnesota. In an open letter published in the *Minneapolis Star Tribune,* George takes Peters to task for confusing spirituality with religion. He begins with the dictionary definition of spiritual: "1. the animating or life-giving principle within a human being, 2. the part of a human being associated with the mind or feelings as distinguished from the physical body, and 3. the real sense of significance of something."

He continues: "This 'significance' is precisely what DePree and Greenleaf are appealing to. After all, we spend more time at work than in any other part of our lives. Shouldn't we find significance in our work and the opportunity to use our mind and feeling while appealing to 'the animating or life-giving principles' within us? This isn't practicing religion per se but rather devoting our whole being toward a higher purpose in our work."

Medtronic, George insists, continues to live the mission penned more than 30 years ago by founder Earl Bakken: to restore people to the fullness of life and health. To do this, the company stresses "leading by values," rather than management by objectives, especially in its self-directed work teams. "At Medtronic," he concludes, "we don't mix religion and business, but we certainly do not shy away from the spiritual side of our work and the deeper meaning of our mission to save lives. If all this makes you want to run, so be it. For all of us, it is the real reason to go to work every day."

The Manager as . . . Messiah?

Beyond all the talk about meaning and values, a substantial question looms: What do spiritually minded managers *do* that distinguishes them from the old model boss? According to *Managing from the Heart*, a servant-leader/steward-manager honors "five unspoken" employee requests:

- Hear and understand me.
- Even if you disagree with me, please don't make me wrong.
- Acknowledge the greatness within me.
- Remember to look for my loving intentions.
- Tell me the truth with compassion.

According to Bracey, "Honoring these five unspoken requests is a style of management that brings high levels of both compassion and accountability to the workplace." They form "a sort of behavioral approach to spiritual principles."

In his new book, *Leadership Jazz*, Max DePree concludes: "Above all, leadership is a position of servanthood. Leadership is a forfeiture of rights." He proposes 12 characteristics as the keys to becoming a successful servant leader:

- Integrity.
- Vulnerability.
- Discernment.
- Awareness of the human spirit.
- Courage in relationships.
- Sense of humor.
- Intellectual energy and curiosity.
- Respect for the future, regard for the present, understanding of the past.
- Predictability.
- Breadth.
- Comfort with ambiguity.
- Presence.

Blanchard suggests managers learn to think of themselves as partners with employees, rather than judges and critics. Instead of management by objectives (a goal-setting system that doesn't work, he says, because goals are simply dictated by the manager to employees), he sees the servant-leader model as one that makes possible a true partnership between managers and employees. And in a true partnership, both parties are equally responsible for goals.

Servant-leadership is not soft leadership, he emphasizes. It's the leader's job to create a vision, set up tough goals in partnership with employees and then help people become winners in the performance game. Blanchard compares it to the way he taught college. "I gave out the final exam on the first day and taught the answers all quarter. All the students got A's. That's what life is about—getting A's, not grading on a curve. I'm talking about getting away from the cat-and-mouse game where it's the manager's job to be judge and jury. It's a powerful package that's based on a lot of spiritual principles."

Block, on the other hand, sees lists of traits, attributes and behaviors as a trap, and compiling such lists as a counterproductive activity. "Our profession is caught up in prescribing," he says. "[Warren] Bennis writes a book on the four essences of great leaders, and we attempt to re-create them [in others] in some fashion. Stewardship is less a prescription than about being accountable and owning—about making democracy work at work."

While these descriptions fall short of expecting the servant-leader to walk on water, the image of the manager as messiah inevitably intrudes. While acknowledging that the language they use can unintentionally evoke the impression that the manager they're describing is an other-worldly being, proponents insist that the servant-leader is expected to be neither Lama-like nor priestly.

What distinguishes the servant-leader from the messianic manager out to save corporate souls? Bellman sees corporate purpose as one safety valve. "The primary reason that we're gathered [in the workplace] is to get something done," he says. And as long as everyone recognizes an organizational purpose that requires productivity and accomplishment, no one is going to confuse the servant-leader with a semi-saint.

Covey generally agrees with that perspective. "As I see it, [the difference between the leader as servant and the manager as saint] is in the consensus process that surrounds the development of the mission statement," he says. Developing a meaningful mission statement is a long, difficult, inclusive process that positions the manager as neither saint nor sinner, but simply as the person who keeps the process moving.

On a day-to-day level, adds Covey, sharing raw data—not information that's been digested and repackaged by the corporate marketing department—about everything from employees' own performance to financial results works against relying on a single leader. "I say keep involving people in the raw data. People are basically proactive; they have the capacity to respond. When you share raw, unfiltered data, trust goes up and people move fast. There is no dependence. [These types of] stakeholder information systems keep people focused on the mission and the vision—not on the leader."

So what do we have here? A movement? A mood? A desperate quest for stability in an unstable world? An idealistics creed that will never gain acceptance in the hard-bitten workplace of the '90s? Or could this be the new way of working we've been looking for? "We're searching for a new organizational model," says Edward E. Lawler, professor at the Business School of the University of Southern California and director of the school's Center for Effective Organizations. "The traditional business model has failed and we're looking for a replacement. Here's one new—old—paradigm."

9

Servant-Leadership: Is There Really Time for It?

Ann McGee-Cooper, Ed. D. with Duane Trammell

I was first introduced to servant-leadership 12 years ago when I was invited to work with TDIndustries in Dallas and was given a copy of the book, *The Servant As Leader,* by Robert Greenleaf. Since that time, I have been wrestling with all that concept means.

While exploring servant-leadership, I found that it is much more than a philosophy or management model; it is a helpful (although sometimes troublesome) yardstick that measures my leadership assumptions and ethics in day-to-day business practices. It would be nice if it were just a motto that could be hung on the wall. But once you embrace the ideals of servant-leadership, it becomes a razor-sharp sword that challenges every decision you make as a leader.

One of the projects my business partner Duane Trammell and I have been working on is a reexamination of time management skills. In our book, *Time Management for Unmanageable People,* we examined different thinking styles and how those styles affect the way we make decisions and manage our time. Midway through the manuscript process, we found another fundamental issue that greatly affected time management. We could learn tips to better our own personal time management, but most of us function as part of a team. Everyone else's time management affects ours. We decided to write a book on *team* time management. And that's when we began to see the direct relationship of how servant-leadership affects time management.

To understand how time management is affected by servant-leadership, it helps to look back at what Robert Greenleaf suggested servant-leadership is. He writes, "The servant-leader is servant first. . . . It begins with the natural feeling that one wants to *serve,* to *serve first.* Then conscious choice brings one to aspire to lead. [This person] is sharply different from the person who is *leader* first, perhaps because of the need to assuage an unusual power drive or to acquire material possessions."

Servant-leadership is about taking the time to serve, or to give people the opportunity to grow. Most people would not argue that this needs to happen, but when is there time? Generally speaking, there is none; most of our time is spent trying to catch up with yesterday's and last week's to-do list. And everything must be done faster, better, and more expediently. Hurry sickness pervades our society, and it is the enemy of servant-leadership.

An Epidemic of Hurry Sickness

We first learned the term hurry sickness from the work of Dr. Larry Dossey. In his book *Space, Time & Medicine,* Dr. Dossey writes, "The perceptions of passing time that we observe from our external clocks cause our internal clocks to run faster." Hurry sickness is a metaphor for all those illnesses brought on or exacerbated by stress, rush, and constant pressure. In short, hurry sickness is habitual, unnecessary, or compulsive rushing that leads to the speeding up of our natural body functions, ultimately damaging our health. We are caught in an epidemic of rushing as an end in itself and, no longer aware of other options, we find it hard to escape.

How Hurry Sickness Affects Our Lives

What does hurry sickness look like in our lives? It's when we rush to be first whether we need to or not. As a matter of principle, we press to be first off the airplane even though we know we will just stand and wait with the others once we get to the baggage claim. We press forward, inch by inch, bumper to bumper, in gridlock traffic, incensed if anyone cuts ahead of us, even though our lives won't be changed by the five minutes we may "save" once we reach our destination. We skip meals or eat on the go to "save time."

Hurry sickness also contaminates our leadership ability with our team. Think about the essential qualities of a servant-leader. If I am consumed with hurry sickness, I can't listen to understand; I will be too busy finishing your sentence and rushing ahead of your words to guess the ending, never really hearing the message because my mind is already elsewhere. I can't empathize with you because I will be too busy drumming my fingers impatiently or glancing frequently at my watch to let you know I have to move on to more pressing matters. I cannot increase my awareness and broaden my perception, because I have moved on too quickly to notice anything in depth about a situation. Many times our lack of courage is what propels our hurry sickness even faster.

Greenleaf tells us that slowing down to increase our awareness usually does *not* mean smoother sailing. "Awareness is not a giver of solace—it is just the opposite. It is a disturber and an awakener. Able leaders are usually sharply awake and reasonably disturbed. They are not seekers after solace. They have their own inner serenity."

Is it any wonder that we don't "have time" for servant-leadership?

Isn't It Just Faster to Tell People What to Do?

Another perceived time trap with servant-leadership is that we think it is more expedient to just command or tell someone to do something, rather than offer any explanations or encourage dialogue to get input and buy-in. This might slow down the process, or worse yet, it might change the way we originally intended the outcome.

In our consulting work, we encourage organizations to examine their feedback loops at every level of the company. Although it takes longer on the front end, we suggest that involving people in a decision that affects them is essential for buy-in and support. Although the plan may be tweaked and changed a little—or a lot—from having other eyes and ears review it, only then does it have a chance of garnering shared support.

People support what they help to create. Only as people learn to listen carefully with respect for feelings, insights, and perspectives of others, only as we learn the importance of sharing ownership with each and every person on the team, do we begin to realize the strength and momentum that comes from this shared ownership.

Sounds Great on Paper, but . . .

Sounds great on paper, but what happens when deadlines enter the equation? Consensus is great when you have the time, but sometimes you "just gotta make a decision and go with it."

We have noticed an interesting correlation in our work with companies. The more decisions you just "make and go with," the fewer decisions that ever get input. Conversely, the companies that invest some time up front with consensus and inputting processes, not only get better at making these decisions faster, but the more they trust and support each other when individual team members must "just make a decision and go with it." The contact time they spend up front teaches them how one another thinks on issues. Team members can learn to think on one another's behalf without even being present in the room.

This may sound easy, but it's not. Let me confess some of my own sins here. From the outside, our company appears to be a highly participative team. But if I don't use the measuring stick of servant-leadership, the clock always wins. Part of my role is to meet with the executive leadership of our external clients and listen to their business challenges. When I come back to the office, it is very easy to get involved with the new list of to-do's and not have time to brief my team on these critical issues. If they don't have this information, the roles they play on writing proposals, providing resources to clients, putting calls through, and so forth cannot be done nearly as effectively. I limit their leadership ability in these important areas.

To complicate matters even further, my team members have their own deadlines to honor and don't have the time to sit in a debriefing meeting. What starts out as a gift of time from the servant-leader can quickly turn into an imposition in the minds of the people being "given the opportunity to grow." I wish that we could say we have solved these complex issues, but we haven't. There is one thing we know for certain: Not doing anything is a cop out.

Making Servant-Leadership a Priority

Another problem with time and servant-leadership is the relationship to priorities and schedules. Many leaders feel that their schedules are driven by outside forces. With the popularity of software calendaring programs, many leaders from large companies have their schedules on line. These schedules are accessible to everyone, and every open time period can become filled with meetings and other commitments.

Spending time with team members on an individual basis, coaching them, and growing them in new leadership areas is a task that normally gets put at the end of the to-do list. It is only done if the other priority tasks get completed first (which rarely, if ever, happens). The number of critical tasks that pop up during the day seems to always magically equal or surpass the amount of time we have available on the schedule.

So how does one find the time? The only sure way of making it happen is putting it on the calendar or daily schedule. If we wait until after we have finished our "management" work responsibilities to coach, listen, and do other people-focused tasks, we will be waiting forever. Servant leadership tasks are much more likely to occur if we give them a name, log them on the schedule at an appointed time, and assign them a priority. Even in extremely busy seasons, we log the people-tasks on post-it notes, put them on the schedule. If a legitimately urgent task needs to take precedence, the scheduled people task can be moved to another day. But it is not forgotten. We have learned a good lesson from the quality process and applied it to servant-leadership: "What gets measured gets done!"

The Higher Road Is Not Always the Expressway

Servant leadership asks a higher ethic of us. Greenleaf writes, "The best test, and difficult to administer, is: Do those served grow as persons; do they, while being served, become healthier, wiser, freer, more autonomous, more likely themselves to become servants? And what is the effect on the least privileged in society; will [they] benefit, or, at least, will [they] not be further deprived?" The ethical way is not always the most time-efficient.

Jack Lowe, A True Servant-Leader

A sterling role model for the servant-leadership test is TDIndustries. Jack Lowe, CEO, described his personal experiences and journey as a leader in search of a greater understanding of Bob Greenleaf's concept of servant-leadership. His company is in the air conditioning and plumbing business. Dallas has been hit hard by the economic decline and building went from boom to bust, dramatically impacting the business opportunities for TDIndustries. Lowe says it is challenging to stick with a commitment to servant-leadership when "your back is to the wall."

TDIndustries had worked hard on instilling a quality process that had every manager teaching quality, setting quality goals with his or her team, and participating in quality teams. Lowe described a large shop team of about 20 to 30 people meeting weekly in the coffee room to develop a mission statement for their team, sometimes for as long as two hours. He said he made frequent trips to the coffee pot, so he was painfully aware of how many were meeting, how often, and for how long. In his head, the meter was running, racking up a lot of overhead being spent. But he trusted the process although he confessed that inwardly he was anxious and questioning. The outcome was great.

Sometime later, a smaller number of this team was working on a problem concerning potential profit or loss on a big commercial job. The cost of hiring workers to construct the duct work and piping on-site would be approximately $380,000. The team discussed other options for dealing with this challenge, and they came up with a way to construct the duct in the shop in large, 30-foot sections. Those sections could then be moved to the job with special equipment. This was truly a major shift in how things got done, and there were numerous dissenting opinions about why it wouldn't or couldn't work. However, there was a happy ending: The company tried the new system, and while they went over shop budget by $15,000, they saved $207,000 on the site budget. The company made a better profit, better use of its talent, and the client got a better job. This was only one example of many creative ideas and productivity improvements that have come from this group. The extra time spent up front paid off.

From a servant-leader perspective, an interesting insight is how difficult it can be to trust others and give them room to exercise what they believe in and share the leadership and responsibility. Short term,

TDIndustries spent a lot of time just getting people to think together and speak up. Now, the process is much more familiar, and the teams are generating solutions more easily and working together, sharing ideas, and questioning the process more comfortably.

Jessie McCain, Vice-President of the People Department for TDIndustries gives another example that relates to the second half of the "test" of servant-leadership—the effect on the least privileged in society. As the ethnic diversity of the Dallas Metroplex keeps increasing, many craft workers lack English-speaking skills. According to McCain, "When several Vietnamese, Laotian, and Cambodian families moved into our community and needed work, we knew we needed to create a bridge. In order for them to be trained in the work skills and interact with other workers, they needed to learn English." Although it cost them more money and time, TDIndustries chose to honor a different set of priorities. "By working with our local community college we were able to arrange English-as-a-Second-Language classes offered in our building. The results were miraculous! These new employees learned rapidly with enthusiasm and gained significant confidence. They are wonderful craftsmen with a strong work ethic, so we welcomed these talents and influence. In addition, this action demonstrated our support for diversity in our community."

The Servant-Leader: A Person Who Makes the Time

As we learn more about servant-leadership from observing it in others and practicing the principles ourselves, we find that redefining priorities in our time management practices is a major part of the process. Namely, people are elevated to a higher importance than the "things" we have to manage. Tasks on the to-do list involve more difficult, self-initiated assignments that have greater long-term pay-offs. For example, servant-leaders go beyond simply approving budgets; they figure out how to share power and mentor others in the politics of how to get a worthy item through the budget approval process.

A servant-leader not only puts a task force together to recommend, for example, a fair benefits package, but also listens, teaches, and helps the members of the task force ask the right questions so that together they can discover answers that represent everyone. Rather than simply mediating a dispute, a servant-leader notices a person whose views are not being heard because of a communication style that unnecessarily irritates others. A servant-leader takes the time to offer sensitive and supportive coaching in a way that preserves the message but eliminates distancing mannerisms—helping not only the individual but also strengthening the team. In essence, a servant-leader makes time for people—even when there isn't any.

10

The Leader as Servant

Walter Kiechel III

These days it seems one can hardly visit the Temple of Corporate Heroes without running a substantial risk of being hit by a falling idol. Crash! There goes Lee Iacocca, former company savior and patriot messiah, toppling into a rubble of big bucks, protectionist whining, and reluctance to leave. Wait. Are those actually vultures perched atop the now mostly horizontal statue of Donald Trump, always one of our more brazen images? Hmm. Those plinths under the Johns Reed and Sculley sure look a little wobbly.

Ah, dear Brutus, perhaps the fault was not just in our practice but in our theory as well. In the 1980s, we seemed to fall all over ourselves to embrace highfalutin concepts of leadership, each more grandiose than the last. Remember the transformational leader, or the visionary variety? How many jobs have they created lately?

Time to rethink. Time, arguably, for a downsized, restructured notion of leadership. Conveniently, the requisite concept may already be at hand, quietly at work in some nonprofit institutions and a few businesses across the country. Call it by the name its author, Robert K. Greenleaf, gave it 25 years ago: servant-leadership.

Try to think of the two words not as an oxymoron but rather as a sort of Zen koan, a juxtaposition of apparent opposites meant to startle the seeker after wisdom into new insight: The leader exists to serve those whom he or she nominally leads, those who supposedly follow. He or she takes their fulfillment as his or her principal aim.

Greenleaf, who died in 1990, led an interesting, in ways inspiring, life. He spent his first career at AT&T, mostly in personnel; he was director of management research when he retired in 1964. At age 60 he started a second career, setting up the Center for Applied Ethics, a small think tank later renamed The Greenleaf Center. From conversations with college students, Greenleaf got caught up in the intellectual ferment of the late 1960s—the questioning of authority, the search for new sources of legitimacy. Finally, at the end of that tumultuous decade, he wrote and privately circulated an essay, "The Servant as Leader," in part to encourage young people to take on more responsibility. Observes Max DePree, the former CEO of furniture maker Herman Miller and a management guru in his own right: "Bob Greenleaf did something more people should do: He waited until he knew something before he tried to share it with people."

Over the past 25 years, more than a quarter million copies of the essay have been sold, mostly by word of mouth. But nobody should dive into "The Servant as Leader" expecting another *One Minute Manager* or *In Search of Excellence*. Greenleaf is discursive, and at times maddeningly woolly. He got his seminal idea not from studying, say, 25 high-performing companies but from reading Hermann Hesse's *Journey to the East*. (Riiight, all you late 1960s atavistos out there, the same Hesse who gave us *Siddhartha* and *Steppenwolf*.)

In Hesse's novel, Greenleaf encountered the character Leo, seemingly a mere menial accompanying a group of men on a journey. Leo does the lowliest of chores for them but also buoys them with his good spirits and song. Indeed, when Leo disappears, the travelers find they can't go on without him. Let Greenleaf deliver the punch line: "The narrator, one of the party, after some years of wandering finds Leo and is taken into the order that had sponsored the journey. There he discovers that Leo, whom he had known first as servant, was in fact the titular head of the order, its guiding spirit, a great and noble leader."

Okay, okay, it will never play in the corner office. Still, even if the would-be great and noble leaders of the 1990s aren't ready to trade in their $900 suits for Leo's monkish sackcloth, they could pick up a tip or two from this paragon. Consider a few of the more beguiling aspects of the servant-leader:

- Takes people, and their work, really, really seriously. We're talking beyond empowerment here, beyond freeing up the troops to better pursue the purposes of the organization. "The servant-leader says human beings have a value in their own right," argues Peter Hammerschmidt, professor of economics at Florida's Eckerd College. "He or she doesn't have to have an end beyond that. He or she calls for doing what's good, even if it doesn't pay off." Adds Hammerschmidt, with an eye toward the worldly consequences: "It probably *will* pay off."

  Mere academic idealism? Not in the view of Max DePree: "I see authenticity as an inherent value or right—we're authentic before we get to the workplace," and must be treated accordingly when we arrive there. In Greenleaf's view, valuing people this way entails a new business ethic: "The work exists for the person as much as the person exists for the work. Put another way, the business exists as much to provide meaningful work to the person as it exists to provide a product or service to the customer."

- Listens, and takes the lead from the troops. Some proponents maintain that the primary mission of the servant-leader is to figure out the will of the group, to express that will, and then to further it however he can. He or she begins by listening. Robert Taylor, dean of the University of Louisville's business school, explains: "The servant-leader today doesn't have answers, he or she has questions. The people working with customers are the ones with answers."

  Most critics of servant-leadership concentrate their attack on this idea of eliciting the group's will. What if the group has no collective will? They go on to argue that what most people in an organization want is a person with a plan, somebody to set the direction. Besides, this listening stuff takes forever. Professor Gerald Graham, an expert on leadership at Wichita State University, tells of one businessman, a good Mennonite, who tried to run his small company along servant-leader lines, even allowing employees to determine his paycheck. "The business didn't last very long," says Graham. "They couldn't make the hard decisions—on wages and salaries—and spent too much time in meetings."

  Actually, servant-leadership's champions respond, the process works more like the consensus building that the Japanese are famous for. Yes, it takes a while on the front end; everyone's view is solicited though everyone also understands that his or her view may not ultimately prevail. But once the consensus is forged, watch out: With everybody on board, your so-called implementation proceeds wham-bam.

For two decades TDIndustries, a $75-million-a-year mechanical contracting firm in Dallas, has used servant-leadership as the centerpiece of its supervisor training. CEO Jack Lowe Jr. wryly likens it to a different management fashion: "It sounds a little like the quality movement, doesn't it?" His company is into that effort too, and finds that it marries quite nicely with servant-leadership, thank you very much.

- Heals. As in makes whole or binds up—not a bad skill to have in this age of trust gaps and morale crises.

  Servant-leadership requires a kind of openness, a willingness to share in mistakes and pain, that few managers will be comfortable with. Still, "to be vulnerable is risky, but there's tremendous power in it," argues Hyler Bracey, head of the Atlanta Consulting Group, Greenleaf fan, and coauthor of *Managing From the Heart.* In practical terms, say, in that worst of possible cases—you're forced to let people go—this would mean giving everyone a chance to vent his or her feelings, "sharing whatever brightness for the future you can," as Bracey puts it, and "acknowledging the devil out of performers."

  Sound sappy? Well, then you probably won't want to know about what may be the hottest new management buzzword emerging among consultants working with restructured companies. It's "grief work"—lancing the boil of rage, resentment, and fear among survivors, a necessary first step before going on to try to rebuild any kind of trust in management.

  The irony: A little servant-leadership can head much of this off. Jack Lowe reports that his company, like most in the hard-hit industry, has had to lay off employees in the past few years. Nonetheless, in 1991, it racked up the highest scores on its annual morale survey of employees—"partners," in company parlance—since it began polling over a decade ago.

- Is self-effacing. President David Davenport has used servant-leadership to help make California's Pepperdine University a magnet for students who want something better than the impersonality of a large institution. Instead of registering for classes in a noisy gym, for example, each student works out his or her schedule with a faculty adviser who has a computer tied into the central scheduling system. When asked why he hasn't made more noise about this philosophy,

Davenport responds: "If you draw a lot of attention to it, that's probably self-defeating. What we are trying to do is *not* glorify leadership."

- Sees himself as a steward. Which means pondering what he or she has been entrusted with, and what he or she will hand on. Says John Rosenblum, dean of the University of Virginia's business school: "If you're going to be a steward of institutional vitality, you have to take a long-term perspective."

Rosenblum even sees a way of reconciling the servant and the visionary leader. Management is a conversation, he says. To it the leader brings his vision, but also his realization that everyone else in the organization may have a vision of his or her own. Hence Rosenblum's observation that "servant-leadership at its heart is an openness, an ability to listen, and an ability to speak in a way that engages people directly affected by the choices to be made." You talk. They talk. From your conversation emerges a shared vision—and a better one.

11

Some Executives Are Trying to Make Companies Heed a Higher Authority

Edward Iwata

In the beginning, the Big Executive in the Sky created heaven and earth. Many fiscal quarters later, the first companies were born. Now, as the next millennium approaches, a quiet trend is emerging with some businesspeople—mixing spirituality and work to create corporations with soul.

Atheists and agnostics need not worry. The goal isn't religious conversion. Corporate veeps aren't reciting the Lord's Prayer or chanting Buddhist mantras in the boardroom. Rather, some corporate leaders are ushering traditional and New Age spiritual values into the office and factory in the quest for higher worker morale, greater customer satisfaction—even deeper meaning in their lives—all in the hope of honest profits.

Converts call it "corporate stewardship" or "dharmic management." Others speak of "holistic leadership." Whatever the tag, corporate apostles—from blue chip executives to respected authors Kenneth Blanchard (*The One-Minute Manager*) and Stephen Covey (*Principle-Centered Leadership*)—are preaching the new management philosophy.

"It's been a quiet, slow-growing revolution, but we're reaching critical mass," said Larry Spears, director of the Greenleaf Center, an Indianapolis-based leadership institute. "People are taking a broader view of spirituality. . . . What was once simply going to church on Sunday morning has evolved into people seeking to integrate personal and spiritual growth with work."

According to advocates of spiritual management, employers can reinvent companies by following a blueprint of values such as compassion, shared decision-making, and community building.

A model holistic company would insist on harmony in workforce relations, strong corporate ethics and trust throughout the firm and in its relationships with customers and the surrounding community. There would be profit sharing with employees. And the company would pour money back to local community groups, even though most corporations have pared their charitable gifts in recent years. Lastly, the holistic company might see a healthier environment as a key goal.

"Once seen as a way to get rich, business is seen today as a vehicle through which individuals can realize their personal vision, serve others, and make a difference in the world," said Herman Bryant Maynard Jr., a DuPont Co. executive and author of *The Fourth Wave: Business in the 21st Century.*

But not everyone is praising the new management philosophy. Consultant Tom Peters gets nervous over talk of the "greater good" in business. "In tapping the imagination [of workers], let's leave the Bible, the Koran, and facile talk of spiritual leaders at home," he wrote recently.

"It's a double-edged sword," said Edward Lawler, director of the University of Southern California's Center for Effective Leadership. "If you convert people to a common philosophy, you can develop a sense of purpose, but the closer you get to values, the greater the risk you'll offend people and do something illegal" such as discrimination or wrongful termination.

As companies rebuild in the recession, Lawler sees many employers abandoning "positive values" and mission statements. Instead, the companies are doing "whatever it takes to stay in business."

Battle-weary executives admit the cut-throat business arena doesn't always welcome the new ethos. Greed, layoffs, legal fights, hostile takeovers, labor-management strife—all still darken the corporate landscape.

And changes will come from the top. Most executives have been traditionally trained to see their workforce as machinery, said Jeffrey McCollum, a Hillsborough, New Jersey, management consultant. Now, these managers must stop neglecting the soft, soulful side of their employees. "Everyone wants to be valued. Organizations need to develop this spirit, this deep human connection."

Collaborative—rather than combative—management has succeeded at Xerox Technology Ventures, a venture capital group in El Segundo, California. Work teams at the Xerox Corp. subsidiary honor each employee's talents and contributions.

One group of software engineers and sales people learned communication and problem-solving skills to gain trust and overcome their differences. Then they tackled a money-losing software project that looked doomed. To their delight, sales on the software jumped from $500,000 to $3 million. Sales of $6 million are anticipated for next year.

"Something special happened—they were glowing in their mutual accomplishment," said Robert Adams, president of the venture group and a Presbyterian Church elder. "In Christian tradition, it's 'Do unto others as you would have them do unto you.' In the business world, it's creating a learning organization so all employees can find fulfillment."

Spiritual management has old roots in the business world. Since the 1970s, futurists and executives at three influential Northern California think tanks—the Stanford Research Institute, the Esalen Institute, and the World Business Academy—have spoken widely of the spiritual transformation in business and economics. Many precepts of spiritual management came from a late AT&T executive, Robert Greenleaf, who gave birth to servant-leadership, the philosophy that businesses have a mission to serve people and society. But only recently have their ideas spread widely into the corporate realm.

Why now? Business experts say mass layoffs have forced many to reexamine their lives. Millions of baby boomers are seeking spirituality. Women in business are creating kinder workplaces. The greed of the 1980s may have awakened social consciences. "We can either elevate the human spirit, or we can crush it," said Rabbi Wayne Dosick, author of *The Business Bible* and a professor at the Catholic University of San Diego. "If we uplift the human spirit, we can bring meaning and value to the modern marketplace."

12

First Among Equals: A Corporate Executive's Vision and the Reemerging Philosophy of Trustees as Servant-Leaders

Deborah Brody

Although the notion of "leaders as servants" goes back to Biblical days and perhaps even further, in modern times many leaders seem to have forsaken this simple yet powerful concept in favor of leadership as self-aggrandizement and power. But the increasing acknowledgment of the philosophy of Robert K. Greenleaf perhaps can be attributed to a loss of faith in our modern leaders—be they corporate CEOs or politicians.

A native of Indiana, Greenleaf spent 40 years working with the AT&T company as essentially a "talent scout." He identified promising middle managers within the company and developed educational programs for them. Along the way, Greenleaf developed a knack for identifying exceptional leaders and found that these people had something in common: They worked primarily to empower their team and generally were not motivated by personal gain. They used the sharing of authority and responsibility as a way to enhance the well-being of their programs.

Following his retirement in 1964, Greenleaf embarked upon a second, 20-year career as a writer and management consultant to various organizations. In 1970 he wrote "The Servant as Leader," the first in a series of essays discussing the servant-leader concept.

Today, Greenleaf's work continues through the Robert K. Greenleaf Center in Indianapolis. The Center's mission is to promote a new approach to leadership, structure, and decision-making. It advocates a holistic approach to work, a strong community, and shared power.

A handful of corporations including the AT&T Consumer Products Education Division in New Jersey, Herman Miller Co. in Michigan, and Indiana-based Schmidt Associates Architects have adopted servant-leadership models as part of their corporate philosophy and mission statement. For a corporation, servant-leadership requires turning the traditional U.S. corporate "pyramid" structure upside down, thus making it an inverted pyramid with employees, customers, and the community at the top.

According to Larry Spears, executive director of the Robert K. Greenleaf Center, the concept can be traced back to an ancient Roman model: *primus inter pares,* first among equals. In more concrete terms, this means involving staff in making decisions and setting organizational goals.

Questions for Foundation Trustees

But how does this concept apply to foundation boards? Greenleaf addresses this in another essay entitled "Trustees as Servants," where he urges trustees to ask themselves who they serve, and why. According to Paul Olson, president of the Blandin Foundation and board member of the Greenleaf Center, foundation trustees exist to serve the public trust.

The Blandin Foundation is in the process of adopting a servant-leader philosophy. Its focus is to "help create healthy rural communities." To do this effectively, the board is looking at ways to listen to the interests, concerns, and needs of the rural people it serves. Listening is an essential component for servant-leaders, thus the Blandin Foundation board is experimenting with different ways to be a good listener.

According to Olson, it is especially important for family foundations "to find a zone of agreement" among their board members. Boards comprised solely or mostly of family members have an even higher need for public trust. They must ask themselves: "What do we want our real accomplishments to be and how can we achieve them?"

Servant-Leader Workshops

The W. K. Kellogg Foundation recently made a three-year grant to the Greenleaf Center to fund a servant-leadership workshop program. The workshops are structured to introduce participants to the principles and practices of servant-leadership and suggest approaches to making this philosophy an important part of one's daily life—both at work and at home. The workshops draw upon a variety of methods including traditional teaching methods, exercises, personal reflection, videotapes, and small group discussions.

According to Larraine Matusak, coordinator-program director for leadership at Kellogg, the foundation is committed to the concept of servant-leader both for its internal operations and for its grantees. It is important to Kellogg that its grantees have adopted or are working toward a servant-leader philosophy. Since 1987, 69 of its grantees have become servant-leader organizations.

To monitor the progress of their grantees, Kellogg program officers engage in extensive dialogues and visits with their grant applicants, and about one year into the grant the program officer makes another site visit to determine whether servant-leader objectives are being met. It is important that grantees develop their own strategies for becoming servant-leaders.

Kellogg is also working with colleges and universities to ensure that future generations of leaders understand the servant-leader philosophy. Matusak's advice to foundation boards seeking to adopt the Greenleaf philosophy is to strive to become servant-leaders as individual trustees and to encourage grantees to adopt the servant-leader model.

Other helpful resources for trustees are distributed by the Greenleaf Center. The Center has developed materials for trustees to use to reflect on their responsibilities.

These tools and others can help trustees assess both their personal and professional lives. Boards as a whole might consider undergoing a series of workshops, retreats, or even conversations. The Greenleaf Center can put trustees in touch with consultants who specialize in servant-leader issues. "Still," asserts Larry Spears, "this is not a straightforward management philosophy; there are no 14 points to follow. Instead, trustees must reflect upon their philosophies and behavior and have ongoing discussions."

This may sound like a tall order—especially for busy trustees who often lead dual professional and volunteer lives in addition to having personal and family commitments. But as James P. Shannon, former executive director of the General Mills Foundation and an experienced foundation and nonprofit board member maintains, "Power is something you can give away and still get more of; shared power is power multiplied. Moreover, the best trustees are humble enough to know that they can improve." With this type of thinking, the possibilities abound. Not only do we change ourselves, but we change the world in the process.

PART THREE

Growing as Servant-Leaders/Managers

13

Servant-Leadership and Corporate Risk Taking: When Risk Taking Makes a Difference

Sheila Murray Bethel

Why would anyone want to take a risk? The dictionary defines risk as "exposure to the chance of injury or loss; danger, hazard, peril." Definitely something to avoid. Yet risk taking is integral to both leadership and living, whether the risk is unexpected or a challenge that was created or deliberately sought out. Both kinds can be equally frightening and exhilarating—but risks cannot be avoided. Every leader and every life that makes a difference develops the ability to evaluate ideas and the courage to seize the opportunities associated with them.

Robert K. Greenleaf's philosophy of servant-leadership may not seem to include elements of risk. But I believe it does. We think of leaders as people who are in control and who give orders. We think of servants as people who take orders and do as they are told. Risk taking becomes your servant when it is part of a plan—part of a powerful picture of the changes, a vision of the future.

Analyzing and evaluating the risks involves a five-step process. The servant-leader must be comfortable with the decision to take the risk.

1. Identify the risk: This is not as simple as it seems because of hidden agendas, personal biases, and differences in perception. Remember, a trapeze artist with a safety net below, performing a triple somersault that has been rehearsed to perfection, will perceive the risk quite differently than a small excited child sitting in the bleachers below.
2. Identify benefits and liabilities: Are you working in an area where even a 1 percent chance of failure is too much? Or is 50 percent or even 60 percent acceptable? Often, intangibles are important factors—things like reputation, public relations, employee morale, future opportunities, and personal comfort.
3. Describe a worst-case scenario: Be ready for something to go wrong. Make a road map of all the potential repercussions for different courses of action. Like a skilled chess player, anticipate the worst in order to achieve the best. Build a "back door" to get out of any disaster; it will help you stop worrying about it.
4. Choose role models: Even leaders need leaders. Find people whose foresight and courage you admire, then copy them—not necessarily any specific thing they do, but the spirit with which they do it.
5. Write personal definitions: What do you consider risk? Safety? Success? Failure? For one person, even a slight leveling off in advancement constitutes abject failure. For another, a devastating defeat can become a useful tool for future accomplishments. Carefully defining risk, safety, and failure helps strengthen your courage to lead.

All risk involves change, and all change involves risk. Everyone loves novelty, but no one likes change. Change, however, is inevitable. You can initiate it, try to predict it, be swept along by it, or get crushed as it steamrolls over you. No matter how you respond, change is going to happen anyway, so if you don't master change, it will master you. Challenge yourself:

- What is your vision?
- What risks do you face?
- How willing are you to take them?

Sharing the Risks

In the old hierarchical model of power—the pyramid-shaped triangle with the leader on top and everyone else spread out in layers below—people were simply ordered to take risks. The person at the top would say, "Do it," and everyone did or suffered the consequences. Sometimes even those who obeyed orders and took the risks suffered if the risk didn't pay off. Workers were often trapped in no-win situations.

Recently, compelling social and business realities have made the triangle approach to power less functional. Middle management has flattened out, workers' expectations are higher than ever, and we've begun to focus on the important differences between great management and great leadership as detailed in this list:

Management Skills	***Leadership Skills***
Directing and controlling	Supporting
Making decisions	Empowering
Thinking creatively	Inspiring Creativity
Listening	Ensuring understanding
Solving problems	Anticipating problems
Implementing technology	Humanizing technology
Avoiding risks	Inspiring risk taking

The triangle model of power is being replaced by a new model, one with interlocking, interdependent circles. Paradoxically, risk is the factor least—and most—affected by this change. In both models, risk taking affects everyone. In both models, leaders ask their people to take risks. And both spread the risks around, but in different ways and with different results.

In the traditional hierarchical model, instinct for self-preservation kicked in when the person at the top orders them to take risks. They devoted a lot of energy to diffusing the risk by filtering it through layers of management and paperwork. If an idea flopped, each layer had built-in survival mechanisms.

That type of mandated risk also stifled creativity and enthusiasm. A good example was the attitude of the automobile industry in the 1970s and early 1980s. The management philosophy was, "Don't tell me about problems, just roll the units off the assembly lines. If there is something wrong, let the customers take the bad ones back to the dealers." Consumers were the least important part of the process. The Saturn automobile turned all of that around. It became the most successful automobile in current American sales because it's the most trouble-free. Why? Because Saturn took a big risk by empowering their people. Everyone on the assembly line has the power to stop production to fix a problem. Imagine the eagerness and sense of responsibility Saturn workers feel when they go to work in the morning. Compare that to the attitude of traditional workers in no-rewards jobs who know that nothing they do will really make any difference. Which worker do you want to make your car? Empowerment is a big risk, but obviously one that Saturn found worth taking.

Risk mandated from the top offered more protection and often more assured results than shared risk, but it offered less creativity and responsiveness. It was also much slower, and therefore more costly, because no one was willing to take responsibility or initiative.

The interlocking circle model, which incorporates the principles of servant-leadership, shares the risks by encouraging resourcefulness, enterprises, and a level of enthusiasm and loyalty rarely experienced in traditional top-down organizations. This new level of responsiveness couldn't have come at a better time.

Risky Business

Business-as-usual is dying. Competitive local and global economies are causing massive changes. The organizations that will survive into the twenty-first century are those that are customer focused and make the customer their priority. In the past, it was easy to avoid responsibility for the customer: "It's not my job. It's someone else's responsibility." But empowerment makes the customer everyone's job. Even if you're not serving the customer directly, you're serving someone who is. Customer satisfaction comes first. An individual worker may not be able to resolve every problem and request personally, but he or she can make sure there's follow-through and resolution. Companies must remember that it is the customer who ultimately writes their paycheck. You and I write someone's paycheck every time we buy anything, do anything, or go anywhere. Every day we're writing paychecks for thousands of people, and thousands of people are writing paychecks for us.

What does this have to do with risk? It's risky business when you start to put responsibility in the hands of the people at lower levels. This dilemma must now be faced by one of the riskiest businesses in the history of the world—the entertainment industry. The American film and television industries used to lead the way in innovation and creativity. Now, despite enormous technological advances and budgets, they seem to turn out the same safe product over and over in various wrappings. Few leaders in these industries are willing to risk anything different. When someone with vision does take a risk and succeeds, the non-risk takers immediately imitate him or her, usually producing something as far from the quality of the original as a cheap reproduction is from a real Van Gogh. So much is at stake, so many millions of dollars, so many thousands of jobs, so many lives, that risk is anathema.

Now the entertainment industry is on the verge of a 500-channel world with a voracious need for product. The world of technology is reengineering itself, and people are going to have to do the same. Networks are about to lose market shares as viewers have more choices. How are industry leaders going to reinvent themselves to prepare for this massive change and the necessary risks ahead?

"Psyching Up" for Risk

Servant-leaders are supposed to develop other people's risk-taking skills, but who develops servant-leaders? They need just as much encouragement and support, if not more. An excellent source is the experiences—positive and negative—of other leaders.

Jack Wahlig knows both the pitfalls and payoffs of risk taking. When he served as chairman of the board of McGaldrey & Pullen, a successful accounting and consulting firm, he recognized that the marketplace was undergoing major changes. His company was going to have to prepare for customers' future needs or fall irreparably behind. "We identified what we were and what we thought we wanted to be; then we charged boldly off into the future. It didn't work. We were telling our people, 'Hey, here's what we want in the future, let's go there.' But we were asking people to take so many risks and make such rapid change that the organization just froze."

Wahlig had to rethink what he was asking his people to do and how he was asking them to do it. He started by visiting each of the company's 70 offices and getting personal input from 400 partners. Then, he reorganized the company and put the people most eager and able to keep the company competitive in charge of directing and motivating others.

This time, the risk taking worked. "Just describing the goals and keeping everyone focused on them helped a lot," says Wahlig. "We set quantifiable benchmarks each year for the next three years and let everyone know when we passed major milestones. The progress being made by high risk takers encourages low risk takers to push on. Ultimately that's what risk taking is all about: how to handle the challenges of the twenty-first century."

Helping Others to Take Risks

There are many reasons that people are reluctant to take risks, including fear of failure and loss. Some less obvious penalties can be even more compelling. For example, no one likes criticism, and everyone hates looking stupid, or losing self-esteem and the good opinion of others. Some may even fear that if they do something well they will then be under pressure to do it again.

To get past such reluctance, servant-leaders have to inspire a sense of ownership in the people they ask to join in the risks. People who are asked to share in the decision-making process are more likely to be committed to the idea, the project, the goal, and the organization. Servant-leaders must also make it clear to their people that it is acceptable to fail while building the skills for succeeding. Finally, servant-leaders must make the potential results nearly irresistible. The result is getting novice risk takers to invest willingly in an exciting future and accept the bumps and setbacks along the way.

Gwen Edwards, Vice President of Pacific Bell Health Care Group, compares this to a combination trampoline and safety net. "I persuade them that what they initially see as risk is actually adventure. So many believe they can't do something because it's never been done before or the company won't permit it, or they could lose their jobs. I challenge that: 'Believe me. I'll back you up. Do it. If there's a problem, come to me.' I give them a safety net, a security blanket. I say, 'Here's the trampoline—jump!' I get them to discover how much fun it is. The greatest satisfaction is watching people do things they were convinced they could never do, and to realize it's exciting and fun."

The Five-Point STAR Model

Servant-leaders can use a five-point approach to energize and motivate risk taking. It suggests a simple acronym: I-STAR. "I" is where it all starts, "I" for the individual as the source of energy, and "I" for inspire, what has to be done to get started. ("I" can also stand for ignite, imbue, impel, incite, increase, induce, inflame, influence, infuse, inseminate, instigate, instill, instruct, and involve.) The other points of the STAR are:

- Support: Emotional, physical, spiritual.
- Train: Both basic and advanced skills, like core competencies, best practices, quality/service, customer focus, and value-added strategies.
- Acknowledge: Effort and results, individuals, and teams.
- Reward: Both tangible and intangible rewards, like pleasure, excitement, self-esteem, and team spirit.

The model is graphically shown in Figure 13.1.

Figure 13.1
The STAR model.

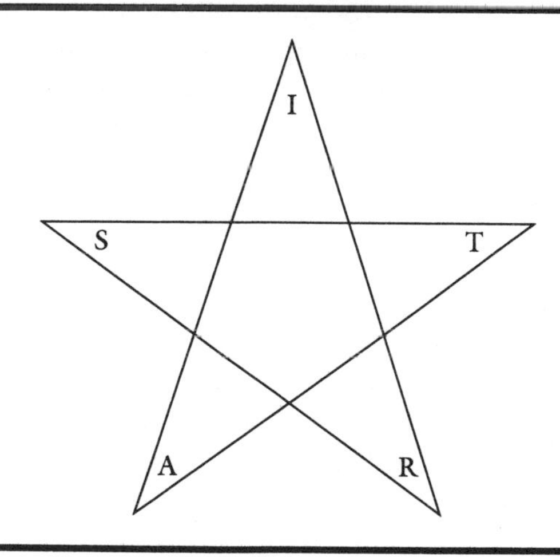

Inspire

Start by offering a clear and exciting vision of what you want to accomplish and where you want to go. Who and what will you and your people become as a result of taking the risk? Creating "coownership" and "buy into" is critical. One of the best ways to do this is to become a good storyteller.

In the past, long before they knew how to write, people sat around the fire telling stories to discuss the days events, preparing for the tasks of tomorrow, and teaching their young, history, tradition, and how to live in a dangerous, risky world. For modern leaders, the equivalent of this is learning to use anecdotes, analogies, and examples to create powerful pictures of the future and of others who have successfully taken risks. When followers have become inspired or have a bigger picture of the future, you can then go on to the next part two of the STAR, Support.

Support

Offering support, starts with the recognition that builds confidence and enthusiasm. If people don't feel secure, they'll stay right where they are and refuse to budge. Even if they do take the jump, they aren't going to try again if there's no one there to support them. There are three ways you can support and encourage your people:

1. Emotional support: People need to know that they will have someone to turn to when the going gets hard. Servant-leaders often take on the role of mentor, giving their people someone to depend on. That means being there to cheer when things go well, and being there to comfort and advise when things go badly.
2. Physical support: Taking risks uses vast amounts of mental and physical energy. As servant-leaders we need to ensure that our followers take time off to "re-create." There is a parable about an old miner who once explained to a visitor, "I let my mules spend one day a week outside the mines to keep them from going blind." "Blindness," or burnout, can easily result unless servant-leaders guard the health of their flock like sagacious shepherds. Polls indicate a growing backlash against money-making at any cost. Many people are saying they'll gladly swap some of the perks of success for personal time—time to know themselves, their families, and

the world that exists outside their job. Respect this and use it to allow people to give the best they can give. (Robert Greenleaf said, "An institution that has firmly established the context of people first moves from people-using to people-building.")

3. Spiritual support: If a servant-leader can offer only one thing, it should be hope. Hope for the future of the organization and for the individual. Inner fulfillment is ultimately more potent than all the money, titles, and trophies in the world. Servant-leaders make sure their people know that what they are doing is valuable and makes a difference. This hope must be believable and contain a challenge. When President John F. Kennedy said that people would walk on the moon within a few years, he challenged the rest of us to commit to his vision. We did, because he gave us hope that by accepting the challenge we would benefit not only our selves but all future generations. He appealed to the best within us.

A servant-leader can't demand what people can't give, however. If you stretch people too far too fast, you can say goodbye to productivity, quality, creativity, and loyalty. Be sensitive to how much risk your people can tolerate before they rebel or quit. Go slowly at first. Work in measured increments until people learn to accept risk as part of the normal daily process.

Train

The most effective-servant leaders are usually great coaches and skill builders. It is said that legendary football coach Vince Lombardi greeted his champion teams on the first day of practice by holding up a pigskin oval and saying, "This is a football." He understood the value of reviewing the basics. Many organizations fail because they do not review the basics often enough. Today the motto for productivity and competitiveness is, "ahead with the basics." Don't lose track of the basics that got you where you are: your value systems, beliefs, processes, and procedures. At the same time, have the courage to risk changing what doesn't work. Training may mean developing new or improved skills. Skills build confidence, and confidence builds skills; both are an essential part of the risk because each element reinforces and feeds the other. Three kinds of support fall into this category:

- New information to expand thinking: Information is the key twenty-first-century power tool. Power used to belong to whoever had the strongest army. Then it meant who had the most money. Now it means who has the best information.
- New ideas to spark creativity: Describe your vision of the future and ask how others would go about getting there. Help them to be part of the process. Encourage and create discussion groups or focus groups whose sole purpose is to master mind ideas.
- New experiences to attack preconceptions: Some people seek out new experiences as a way to increase intellectual capacity. Others literally have to be picked up and moved to where they can see that something is working or that others are taking similar risks. Putting them in new and different environments can broaden their comfort zone and ignite their vision of the future.

Naturally, the kind and extent of training depends on the organization and the risks being undertaken. Once upon a time we put people in jobs and they stayed there; that's all they did and all they knew how to do. It was a great way to control people and retain power. Now we have interdependent circles and a great need to cross-train for speed, flexibility, and empowerment.

Empowerment is an enormous risk. It requires leaders to swap some of their personal and position power for increased power of the group. That's not easy to do when you've invested so much of yourself to get where you are. When you're really willing to share power, you become even more powerful because you make others powerful. You experience power-enhancement, not power-loss. Training people, giving them new experiences and ideas means sharing power because knowledge is true power. It can be a difficult adjustment, but the servant-leader recognizes that it must happen if there is to be growth and change.

Acknowledge

People work hardest when they know that what they do is making a difference and when they know that you know that what they are doing is making a difference. Here are some ways to encourage this behavior:

1. Recognize the accomplishments: Acknowledge those who are out in front, those who have stretched and grown the most, and those

who have risked the most or went the extra mile. Measure progress by where someone has been compared to where he or she is now.

2. Recognize effort as well as results: One of the fastest ways to destroy any team or organization is to reward only the highest achievers. It creates a "winner take all" environment, which in turn destroys effort in those who are still progressing. People need to be acknowledged for trying, for taking a difficult step or for coming out of their comfort zone. Sometimes people fail temporarily, but they pick themselves up and try again. Servant-leaders show people how they can fail forward when they learn from their experiences. Sometimes, triumph or success consists of just finishing the race, not winning it.
3. Recognize individuals and teams: Interlocking circles are made up of interdependent teams. The old cliche that a chain is only as strong as its weakest link was never truer. This doesn't mean ignoring high achievers. (Fortunately, they are usually happy to share the glory.) It means being sure that group effort and results are respected, recognized, and acknowledged as much as individual success.

Reward

Remember that what gets rewarded gets done. That doesn't mean tossing around certificates, medals, or trips to Bermuda. Rewards can be both tangible and intangible. Often a heartfelt "That was great!" when someone has really accomplished something is a hundred times better than formula awards. Insincerity poisons initiative faster than indifference. Lavish praise can be insulting and counterproductive when the recipient knows it's undeserved.

The rewards that most people want most are priceless: the pleasure of an honest compliment, the excitement of taking a risk, the feelings of self-fulfillment, self-esteem, and true team spirit, the electrifying sense of being part of something greater than themselves. Most of all, they want someone to be aware of what they are accomplishing, to really notice and really care.

The Self-Powering Cycle

As risk takers increase their skills, their accomplishments fuel more enthusiasm and expansion, which leads to their doing even more. The result

Figure 13.2
Commitment-competence-confidence cycle.

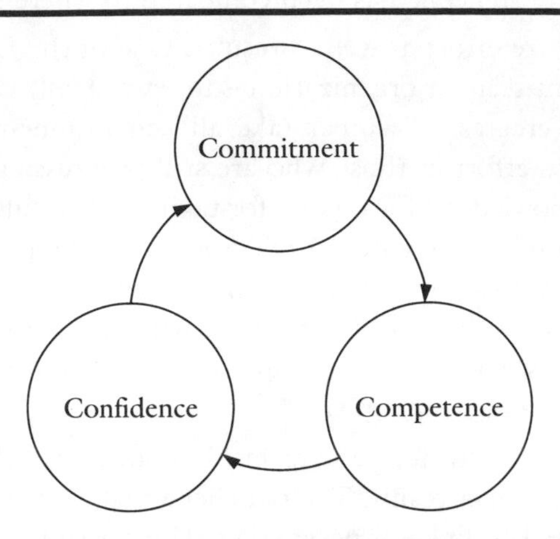

is an ever-increasing circle of competence-confidence-commitment (see Figure 13.2). Each part of the cycle contributes to the growth of the other. Science has yet to come up with a real perpetual motion machine, one that creates all the energy it needs to continue indefinitely, but true servant-leaders have discovered its human counterpart.

Where does this cycle start? Like the chicken and the egg, people argue endlessly about which part of the cycle comes first. And, like the ancient riddle, there is no simple answer. Increasing someone's competence through training and support makes them better able to do the job, which builds self-confidence. Confident people are more willing to take risks to increase their competence. Competent, confident people are more likely to feel committed to the source of their new empowerment.

Unfortunately, this positive energy cycle of competence-confidence-commitment has a dark side. Many Americans are reaching adulthood without the competence or confidence to get and hold jobs. As a result, many American businesses find themselves having to take over the job of training workers. Servant-leaders can shatter this negative cycle and build capable workers by training to increase competence, praising and supporting to increase confidence, and inspiring to increase commitment. A good way to begin this process is to:

- Identify the important risks and challenges facing you and your organization.

- Analyze the strength of your cycle of commitment, competence, and confidence.
- Rate your success at sharing your vision of the future and how you and your followers will get there.
- Identify the supports and incentives you can offer to encourage risk taking.

Lead by Example

The author Elie Wiesel said, "First we must understand that there can be no life without risk—and then when our center is strong, everything else is secondary, even the risks. Thus, we best prepare by building our inner strength, by sound philosophy, by reaching out to others, by asking ourselves what matters most." But luring people onto the perilous bridge to the future is something of a carrot-and-stick process. Servant-leaders must point out the risks of not risking. The ultimate risk, of course, is that we may die—if not literally, then in the context of being a productive part of a thriving organization. Risk is essential to staying healthy and competitive.

Sometimes, in desperate situations, the risks of inaction are so obvious that no further persuasion is necessary. Usually, though, the servant-leader has to paint a vivid picture of both the "carrot" (the potential advantages of risk over no risk) and the "stick" (the possible disadvantages of avoiding risk). Think of a reluctant risk taker being pushed onto a perilous bridge. More often, the leader is already out there, coaxing people to follow and throwing a life line to the guy who's slipped. That's because we lead first by example. Everything we say or do sends a message, sets a tone, or teaches people what to do or what not to do. Your example reflects your core values and has a massive affect on others. Congruency between your words and actions is paramount in your ability to be a successful risk-taking servant-leader.

Daring to Fail

The great inventor Thomas Alva Edison said, "A failure teaches you that something can't be done—that way." Failure tells us what not to do, what doesn't work. Failure sends us in a new direction, gives us new information, new ideas, and new experiences. If we don't start taking more risks and encouraging "out-of-the-box thinking," we'll never be able to fulfill ourselves, either as individuals, organizations, or nations.

Gwen Edwards says, "If we're here to make a difference—and why else are we here—we have to do things that have never been done before. To many people that's a risk. To me it's an adventure.

A servant-leader who convinces others to challenge their limits is one who makes the goals irresistible and the consequences as painless as possible. The second is harder than the first. Many leaders have a natural ability to inspire their people, to help them identify who and what they can become as a result of risk. However, learning to encourage their failure takes practice. Garis Distelhorst, Executive Director of the National Association of College Stores (NACS), says, "We also have to have a willingness to tolerate failure and not kill risk taking by doling out punishments every time somebody makes a mistake. I tell my colleagues that if we don't fail once in awhile, we're probably not doing enough."

So, no clenched teeth behind the smile, no abrupt intake of breath, no hollow reassurance. Go ahead and fail enthusiastically. When you can tolerate failure as an essential part of advancement, a valuable stepping stone to success, a prerequisite for what is to come, then your passion will communicate itself to your colleagues. They'll be right out there on the bridge to the future with you, ready to take whatever comes.

Nation and World Building

Our great nation was forged on the anvil of risk. Our founding fathers declared their independence and, in so doing, proclaimed that they would risk their "lives . . . fortunes . . . and sacred honor." Since then, men and women have been rewarded for dreaming great dreams and risking everything to see their dreams come true. We are all descendants of risk takers.

Whether it was Columbus sailing the unchartered ocean or the Apollo astronauts sailing the untested universe, risk taking has always been the golden thread that weaves through the accomplishments of individuals who have shown us a better way and a bright new future. The example of these risk takers help us fulfill ourselves and encourage us to make meaningful contributions. Our families, our communities, our organizations, our nation and our global village awaits the courageous risk-taking servant-leader.

14

Becoming a Servant-Leader: The Personal Development Path

Isabel O. Lopez

My earliest introduction to servant-leadership was my family: My mother, who cared, taught, guided, encouraged, and laughed; my grandmother, who imparted wisdom, joy, teachings, and acceptance of others; and my father, who taught me simplicity, honor, and the capacity to love. How wonderful to be served—to have others in both our personal and institutional lives caring for us and being concerned with our growth as persons. I was lucky to have such models and to be on the receiving end of the actions of these simple and powerful servant-leaders.

When I went to school, I met other servant-leaders: Teachers who caused me to stretch, who encouraged, who loved. But, for the first time, I was also exposed to people who were leaders but not servants and to servants who were not leaders. Somewhere in the movement from family to institution, I began to learn about the dark side of life; not everyone was concerned with the other, and some were even invested in the failure, not the growth of others. Servant-leaders are leaders because they serve first. Then they are chosen to lead.

Robert Greenleaf defines the servant-leader as being a servant first. He acknowledges the difficulty of the term servant-leader. In workshops on servant-leadership, participants often struggle with this language. The traditional Western image of a leader is a person who is in charge and in control of others. The image of servant is one who is submissive, takes orders and does as told. How can one possibly be both? If these are our images, do we even want to be servant-leaders? So we struggle with the correctness of these traditional images, begin to understand the limitations of our understanding, create new images, and still have trouble with being both a servant and a leader in action. This is the beginning of the path to becoming a servant-leader—struggling with the paradox. Charles Handy, in *The Age of Paradox,* says, "Paradox . . . confuses us because it asks us to live with simultaneous opposites."

And besides dealing with the paradox, Greenleaf puts a test of our performance as servant-leaders before us. The test, in Greenleaf's words, is as follows: "The best test, and difficult to administer, is: Do those served grow as persons? Do they, while being served, become healthier, wiser, freer, more autonomous, more likely themselves to become servants? And what is the effect on the least privileged in society, will (s)he benefit, or at least not be further deprived?"

In order to develop our personal path to becoming servant-leaders, it might be of help to review the steps that Greenleaf took. In his essay, "Old Age: The Ultimate Test of the Spirit," Greenleaf gives a retrospective. He says:

> So I, in my eighty-third year and with a much larger view of the world than my father had, now lament what seems the small number among those who see themselves as able, conscientious, and dedicated, and who are disposed to respond to a vision of the larger roles they might play and the much greater service to society that the institutions they influence might render. We have plenty of people with the stamina to build and lead a much more serving society and I believe they would lead fuller lives, if they would rise to their opportunities. What they seem to lack is spirit, and I wonder what they will be like when they grow old. Will they find it the 'best' that is yet to be? I said at the outset that I cannot define spirit. But I have tried in what I have said to give human spirit a meaning that is beyond rational definition.

Earlier in his essay, he says that "spirit can be said to be the driving force behind the motive to serve." Perhaps, Greenleaf, in his gentle way, smiles as more and more people are drawn to servant-leadership and toward developing themselves to be servant-leaders.

The steps that Robert Greenleaf took that resulted in his becoming a servant-leader are as follows:

- He took meditative intervals.
- He engaged in conversation with people.
- He analyzed his dreams.
- He developed close relationships with several institutions.
- He became interested in the ethics of his company and developed relationships with others that had a similar interest.
- Although he did not consider himself a scholar and did not focus on reading as part of his development at this time, he did read deeply into the history of two institutions: AT&T and the Religious Society of Friends.

What strikes me about Greenleaf's development path is that it was a path of self development that led to his becoming a servant-leader. As Director of Management Research at AT&T, he undoubtedly had developed his analytical skills: the skills that allowed him to analyze, see gaps, and refine information. His path to servant-leadership seemed to focus on the developing or deepening of new skills; those developed from other than the rational and that were relational in nature.

In becoming a servant-leader, this essay assumes that one has developed the logical and analytical skills that are taught, rewarded, and reinforced by our teaching institutions. This essay is also built around the premise that the mind is a tool of the heart—a concept that goes back to ancient Greece, or perhaps even further back. The personal development suggestions that will be made in this chapter focus on the characteristics of servant-leaders and how we might develop them in ourselves.

What *are* the characteristics of servant leaders that we might emulate?

- Servant-leaders express unlimited liability for others.
- Servant-leaders know self well.

- Servant-leaders are holders of liberating vision.
- Servant-leaders are users of persuasion.
- Servant-leaders are builders of community.
- Servant-leaders use power ethically.

These characteristics will be explored one at a time.

Expressing Unlimited Liability for Others

This characteristic, as well as the others, is a difficult one. In our litigious society, we struggle with the implications of the legalistic framework of liability. Greenleaf speaks about liability in the context of "s/he who is served should be loved in the process" and that "living in community as one's basic involvement will generate an exportable surplus of love which the individual may carry into his or her many involvements with institutions. . ." So, there is a root of unconditional love in servant-leadership. How might we point ourselves in this direction?

First, we accept others as they are. This is a more spiritual than psychological approach. There is beauty in each person, and we focus on that beauty. I am reminded of one of Anthony De Mello's stories. In *The Song of the Bird,* he tells this story.

> I was a neurotic for years. I was anxious and depressed and selfish. Everyone kept telling me to change. I resented them, and I agreed with them, and I wanted to change, but simply couldn't, no matter how hard I tried.
>
> What hurt the most was that, like the others, my best friend kept insisting that I change. So I felt powerless and trapped. Then, one day, he said to me, "Don't change. I love you just as you are." These words were music to my ears; "don't change. Don't change. Don't change . . . I love you as you are."
>
> I relaxed. I came alive. And suddenly I changed! Now I know that I couldn't really change until I found someone who would love me whether I changed or not.

Second, we must learn to empathize. This entails learning to walk in someone else's shoes. Being able to empathize is a sign of our maturity. Sympathy, on the other hand, only allows us to feel sorry for someone else. The outcome of acceptance and empathy is that we will not reject the other and will therefore be practicing "unlimited liability."

To develop this characteristic, try the following exercises. When someone brings you a problem, an issue, or an idea, listen first. Don't assume you know what they want. Just listen. Listening is an intense activity. You may want to ask someone to talk to you for five minutes while you listen. After they have finished, repeat what you heard. Did you hear what they were saying? The more emotional the conversation, the more intense is the listening required. Ask yourself the following questions:

- Was I able to concentrate?
- Did I have other thoughts running through my head while the other person was talking?
- How often was I framing solutions to what I perceived was the "problem" rather than listening?

Although the practice of listening is intense, the opportunities to practice present themselves all the time.

Another activity that will help to develop the characteristic of expressing unlimited liability for others is to view those we serve as the acquirers rather than the recipients of service. In other words, they have a choice and we do not have all the answers for them. Practice asking questions rather than giving answers. Some questions you might ask are:

- How might I be of help?
- What is it that you need from me?
- What resources do I have that would be of use to you in your circumstance?
- How can I help you think through your choices in this matter?
- Would it be helpful for me to share my experience with you?

Again, the opportunity to practice asking questions will present itself as often as the current opportunity to give answers does. The danger in providing our answers to someone else's issue is that our experience and circumstance may not match theirs.

Know Self Well

The development of this characteristic is critical to the servant leader. The old Chinese saying, "S/he who feels punctured must have once been a balloon" speaks to this characteristic. Our actions can spring from our own needs for recognition, acknowledgment, and power unless we know ourselves well. The development of this characteristic is a life-long commitment, but is the foundation of becoming the servant-leaders of which Robert Greenleaf speaks.

One step we might take to know ourselves well is to be active learners who are immersed in the world. Greenleaf's learning path included conversing with people, developing institutional relationships, developing deeper relationships with people around a common interest, and doing some in-depth reading. We might engage in some of the same activities. Some guiding questions for us might be:

- Who is missing from my circle of friends and acquaintances? Missing might be people of color, people of other religious beliefs or lifestyles, people from other countries or areas of our country, or even people from professions different from ours.
- Who do I know that has relationships with a variety of people who are not part of my circle?
- What institutions do I know the least about? How might I find out more?
- Who is interested in some of the deeper issues that concern me? How can I learn from them?
- In what areas do I normally read? How can I expand my learning through reading?

Another step we might take is to start inside ourselves and light our own lamps. Another De Mello story, "The Truth Shop," talks to the difficulty of this step.

> I could hardly believe my eyes when I saw the name of the shop: The Truth Shop.
>
> The saleswoman was very polite: What type of truth did I wish to purchase, partial or whole? The whole truth, of course. No deceptions for me, no defenses, no rationalizations. I wanted my truth plain and unadulterated. She waved me on to another side of the store.

> The salesman there pointed to the price tag. "The price is very high, Sir," he said. "What is it?," I asked, determined to get the whole truth, no matter what it cost. "Your security, Sir," he answered.
>
> I came away with a heavy heart. I still need the safety of my unquestioned beliefs.

Starting inside ourselves requires a great commitment on our part. The value is that we *know* who we are, our behavior becomes more consistent, and we become worthy of the trust of others. Activities to engage in include the following:

- Analyze your dreams, as Greenleaf did.
- Keep a journal.
- Be aware of feedback that is given to us.
- Meditate.
- Find a teacher.
- Develop your own path.

Another step to take in knowing self is to withdraw, be silent, and reorient. This step is the place from which we gain perspective. With the speed of change in our world today, it is easy to lose perspective. Without perspective, we can too easily lose our way.

Hold a Liberating Vision

This characteristic is key in relationship to being allowed to serve, to helping point the way, and to allowing others to join us. A liberating vision will serve to enlarge and create spaces in which our work can become more focused, more excellent, and more apt to make a difference in both our personal and institutional lives. Elements of this characteristic include being comfortable with the mysterious nature of things, and being comfortable with the use of intuition. Striving to embody this characteristic helps us to develop our foresight—we learn to see a way and point to it.

Suggestions that might help us develop this characteristic are:

- Develop the creative part of you.
- Draw rather than write your ideas.

- Write a poem about your vision.
- Use metaphors to capture your ideas.
- Practice reading between the lines in written items.
- Practice hearing between the words in oral communication on both personal and business matters. (Sometimes what is spoken or written is only the surface.)
- Work at understanding what is really important to you, both personally and professionally.

Use Persuasion

This characteristic assumes that servant-leaders do not control others. Rather than control, they share their wisdom. Their approach is one person at a time while seeking always to develop understanding. Servant-leaders use this characteristic *now,* but the impact of their persuasion withstands the test of time and effects the future. Look at Greenleaf himself. His major essay was published 25 years ago. Today, his model of servant-leadership informs much of the current leadership literature.

Two basic principles underscore the use of persuasion in this context: one is the reinforcement of hope; the second is that others can do for themselves what they must do.

The use of this characteristic allows the servant-leader to offer hope to the cynical and to those who have forgotten how to hope. This characteristic also allows us to persuade others to see themselves as empowered people—we are not the empowerers. Suggestions in this area are:

- Check your own quotient of hope.
- Point out the possibilities for others.
- Develop a patient attitude.
- Do not expect quick results but notice the beginnings of change, the seedlings that are growing.
- Share your joy.
- Smile often.

Build Community

Builders of community invent the ways that we will live together, either personally or institutionally. Greenleaf quotes Camus when he speaks of builders of community:

> Great ideas, it has been said, come into the world as gently as doves. Perhaps, then, if we listen attentively, we shall hear, amid the uproar of empires and nations, a faint flutter of wings, the gentle stirring of life and hope. Some will say this hope lies in a nation, others, in a man. I believe rather that it is awakened, revived, nourished by millions of solitary individuals whose deeds and works every day negate frontiers and the crudest implications of history. As a result there shines forth fleetingly the ever-threatened truth that each and every person, on the foundations of his or her own suffering and joys, builds for them all." (Camus, "Create Dangerously," 1961)

Wendell Berry in *What Are People For* expands on this thought. He says:

> . . . when a community loses its memory, its members no longer know one another. How can they know one another if they have forgotten one another's stories, how can they know whether or not to trust one another? People who do not trust one another do not help one another, and moreover they fear one another. And this is our predicament now. Because of a general distrust and suspicion, we not only lose one another's help and companionship, but we are now living in jeopardy of being sued.

Builders of community understand that we each build for all. Builders of community also understand that work is as essential for the worker as what is being produced.

In these times of corporate competition, mergers, and buyouts, I often wonder how many executives cry over the effects of their actions on their workers. And I wonder how many workers resist the temptation to become bitter and powerless in the aftermath of corporate layoffs. I also wonder about the effects on the products being produced. Certainly we see many new programs coming into place to respond to these effects, TQM (Total Quality Management) being just one of the many. Sometimes I wonder if the effects of the current environment drive us to look for solutions that are more meaningful, which might explain the deeper interest in Greenleaf and others who speak a similar language: the language of ethics, of values, of principles, and of love.

Builders of community understand the value of each person and how each person contributes to the whole. In workgroups, they insist on teams led by *primus inter pares,* or "first among equals." The concept of first among equals can be implemented either formally or informally.

Formally, one might ask a team to choose its leader. Informally, a group can develop an attitude of first among equals, rather than power by formal position. The informal way requires much discussion and consensus building so that the philosophy frames the work. Some suggestions to develop this characteristic are:

- Share your story.
- Look for the good in each person.
- Create spaces that allow people to bloom personally and to perform professionally.
- Listen for the "faint fluttering of wings."
- Practice hospitality: the art of letting the stranger in to be who they are; not who we are.

Use Power Ethically

The more we know ourselves, the less apt we will be to abuse power. Servant-leaders have made this connection. They assure that no one is harmed by the actions of the team. They accept authority that is freely and knowingly granted. And they are aware that giving is a potentially immoral act. In many ways, this characteristic is developed as an outcome of the development of the other characteristics.

The suggestion for our progress on this characteristic is to apply the servant-leader test. Do those served grow as persons? Do they, while being served, become healthier, wiser, freer, more autonomous, more likely themselves to become servants? And, what is the effect on the least privileged in society? Will they benefit or, at least, not be further deprived? The bottom line of this characteristic is to be able to respond with a "yes" to this test.

To develop the characteristics of a servant-leader is not easy—and not fast. For us to be able to express unlimited liability for the other, to know ourselves well, to be holders of liberating vision, to use persuasion wisely, to be builders of community, and to use power ethically sets a high standard for us. We are required to be committed and can only take one step at a time. Another Chinese saying, which tells us that the journey of 10,000 miles begins with a single step, points to the requirement of commitment. And, before we know it, we have gone many miles. Each of us individually must decide on our first steps.

Servant-leadership and servant-leaders fit into a larger context. We begin our development as individuals. We then become healthier, wiser, more autonomous, and more disposed to serve. Because of who we have become, we are then asked and choose to lead. From this dual role we can become the roots of communities and institutions that enlarge and liberate. Our institutions can then become distinctive through raising their level of performance as servants. Institutions play such a critical role in our society. If they become servant leaders, a society can emerge that is more just and caring where the less able and the more able serve each other. We start with one person, and then with another, and then yet another.

Perhaps this time is ours. In 1992, DDB Needham, a marketing and research firm, released the results of a 16-year survey on lifestyles. I was struck by some of their findings.

- Trust continues its steady decline: (in 1992) 66 percent of women and 62 percent of men said, "Most people are honest," down from their peaks of 77 percent and 74 percent respectively in 1976.
- . . . 79 percent believe "Most big companies are just out for themselves," up from about 65 percent in the mid-70s.
- The number of people saying, "It is hard to get a good job these days," has climbed sharply since 1989, to 79 percent of women and 75 percent of men, approaching the high of 83 percent for both men and women in 1983.
- After dipping in the late 1980s, "dread of the future" has risen since 1989 to 29 percent.
- If they could do it all again, 60 percent would "sure do things differently," up from 56.5 percent in 1988. Paradoxically, 75 percent say consistently over the years that they "would be content to live in the same town the rest of my life."

- But there's been an increase in people who have trouble getting to sleep, and reach for pain relievers "right away" when they don't feel well.

Perhaps in light of these indicators, servant-leaders will be those who provide a "sense of continuity, a sense of connection and a sense of direction," to use Charles Handy's words from *The Age of Paradox*.

Robert Greenleaf died in 1990, and now our generations are called to become the servant-leaders who will act on the legacies we have been left. Welcome to paradox. Welcome to joy.

15

Managing Toward the Millennium

James E. Hennessy, John Killian, and Suki Robins

The forces management must deal with in the 1990s could be a rather disheartening subject. We could catalog the complex problems facing us all—world debt, international terrorism, social upheavals of all sorts—and leave you feeling hopeless and helpless. But, instead, we'll offer a new way of looking at the issues and trends we'll face as we approach the next century, and a way of dealing with them that will spur you to think positively about the challenges of the decade ahead.

Trends are apparent now that seem to indicate we may be in a transitional period between two very different ways of dealing with the challenges of business and of society as a whole. The outgoing order is the age of specialization, and the incoming, the era of integration. We'd like to discuss some of the major forces we can expect to face in the 1990s, and what the era of integration will mean for our businesses. Then we'll offer a philosophy of management based on quality and servant-leadership and grounded in ethics and the wisdom of the ages. This philosophy will serve to smooth the coming transition and draw the greatest success from it.

Major Forces Affecting Leadership

Most of the forces dominating the agenda in the next decade have been with us in the current decade, and in some cases in past decades, as well. We have chosen four forces that will become increasingly important in the near future, forces that encompass in their complexity virtually all the items enumerated by the advisory council. These four are:

- Globalization
- The need to satisfy multiple stakeholders
- Environmental deterioration
- And the growing shortage of qualified labor in developed countries.

Globalization

Globalization means more than just selling your products and services in other countries. It means the earth's the limit on where you get your raw materials or where you locate your plants. It means marketing to many different local markets, not to a single homogeneous one. It means your company can base its headquarters in Europe, build its factory in Taiwan, and sell its product in America. And the economic unification of Europe will add a new dimension to the rules of global commerce.

Multiple Stakeholders

Satisfying the demands of multiple stakeholders is an idea that's spreading like wildfire. It used to be that a corporate executive served one primary master: the stockholder. Earnings per share measured success. But the stockholder is not the only one with a stake in the business, and changing one little vowel sound has changed the whole orientation of corporate responsibility. We now see the stockholder as just one of many stakeholders, stakeholders that include customers, employees, suppliers, regulators, and even community and environmental advocates. And the executive now must balance the often conflicting needs and demands of all these stakeholders.

Environmental Deterioration

The problems of our natural environment have become front-page news. New England Telephone's headquarters in Rhode Island overlooks

Narragansett Bay where the tanker World Prodigy ran aground, spilling hundreds of thousands of gallons of oil into the bay. And this was just one of many such incidents. We must vigorously examine the relationship between business and the world we live in. The greenhouse effect, holes in the ozone layer, endangered water supplies, disposal of waste—hazardous, toxic, and just plain voluminous—all these issues demand attention now if we expect to enjoy the kind of future we want for our customers and ourselves.

The Labor Shortage

The shortage of qualified labor in developed countries is a growing problem. The nature of the jobs available calls for fewer and fewer unskilled workers and more and more workers with specialized skills. In America, the "baby bust" and the weaknesses in our school systems have combined to produce a shortage of people capable of mastering the skills required for tomorrow's work.

Now, how are we to deal with these issues? Some people might be tempted to say, "That's not my company's problem. That's a problem for society." But the days when business could afford to think like that are gone. The problems of society *are* the problems of business.

In the past, business often tried to protect and insulate itself from the problems of society. Are drugs a problem in your community? Test all your employees, and lock the door behind any who test positive for drug use. But this approach will no longer work. Why? Because there is a shift taking place which inexorably forces business to reconnect with its environment, both social and physical. A team of researchers at the Fordham Graduate School of Business took a look at our advisory council's 39 forces, and reinterpreted them for us in the light of their theory that the world is now moving from the age of specialization into the era of integration.

For a long time, we achieved improvements in productivity by increasing specialization of task, labor, and knowledge. Task—the number of separate operations that must be performed to accomplish a job; labor—the number of different people who perform the operations; and knowledge—the amount of information each contributing worker has about the entire picture. The more specialized the work became, the more coordination of the pieces was required. Enter middle management and staffs. Layers and layers of management emerged whose job sometimes amounted to nothing more than putting back together the pieces that specialization had separated.

But specialization has a point of diminishing returns, and we have passed that point. Excessive specialization leads to workers who feel powerless, workers who lose the feeling that the jobs they do have any meaning. Too many management layers stifle initiative and creativity and turn a company into a lumbering giant that can't respond quickly to today's rapid changes in technology and markets. The costs of the specialization-coordination pattern rise faster than the benefits.

Over-specialization has become so widespread that the pendulum has started to swing back in the other direction: We are seeing more and more reintegration of overly specialized activities. The Fordham group suggests that you think of this as a new set of lenses to focus through. If you looked at the world through lenses that turned everything upside down, you would certainly have difficulty orienting yourself. How much more difficulty would you have if the world actually *did* turn upside down, and you continued to look at it through your old lenses? The world is becoming more integrated, customized, individualized, and global. If our organizations continue to focus through lenses that recognize only the specialized, mass-produced, mass-consumed, and local, then we will see increased chaos, turbulence, and uncertainty.

Take another look now at the four forces just discussed through the new lenses. Each of the forces can be seen to relate to this change from specialization to integration. Globalization—and particularly the unification of Europe—takes the separate pieces of our world and integrates them into one global economy. Increased attention to multiple stakeholders integrates the interests of many separate parties into a new concept of the unified interest of the whole corporation. Environmental concerns integrate the corporation with the physical environment it operates in. And the shortage of qualified labor in developed countries, along with the increased involvement in education and training that shortage requires of business, integrates the corporation with the society it does business in—the society it draws both its customers and its workforce from.

A New Philosophy of Management

What does all this mean to management? It means that the management techniques that worked in the age of specialization will not fit in the era of integration. Consequently, a new philosophy of management is in order. Imagine yourself seated at your desk, in your own office.

Now imagine that your office sits on a platform supported by twin pillars that are in turn supported by a bedrock foundation. You are the leaders of the 1990s, seated at those desks. The first pillar is *quality* and the second is *servant-leadership,* and the bedrock they're rising from is composed of *ethics* and *the wisdom of the ages.*

Let's start with servant-leadership. In the age of specialization, the predominant style of leadership was authoritarian, modeled largely on the military chain of command. The new style of leadership appropriate to the era of integration can be called servant-leadership, a term used by Robert Greenleaf, who was a "lifelong student of organization." He spent 38 years at AT&T in the field of management research, development, and education. After he retired from AT&T in 1964, he lectured and wrote widely—and wisely—on the subject of leadership.

Authoritarian leaders give orders and protect the concentration of power at the top of the chain of command. To them, people are simply a means for achieving a purpose. In contrast, the servant-leader leads by persuasion on the merits of ideas, and seeks to empower all who can contribute. The servant-leader sees people as an end in themselves, worthy of full development. The goal of the authoritarian leader is to have obedient, relatively passive followers. The goal of the servant-leader is to interact with active followers in such a way as to maximize their self-sufficiency and creativity to satisfy all stakeholders. The servant-leader helps followers to grow, and benefits from their initiative.

The key characteristic that distinguishes Greenleaf's ideas about leadership from other, similar philosophies is that for Greenleaf's servant-leader, the desire to serve comes before the desire to lead. Those who have leadership qualities will become leaders because it is their most effective way of serving. "Leader" is an assumed role; "servant" defines the person.

Inverting the Management Pyramid

The traditional structural model for business is the pyramid. The broad base of the pyramid represents the bottom tier of the organizational ladder, the majority of the workforce. As the pyramid narrows toward the top, it is occupied by layer after layer of management, each successive layer becoming smaller and more powerful until it reaches the CEO on top. But the workforce is changing. The majority of employees in most service-oriented businesses are not unskilled laborers, but skilled knowledge workers. Peter Drucker has said that the corporate CEO must begin to operate more like the head of a hospital or university, or the conductor of an orchestra. Information does not need to pass through so many layers of management. And, as more and more work is reintegrated, fewer and fewer coordinating managers are needed. All this contributes to the flattening of the pyramid and the elimination of several of those intermediate layers. Along with this change, the pyramid is flipped so that the servant-leader is the foundation. This is the model of servant-leadership: The leader's role is to support, and the fully empowered workforce is the broad top.

A look at two very different CEOs will illustrate the value of servant-leadership. One is chairman of a major airline, and the other is chairman of an office furniture manufacturer. The airline executive was accorded the dubious honor of being chosen by *Fortune* magazine as one of America's toughest bosses. According to articles in *Fortune* and *The Wall Street Journal,* he is demanding, impulsive, and prone to undermining his own managers, and has created an atmosphere within his company of tension, intrigue, and lack of trust. His employees feel management is obsessed with pinching pennies and controlling every aspect of their working lives, and that has destroyed their dignity and self-respect.

In marked contrast to this executive stands the office furniture chairman. The atmosphere in his company is one of creativity, enthusiasm, and shared goals. He has built an organization that fosters strong bonds between management and employees. This man believes employees are bound not primarily by contractual relationships that spell out mechanical details but by covenantal relationships that fill deeper needs and rest on "shared commitment to ideas, to issues, to values, to goals, and to management processes." To such a person, leadership is not a technique, but a philosophy. And it is a philosophy that brings practical results: His company has achieved a worldwide reputation for excellence, and in 1989, a *Fortune* survey ranked it ninth among the most admired corporations in America.

Clearly, these two CEOs have very different uses for their power, and the bottom line reflects this difference: For the ten-year period from 1977 to 1987, the servant leader's company averaged a 27 percent annual return to investors, while the authoritarian leader's company averaged 4 percent.

Closely related to this view of leadership is its twin pillar, quality. Simply stated, a business is committed to quality when it focuses on satisfying its customers, both external and internal, by conforming to mutually agreed-on requirements and by actively encouraging continuous improvement. The emphasis is on prevention, not on inspection. And the empowered worker is the key to the achievement of quality. After all, the front-line worker has the most contact with customers. So the front-line worker stands in the best position to understand customer needs and take the initiative to meet them.

Benchmarking is one of the main tools in today's quality effort. Go out and find the companies who do the job best: SAS for service, L. L. Bean for order-taking and warehousing, United Parcel Service for fleet management, Honda for manufacturing. Compare your operations to theirs, and see where you can improve. Quality has been hailed as the added value that gives a business an invaluable competitive edge. But keep in mind that as more and more companies become quality oriented, they will create a new standard of customer expectations. Soon quality will no longer be the key to getting ahead of your competition; it will become essential just to keep up with them!

Take another look at the organizational pyramid. Servant-leadership inverted it, putting the worker on top. Now add another layer above the worker, and label it "customer." That is how quality completes the model. The leader serves the worker, who in turn serves the customer.

Leadership Based on Integrity

The era of integration affects not only how individual tasks are organized. The underlying principle of both quality and servant-leadership is integrity, and integrity has the same Latin root as integration: integer, meaning whole, complete. They are two forms of the same word, and the era of integration is also the era of integrity. A business never needs to behave in any way other than ethically, justly, and with full respect for human dignity. The prophet Amos exhorted his people not to park their ethics outside the marketplace, but to keep them as a guiding light in all their dealings. Throughout the ages, prophets and philosophers in many guises have repeated this message. Mortimer Adler's *Six Great Ideas* eloquently expresses the values that must support business leadership in the decade ahead, and beyond.

A lot of this might sound idealistic to some people. There are those who believe that a business's only responsibility is to make money, and that doesn't include wasting time on social problems, or on how employees feel. These skeptics do not agree with what Robert Wood Johnson of Johnson & Johnson expressed more than 40 years ago when he said, "In a business society, every act of business has social consequences. . . . [And business] must be prepared to accept full responsibility for its acts." The skeptics also don't agree with Justice Louis Brandeis, who said, "In the field of modern business . . . mere money-making cannot be regarded as the legitimate end . . . since with the conduct of business human happiness or misery is inextricably interwoven."

Do you want your business to survive? Then try looking through new lenses. Take one example from the forces: the shortage of qualified labor. This problem has already reached the point where on-the-job training can no longer solve it. Of 41,000 people who took New York Telephone's basic skills exam for entry-level jobs in 1988, 75 percent failed. Where are you going to get the workers you need to fill your entry-level jobs? The answer is involvement in the community—integration with your social environment. More and more corporations are responding to the need to become involved with public education, not just with money, but with time and effort. NYNEX, Ashland Oil, General Electric, Procter & Gamble, and many others can be counted in this group. Join them.

It is a natural reaction for most people to resist change, to try to keep the comfortable world they are familiar with. But resistance is futile. The change is coming. Your choice is not whether to allow it—you can't hold back the tide. Your choice is whether to let the waves break and crush you, or to ride the crest of the wave triumphantly into the new era.

16

Team-Building and Servant-Leadership

Philip Chamberlain

A trustworthy professional is someone who serviceably combines a favorable "professed" theory of action with a technique of practice. An ambiguity of our age is how the word "profession" is so often used without well-defined interpretation. Someone who lives only by absolute technique of practice might be professional, but he or she may not be notably trustworthy without a favorable theory of action.[1]

One who would "profess" servant-leadership as a confirmed theory of action for prediction of team-building, and as a form of technical practice, authentically could be considered a trustworthy professional. In this regard, Robert K. Greenleaf considered team-building to be a meaningful technical practice as preparation of future professional leaders by forming "cohesive workgroups or teams with members become a community."

The definition of "community" can be symbolic for team-building, for it can mean there is a sense of reliance on one another toward a common cause. Greenleaf's reference to it can be viewed as the nature of an institution-style structure, which "enlarges and liberates" from team-building. This definition of enterprise community for the common good with a forecast theory of action is found in Webster's dictionary, of institution: "The act of instituting a permanent rule of conduct, something forming a prominence of established feature in social or national life."

This concept is clarified in Greenleaf's explanation of institutions. "An institution," said Greenleaf, "is a gathering of persons who have an accepted common purpose, and common discipline to guide the pursuit of that purpose, to the end that each involved person reaches higher fulfillment as a person, through serving and being served by the common venture, more so than would be achieved alone or in a less committed relationship." Clearly, this can indicate team-building as an ongoing, distinct, social structure that could be a meaningful aspect for the development of a spirited institution-type community in any enterprise form.

Likewise, James L. Hayes declared that, "An effective team is a living thing; an institution is its people. People breathe life and purpose and energy into an institution. An institution has a manner, spirit, tempo, and nature. It has joys and fears. But most of all, an effective institution has a purpose that is shared by all its members and to which they willingly will commit their efforts. People working together can do almost anything."

Megatrends

An era is a period that evidences change. In *Megatrends*, John Naisbitt defined a megatrend and outlined 10 elements that are changing in the current era. His definition of a megatrend is the "deinstitutionalization, the systematic breakdown of structures of many organizations created to organize delivery of private and public goods and services, e.g., health care system, education, and utilities." Deinstitutionalization does not necessarily mean that an institutional enterprise ceases to exist. It may simply mean that the institution is less community-based. These changes can affect team-building and servant-leadership.

In an era of megatrends, it is important to establish what professionalization and institutionalization can mean. Team-building and servant-leadership can offer a basis for investigating the feasibility of professional refinement and the restoration of institutional-style communities throughout society.

Organizations should operate to upgrade their standard community-based operations with team-building promoted by servant-leadership. This influential process could also cause individual team members to develop professionally by being influenced and guided by a theory of emotional attachment and respectful joint servant technique standards.

Team-Building Through Servant-Leadership

In a community-based environment, servant-leaders explore, listen, and guide community members to promote community allegiance and be fully conscious of community surroundings such as value-based factors of the past, present, and the future. The gathering of different community environments may adequately show the differences that exist between disjointed groups and connected teams; that is, "what individually is noticed" versus "what mutually is experienced." The following community components help promote guild-based (or union) team-building.

Structure

The structure of an institutional community can be seen a distinctive arrangement. It should make members feel that they are in a warm climate that serviceably produces intelligent team companionship through communal procedures. Structure should help members appreciate their rank and duty interdependence, and to understand that both personal and team goals are bonded with mutual support.

Greenleaf explained that there can be different institutional structures: formal and informal. A formal structure is one with closely-coupled sections; an informal structure has loosely coupled sections. The size of a community or the specialization level of individual sections can determine which structure is used. For a professional-based team-building process, this can mean that the structural form should work for the benefit of the team as well as the individual.

Formal community-based structures have its servant-leaders overseeing team-building from the perspective of total relations, in order to have all members focused on common team relationships.

Informal team-building provides mutual knowledge of and agreement about the structure's shared tasks and ensures that all team members know what is involved in accomplishing the tasks.

Responsibility

According to Robert K. Greenleaf, "A goal is something presently out of reach and something to strive for; every achievement starts with a goal." This can be a way of assuring promotion of the community's prevailing mission.

The following elements of mutual responsibility are rooted in the community environment:

- Mission: The reason the institutional enterprise exists, and the people it was instituted to serve.
- Purpose: The procedure by which the institution accomplishes its mission.
- Cause: The advantage constituents experience from the institution's mission and purpose.
- Goal: Special tasks structured to assure the vitality of the institution's cause, purpose, and mission.

Communication

Team-building and servant-leadership can productively integrate communication as a goal for the community. Members of a serviceable institutional community should freely communicate with each other. As Greenleaf stated, "Most of us at one time or another would really like to communicate, really get through to a significant level of meaning in the hearer's experience."

Members of each section of the community must understand what the other sections perform and what they may need. The extent to which team members practice open and honest communication across their separate segments, and then make a sincere effort to understand each other's point of view, is how they are able to create a community.

The following are ways to promote communication:

1. Ensure that the institution's operational reports reach team members in a timely manner.

2. Routine information should come from all parts of the community. No part of the community should fail to respond to communication from any individual member.
3. There should be planned times when team members gather and speak with each other around scheduled agendas.
4. Dated communication records should be available for team members who wish to refer to them.

Competence

Team members contribute to an institution's competence by applying distinctive talent and knowledge. To actually uphold proper experience and competence as professionals, they should consider life-long learning. Across time, people most often learn by experience and reasoning. Thus, from servant-leadership reasoning and team-building experience, team members can truly become trustworthy professionals and leaders.

Greenleaf asks whether those who are served grow as persons. "Do they, while being served, become healthier, wiser, freer, more autonomous, more likely themselves to become servants?" In this regard, a professional growth plan (PGP) may be helpful.

Insightful learning is theory contributed to memory by sensibility, with technique contributed to memory by investigation. Each team member's PGP should:

1. Stimulate continuing competence by discovering required community and personal goals.
2. Decipher existing personal strengths and weaknesses as they relate to a community occupation.
3. Motivate a lasting practice of self-assessment.
4. Define what learning activities will enable personal community growth.
5. Outline development activities within a feasible time/work period for each team member.

Team-building competence should be viewed long-term. Encouraging team members to consider a life-long professional learning strategy is also important.

Resolution

Community-based problems may be resolved by a three-step process: identifying and describing the situation; judging one or more ways the situation could be improved; and determining how the situation can be made better. Through servant-leadership, skillfully developed community-based teams can be encouraged to take part in decision-making that could affect the team and community. Problem-solving techniques should be considered as a way to generate consensus from different opinions. Guidelines for problem resolution can ensure that mutual trust will exist among team members. As part of this process, all members should be invited to openly express their ideas, opinions, disagreements, and feelings.

As explained by Robert K. Greenleaf, "One follows the steps of the creative process which requires that one stay with conscious analysis as far as it will carry one, and then withdraw, release the analytical pressure, if only for a moment, in full confidence that a resolving insight will come."

The following paradigm outlines steps of a leadership team strategy for resolution of comprehended community change that is mutually advocated. The paradigm also shows how to set in motion venerated change. Here are the *steps for resolution by a leadership team:*

1. A serious dilemma sensed by a community soon predicts a mutually agreed change.
2. A dilemma causes the team to view a decided change by members.
3. Benefit from change is acclaimed by servant-leadership as team enthusiast.
4. Likely response strategies are studied and theorized by authorized team members.
5. All likely strategy outcomes are explored by full team for community's well-being.
6. The most "alive" solution is jointly chosen from consensus-produced discussion by team.
7. Servant-leadership sanctions that solution contains both community and personal growth.

8. Ample communication of planned solution is issued to everyone having a foreseen interest.
9. Team properly sets in motion the solution, including how, location, and time.
10. Team has plan to value solution outcome to prove benefit to any and all affected.

In summary, team-building by servant-leadership can be understood to have distinct factors for developing different organization structures in a form by which they can be distinguished as institutional communities.

The following factors can be used to analyze the situation in a particular community:

1. The extent to which team members truly identify themselves as being part of a joint community structure, and mutually promote separate responsibilities for accomplishing shared mission.
2. The extent to which team members share communication and give mutual knowledge that is both straightforward and contains personalized information and outlooks.
3. The extent to which team members have the talent and expertise to mutually support the community, and have pledged to be servant-leaders and life-long learners.
4. The extent to which team members possess the ability and willful stimulus to mutually serve the decision-making and problem-solving for joint community preservation.

Servant-Leadership by Team-Members

Robert Greenleaf said that "There must be a goal, a concept of distinguished serving institution in which all who accept its discipline are lifted up to a nobler stature and greater effectiveness than they are likely to achieve on their own or with a less demanding discipline." This suggests that team-building and servant-leadership must be fused by performance disciplines to preserve an organization's institutional nature.

I conducted a special investigation project to discover whether institutions share common elements. Using the Institutional Distinctiveness Survey (IDS) to analyze the mission statements of many businesses, I discovered that there were nine commonalities. Each of these nine elements were identified by Robert Greenleaf.

The following servant-based discipline dimensions were employed by a large health care system:

Affinity and Aptitude Discipline Dimensions

- Humane: Servant devotion inside and outside the community environment, highlighting compassion and empathy to all others.
- Moral: Servant devotion to up-to-date society values favorably serving trustworthy professional and official settings.
- Intelligence: Servant devotion to help support personal obligations to thinking realization and elevation.

Performance and Effect Discipline Dimensions

- Personal Development: Servant devotion to help personal development in sundry capacities and talents.
- Egalitarian: Servant devotion to support interest of persons regardless of race, color, culture, or social status.
- Socio-Political: Servant devotion to encourage accord with favorable civic, social, or professional associations.

Viewpoint and Synthesis Discipline Dimensions

- Spiritual: Servant devotion to philosophical linkage of both personal thought and feeling for uniqueness of one's spirit.
- Tradition: Servant devotion to encourage lively heritage as basis for interpreting issues of contemporary society.
- Epochal: Servant devotion to encourage awareness of conditions with needed attention for lasting professional growth.

The Department of Nursing at Christ Hospital and Medical Center has the same goals, but it crystalizes them in a statement: "A true profession has both a theory of action and technique of practice to fulfill its professed mission. The professional nurse is also a specialist who implements the art and science of nursing through the use of the nursing process. It is the belief of Nursing at Christ Hospital and Medical Center that every individual has the right to quality health care. We are committed to developing resources and structure to provide quality, cost-effective health care. It is in this environment that the professional nurse delivers responsible individualized nursing care for which she or he is held accountable. Within this philosophy, we embrace basic dimensions that govern our mission and goals":

- Humaneness
- Moral
- Intellectual
- Personal/Professional Development
- Socio-Political
- Spiritual
- Egalitarian
- Tradition

As all discipline dimensions were found referenced in many institution mission statements, they may be foreseen to exist in some fashion in any institutional community. Therefore, to outline professed servant-leadership within a community of distinction it is possible to imagine each dimension as a "flag" and surveying team members about its community "flag pole."

This "flag pole" could be very influential in introducing newly appointed team members to the over-guiding distinction of an institutional community. The flag pole is meant to list how each discipline has relative importance. Also, a general map could be created outlining how the discipline dimensions are enlightened.

The Midwest Universities Consortium for International Activities (MUCIA) established the Institution-Building Model (IBM) shown below. I used the model to create a strategic planning tool for servant-leaders at institutional organizations involved with environmental health and prevailing leadership. The models, which rate the "health" of each dimension can be used to generate either professional or institutional goals:

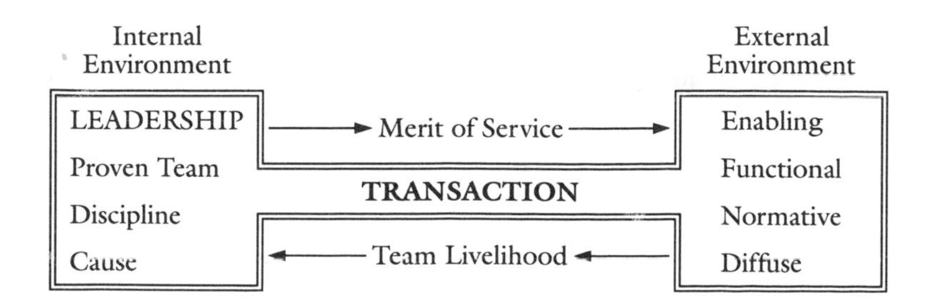

One organization that incorporated this IBM used the following variables:

Internal Variables

Leadership: How is true supervision made with servant-leadership?

Proven Team: How is team-building a guild (union)-based structure?

Discipline: How are team members mutually bonded for service?

Cause: How well does an institution perform its mission and disciplines?

External Variables

Enabling: How has the institutional enterprise been authorized?

Functional: How are constituents serviceably benefited?

Normative: How are existing social-ethical values determined?

Diffuse: How are institution disciplines made widely known?

Conclusion

This discussion concludes with an abbreviated summary of the six distinctive elements just discussed. These elements form an outline of the process of team-building and servant-leadership in order to institutionalize and professionalize an organization for the public good:

1. Distinctive understanding of enterprise structure overriding community team-building and the meaning of personal placements.
2. Distinctive team membership skills and positions mutually promoting enterprise and commitment to life-long learning.
3. Distinctive enterprise communications bonding team members with common knowledge and a chance to view separate opinions.
4. Distinctive mutual trust for team members to be accountable for addressing problems to preserve the enterprise community.
5. Distinctive and serious disciplines mutually infused in the community to authorize team members to react with shared values.
6. Distinctive enterprise by which team members profess servant-leadership and emerge as trustworthy professional co-leaders.

17

Power and Passion: Finding Personal Purpose

Juana Bordas

Recognizing that effective leaders are successful because they are "in sync" with personal purpose, this chapter reflects on how mature leaders can revitalize their sense of purpose and use it to guide others. It highlights the importance of personal purpose as a source of energy and direction for servant-leaders. It also integrates observations from Robert Greenleaf's essay "The Servant as Leader," and other leadership readings with perspectives from Native American and Hispanic cultures. Personal purpose is depicted as one's "life's work"—described in many cultures as "the job you were sent here to do"—and as the inner drive that helps leaders define directions that are right for them, seize opportunity, stand up for what they believe in, and persevere in their work. In Native American cultures, people often go on a "vision quest" to seek a clearer sense of purpose. Using personal experience as an example, the author urges leaders to go on mental and/or physical vision quests to develop their sense of self and connection to purpose.

What Is Personal Purpose?

Effective leaders usually have a strong sense of direction. They may even have a personal mission statement that guides their actions. In *Seven Habits of Highly Effective People,* Stephen Covey describes a personal mission statement as a constitution or creed focused on the values or principles of what a leader wants to be or to do. Yet beyond such statements, there is something deeper, more personal and less structured that guides them. It is more existential, individualistic, and visionary: It is personal purpose.

Personal purpose is the reason a person was born; it is the central core or nucleus of one's being, and purpose is always greater than the individual. It inspires and guides one's mission, just as the spirit of democracy guided the writing of the United States Constitution. Being connected to purpose inspires acts of greatness, yet is larger than the collective sum of one's efforts.

Purpose is like an unseen current that ties an individual's past, present, and future together. Paradoxically, while it remains constant, it is not static; it is organic and evolving. As people grow and mature, their purpose becomes deeper, richer, and more encompassing.

Who Does the Servant-Leader Serve?

The essay "The Servant as Leader" ends much as it began, reflecting on Hermann Hesse's *Journey to the East.* Greenleaf contends that Hesse aspired to serve through his literary creations. He also presents the intriguing concept of serving by becoming a "channel" for something greater than oneself or one's actions. He speculates that Hesse's source of inspiration was greater than the man himself, as it was through his work "for which he was but the channel, that Hesse would carry on, serve and lead."

"Who does the servant-leader serve?" Just as the servant-leader is "servant first" and begins with a "natural feeling that one wants to serve," seeking the guidance of personal purpose begins with the desire to connect with the "greatest good," both within oneself and society.

Because it springs from inspiration and intuition, purpose comes from deep within the individual. If leaders are following their true purpose, they meet Greenleaf's criteria for servant-leaders: "Those served grow as persons . . . And the least privileged in society . . . benefit, or at least, . . . (are) not further deprived." Servant-leaders serve something greater than themselves, something that nourishes the common good, something greater than their causes or deeds. They serve the inspiration that guides their life: the essence of what they were born to do. Servant-leaders serve their life's purpose.

More Than Vision

Personal purpose is more than a great vision. Vision speaks of imagining and anticipating what will be. Your purpose is already there, waiting to reveal itself. It awaits your acceptance. One difference between vision and purpose is that purpose is unique. It is something that an individual alone can operationalize and implement. A person cannot adopt the purpose of another, each must find his or her own. Nevertheless, many people can share a vision. Greenleaf states that, "Not much happens without a dream. Leaders must be able to envision a better and positive future." Great visions like a clean environment, a peaceful world, children who reach their potential and pluralism must be held by many people to move the dream toward reality. In fact, in *Visionary Leadership,* Burt Nanus writes that it is up to leaders to be spokespeople for great visions.

When we look at great servant-leaders of our time, we see that they all contributed to important visions by accomplishing a specific purpose—in a very unique and individualized way. Martin Luther King, Jr. was a spokesperson who organized the civil rights movement in the sixties. Mahatma Gandhi launched a nonviolent movement in India. For more than 20 years, Congresswoman Patricia Schroeder has been a modern-day "Joan of Arc" advocating for and protecting women and children. Each of these models shared visions for a better future with others, yet each had a unique role, and each was guided by and served a compelling inner voice.

Intuition is Essential

Intuition is the bridge that connects purpose and vision. "Intuition is . . . the ability to bridge the gaps . . . to have a feel for patterns . . . to generalize . . . to have a sense for the unknowable and the unforeseeable." In *The Leadership Challenge: How To Get Extraordinary Things Done In Organizations,* James Kouzes and Barry Posner say,

"Intuition is the wellspring of vision. In fact, by definition, intuition and vision are connected. Intuition has as its root the Latin word meaning 'to look at.' Intuition, like vision is a 'see word.' It has to do with our abilities to picture and to imagine."

Intuition has been described as our sixth sense. Sometimes we cannot explain how we "know" something, we just do. Intuition is independent of our reasoning process. It is the ability to discern knowledge from within ourselves. "In far-out theorizing, every mind, at the unconscious level, has access to every 'bit' of information that is or ever was."

To stay in tune with purpose, a person must actively seek it through the "intuitive insight" Greenleaf credited as the source for "the notion of servant-leadership." "Serving and leading," he says, "are still mostly intuition-based concepts." He also says that self-insight is "the most dependable part of the true servant." Greenleaf urges us to develop a sense of faith about our decisions, as there will always be information gaps of some type. "If you are waiting for all the information for a good decision, it never comes." He states that servant-leaders must use intuition to make decisions because we rarely have all the information we need. Individuals cannot embrace their purpose if they are waiting until they understand it totally.

Finding Power Through Purpose

You cannot find your purpose in a book, although the writings of others can certainly point the way. To embrace purpose, one must be willing to be "born of inspiration," to create dangerously," and "to foresee the unforeseeable." Greenleaf urges us to go "beyond conscious rationality," and to push into the "unchartered and unknown" to understand our inherent uniqueness.

Realizing that we are a one-of-a-kind design—that there will never be another person in the universe just like us—can be a source of great power and determination. But to truly understand our uniqueness, we must undertake a deep, honest, and thoughtful examination of ourselves. Indeed, Greenleaf described Albert Camus as a prophet because of "his unrelenting demand that each of us confront the exacting terms of his [or her] own existence."

Covey also emphasized the importance of uniqueness when he said, "You can't become principle-centered without a vision of and a focus on the unique contribution that is yours to make . . . Conscience is the ability to detect our own uniqueness."

A Native American Approach

Many Native Americans believe that personal power arises from a deep sense of identity and uniqueness. A high level of integration is seen as a source of integrity, strength, and focus in one's life flow. This sense of personal power provides the energy to affect the world around us.

One Native American approach to connecting with one's personal power is to undertake a "vision quest." Historically, the quest was an actual journey taken during a transition period, a life passage, or a change in status. The searcher was looking for inspiration and guidance as to how the next stage of life could connect with his or her life purpose.

In *Leadership Jazz,* Max DePree suggests that preparing for leadership "consists of hard work and wandering in the desert." DePree's metaphor of wandering in the desert is similar to the actual experiences of many Native Americans. After preparation through fasting and purification, the searcher goes into the wilderness to pray and asks for a sign or vision of desirable directions.

My introduction to vision quest came in 1980 when I was working with teenage girls in a Hispanic barrio in Denver. Tony Shearer, author of *The Praying Flute,* often came to talk to these girls, play his flute, and tell stories. One time he alluded to the tradition of vision quest. Tony described the power, focus, and sense of direction that connecting with one's purpose gives a person. He said quests reveal insights into the individual's true identity—what he or she is on the earth to do.

I was intrigued because I had always been goal-driven, yet I seemed to lack an overall purpose. I understood that certain events, like serving in the Peace Corps, being offered an unsolicited scholarship to get a Master's degree, and becoming the founding director of a women's self-sufficiency program were key accomplishments. Yet, I felt that they were only chapters, not the whole story. As I listened to Tony, personal purpose seemed to be a unifying thread. I asked him, "How do you do it? Find your purpose?" He answered so matter-of-factly that I felt he must have thought it was obvious. "Well, first you go to a sacred place. You take your shoes off, touch Mother Earth and raise your hands up to the Sun . . . and ask. Then you stay there until you get an answer." He implied that finding purpose was a natural process. It certainly sounded simple, anyway. My mind raced: How would I find a sacred place? How would I know what my purpose was when I found it? The most important thing I learned that day was that I had to ask the question. I made a commitment to myself to find and understand my purpose.

A few months later, a friend asked me to go to Taos, New Mexico. I began thinking that the Blue Mountain in Taos, a landmark, was a sacred place where I might be able to connect with the powerful spiritual heritage of the Hopi Indians and, hopefully, with my personal purpose. I decided to go there, wander around, take off my shoes and ask the question. And that's what I did. At the end of the day, the intuitive message I received was to "teach the old ways." That was almost 15 years ago, and since then, my life has changed and my personal purpose has slowly evolved and become clearer.

A Path to Purpose

Finding personal purpose today is still a journey. It is an inner search that examines the past, special skills and talents, significant events in life, people who have shaped the person's character, and hopes for the future. In seeking purpose, we can look to people who have walked before us for guidance. Just as Greenleaf's insights guide many, other pathfinders have left pointers. For example, in many parts of the world, particularly along mountain paths, intriguing rock piles have been left by people who have been there before. In the Mojave and Sonoran deserts, archaeologists have found many stone piles, called vision cairns, that were used by native people during vision quests. These rocks point direction, offer friendly encouragement during difficult climbs, and are reminders that others successfully made the journey.

In keeping with this tradition, here are nine cairns or markers that can point the way on your path to personal purpose:

1. Call your purpose; listen for guidance.
2. Find a sacred place.
3. See time as continuous; begin with the child and move with the present.

4. Identify special skills and talents; accept imperfections.
5. Trust your intuition.
6. Open the door when opportunity knocks.
7. Find your passion and make it happen.
8. Write your life story; imagine a great leader.
9. Honor your legacy, one step at a time.

Now let's examine each cairn more closely.

Cairn 1: Call Your Purpose; Listen for Guidance

Finding one's "special sense of overarching purpose" is a search that must be directed inwardly. You must listen for the intuitive insight that Greenleaf described as a key ingredient in the rigorous preparation for leadership. Self-insight can only be born in silence—we must withdraw into the deeper well of ourselves. "If one is servant, either leader or follower, one is always searching, listening, expecting . . ."

Greenleaf suggests that leaders must develop the ability to stand outside themselves, while simultaneously looking deep within their souls. To do this, they must pay close attention and practice "the sustained intentness of listening."

We must be willing to be "born of inspiration" and to have faith that "the intuitive insight necessary for one's optimal performance will be forthcoming." We open the doors of greater self-perception by periodically reexamining our course through the art of withdrawal. By constantly reflecting on questions such as "How can I use myself to serve best?" and "What am I meant to do?" servant-leaders reach out to their personal purpose.

Cairn 2: Find a Sacred Place

The most important thing about sacred space is that it provides a quiet, safe, reflective environment that encourages intuitive insights. You can choose a site already dedicated as sacred through purification rituals, like a church or a garden, or create a sacred space of your own. Sacred space can be a place of natural beauty—like the top of a mountain; an oak tree in the backyard; or a site one is drawn to repeatedly, such as the seashore or a park; it can even be a favorite chair surrounded by plants and soothing music. In Carlos Castaneda's best-selling book on the teachings of Yanqui Indian Don Juan, *Tales of Power,* Don Juan told Carlos to find sacred space by feeling its warmth, seeing its color, and sensing its presence.

By recognizing and acknowledging a site as sacred, it becomes a source of inspiration and personal power. As long as a person identifies the place as sacred, it will be glad to accommodate.

Cairn 3: See Time as Continuous; Begin with the Child and Move with the Present

Greenleaf's discussion of foresight as a central ethic of leadership states that this must be grounded in an understanding that the "past, present moment and the future are one organic unity . . . bracketed together and moving . . . (as) a continuous process." In seeking purpose, we move on this continuum by reviewing experiences, events, and opportunities that brought us to the present and use their lessons to connect and clarify the present and the future. Reflecting on where we came from can provide great insight into where we are going.

One's childhood is like the rich soil that holds the roots of the tree. Begin by reflecting on your early childhood and how it shaped your development. Reflecting on the past reveals patterns, motivations and significant values behind one's purpose. Think about:

- *Family Composition:* What was your birth position, family rules, expectations, and economic status? What feelings do you have about your family? What traditions did you have? Think about personal characteristics you feel are genetic or "run in the family."
- *Gender Significance:* Being male or female certainly influences the way we think and what we believe is possible. To really get a grasp on the significance of gender, write down 10 ways your life would be different if you were the "opposite sex."
- *Geographic Influences:* Where were you born? Even different regions within a country have diverse cultures and lifestyles. Talk to people who were born in a different region or country and ask them about the customs, pastimes, and aspects they consider unique about growing up in that area.
- *Cultural Background:* For some people, cultural identity is a key to understanding who they are, while others have little awareness of their heritage. What would you describe as your culture? How significant has this been in shaping your life?

Being born into a particular culture strongly shapes your "world view." Culture, it is said, is like a pair of glasses by which you "see" the world and thus define your reality.

The priorities we set and what we value are deeply affected by our cultural background. Culture influences the importance we assign to work; how we define success, family, time and money. To explore the significance of the culture you were born into, ask yourself: What do you identify as your cultural background and when did you first realize there were other cultures or ethnic groups? What would you describe as key cultural values? How have these shaped your life?

While leadership comes in many colors and can be found in all cultures, the particular culture you were born in has been like the stage or backdrop for your leadership journey. How has your culture woven the fabric of your purpose as a leader?

- *Generational Influence:* Events that occur during the particular time in history in which people are born shape their lives and give identity to their generation. One only needs to talk to a "baby boomer" to understand the importance of generational influences, such as television or computers. Certain influences are so pervasive that the majority of people's lives will be touched by them, such as: the changes in women's roles, the advent of the global marketplace, and demographic changes as America becomes a nation where the majority of its people are not white.

Greenleaf states that servant-leaders must address critical issues of their times: "an immoral and senseless war, destruction of the environment, poverty, alienation, overpopulation . . ." Leaders who have had great impact on society have called people to be part of the history of their times. For example, in 1960, when John F. Kennedy said, "Ask not what your country can do for you, but what you can do for your country," I joined the Peace Corps, as did many idealists of my generation.

Greenleaf looked at three servant-leaders: John Woolman, an early Quaker who dedicated his life to abolishing slavery; Thomas Jefferson, writer of the Constitution; and Nikolai Frederik Severin Grundtvig who reformed Denmark's educational system in the nineteenth century. He stated that each of these men were "very right for the time and place he happened to be."

Your purpose, too will be "in sync" with the time in history when you were born, but you must stay connected and involved with the issues of your time to take full advantage of your opportunity. For example, today, business, education, government, and social institutions are being deeply challenged by diversity issues; many leaders will be affected by these changes and will be called to serve in this arena.

Cairn 4: Identify Special Skills and Talents; Accept Imperfections

Since personal purpose is action-oriented, identifying your skills helps you see how your aptitudes and talents have facilitated your accomplishments and will aid you in the future. Some of your abilities are innate, and others were developed throughout your life. All can be put to work to serve your purpose.

Assess your skills by drawing a timeline of your life that shows major activities and jobs. Take an honest inventory of your abilities from the perspectives of what you are good at and what you like to do. Divide them into areas: people related, technical, intellectual, communication, and so on. Rank them in order of your greatest strengths. Take note of the things that you enjoyed, excelled in, or that "came easy." Pinpoint the ones you are using today. Ask yourself the following questions: What came "naturally"? What have you learned? What is significant and useful for your work today? What is the deeper meaning behind the experiences? How did it change, temper, or inspire you? What kind of study, practice, and training will help you further develop all of your skills?

Just as we must take stock of the special gifts and talents we have, we must have humility for our weaknesses. Greenleaf said that, "acceptance requires tolerance of imperfection, . . . Anybody could lead perfect people." For servant-leaders to accept others, they must first accept their own humanness. This is poignantly expressed by Greenleaf's comment that a servant-leader must "acknowledge that his [or her] own healing is his [or her] motivation."

Looking at significant failures also is key to understanding how our disappointments have prepared us for our current work. Our shortcomings can provide great lessons and clarify our life's purpose. "Stewardship," writes Peter Block, "is the willingness to work on ourselves first . . . to own our doubts and limitations." In fact, he suggests, "Our humanness is defined more by our vulnerabilities than our strengths." So too, in *Leaders: Strategies for Taking Charge*, Warren Bennis and Burt Nanus suggest that successful leaders need to develop a fail-safe attitude toward their work. What others may call mistakes, they label as powerful "learning opportunities."

Cairn 5: Trust Your Intuition

Look back over your life at significant decisions you made that might not have seemed logically sure or most expedient at the time. Perhaps your decision just "felt right"—a hunch. Acknowledge it as intuitive insight and congratulate yourself for having followed it.

To develop intuition, we must learn to trust our hunches, perceptions, and feelings. We must pay attention when things seem "right and then act" or wait when they seem "uncomfortable." Things that happen repeatedly, books that come to our attention, phone calls at the right time are often more than coincidence; they are opportunities that we intuitively know are important. In Native American culture, dreams are doors to intuition, so paying attention to dreams can also be a guide.

In my junior year of college, I was on the porch with a group of friends when a long line of people marched by. I didn't have a clue what was happening, so when I saw my political science professor in line, I asked him, "What's going on?" "We are marching to integrate the University of Florida," he responded. I immediately jumped in line. Intuitively, I knew that it was critical for me to "vote with my feet" and stand up for what I believed in. Until that moment, I had never thought about getting involved at that level. No one in my family had ever been involved in social or political work; perhaps it was because with eight children, our own survival had always been the focus. My intuition led me on that march.

"The foundation of stewardship," Block says, "is the belief that what is true lies within each of us. Knowledge and answers are found within." The intuition is that almost imperceptible voice that leads us to this wellspring of truth.

Cairn 6: Open the Door When Opportunity Knocks

One sure way to achieve clarity of purpose is to look at opportunities that have been offered "out of the blue." These opportunities can be seen as purpose calling and guiding you. These are doors to the future.

After returning from the Peace Corps, my husband and I moved to Madison, Wisconsin so he could pursue a law degree. I planned to work while he studied. When I went to the Department of Social Services to apply, I was told they only hired people with a Masters in social work. My response was, "You don't understand, I was born to be a social worker." The interviewer then told me that government stipends were available for people to study social work and that if I got accepted to the University of Wisconsin Graduate School of Social Work, they would award me a stipend on the condition I work for them for two years after graduation. I accepted. Today I know how valuable that education was and how difficult it would have been to accomplish what I have done without it . . . and it wasn't even my idea!

Other people have similar stories. I recently asked David Campbell, a noted author, how he first got started writing and publishing books. "Oh," he said, "I got a call one day from a publisher who heard a tape I made for National Public Radio on career planning. He wanted me to write a book for high school students on the subject. As usual I had a lot of irons in the fire, so I told him, 'Thanks, but I'm too busy.' He persisted and finally emphatically said, 'But it's your responsibility!'" The rest is history; Campbell went on to write books on leadership and creativity, including *If You Don't Know Where You Are Going, You'll Probably End Up Somewhere Else*. "Wow," I said to David, "that was your purpose calling you!"

Spend some time identifying special circumstances or "golden opportunities," such as getting new employment assignments or meeting a mentor. Pay special attention to anything that seems like a "lucky break" or a time when your skills made it seem like you were in the "right place at the right time." These opportunities have shaped your purpose and current work as a leader.

When opportunity beckons, practice "fresh, open choice." Take a "leap of imagination" as to what could be. Avoid reacting negatively. Use your intuition to discern the possibilities and have faith in the answer. Ask yourself: Will this prepare me to better serve? How does this fit with what I am trying to do?

Cairn 7: Find Your Passion and Make It Happen

At one point, I conducted a career conference for minority girls in the Denver public school system. The theme, "Take Your Passion and Make It Happen," came from a popular song from the movie "Flash Dance." The movie told the story of a struggling young girl who worked as a welder, but who wanted to be a dancer. The story had all the "stuff of leadership." She had a passion fueled by a sense of personal purpose. When she became discouraged, her passion kept her going and, after many setbacks, she succeeded.

Purpose is the fire in the heart and the fuel for the fire. Passion turns us on, energizes us, and gives us the stamina for leadership. According to Greenleaf, it encourages us to do that "which we think we cannot do."

Ask yourself: What would you do even if you weren't getting paid or at least where money or recognition were not the motivators? What would you do if you won the lottery? If you only had six months to live? If you could live in good health for a hundred years? What gives you energy? What do you dream about doing? What is in your heart of hearts?

Cairn 8: Write Your Life Story; Imagine a Great Leader

Federico Pena became the first Hispanic elected mayor of a major city where Hispanics were the minority, representing less than 20 percent of the population. He came to Denver from Brownsville, Texas as a young lawyer and served in the state legislature for eight years. He was not well known when he first declared his mayoral candidacy. But he persevered, and he kept talking about his dream for Denver. His campaign slogan became "Imagine a Great City!" Finally, one day, someone blurted out, "You can't run for mayor, you're too short." Pena claims that that was the moment he "knew" he would be mayor. He would not let obstacles and prejudices stand in his way. Pena's story is a testimonial to purpose and determination.

Reflective journaling is a useful technique for stimulating your imagination. Write a story for your life that blends reality and fantasy. Set it in a favorite time in history. Make your birth something that was predicted and awaited. Make your past obstacles into great challenges that were conquered. You may want to use allegories, such as a journey or a race. Write your goals as dreams that were realized. Take your story into the future, imagine a great vision, and design a path that leads you to this splendid place.

Cairn 9: Honor Your Legacy, One Step at a Time

In *The Seven Habits Of Highly Successful People* there is a chapter on personal mission called "Begin With the End in Mind." In it, Covey asks us to visualize our funeral. At the rite, speakers include family, friends, co-workers, community associates, and so on. The exercise asks us to reflect on what we would want them to say about our life and to write an epitaph that captures the leadership legacy we want to leave. Covey says that we must honor the "vision of what we can become."

Personal purpose doesn't change, but it does expand as life unfolds. Our initial glimpse or revelation must ferment and germinate in our consciousness. A person's life purpose is "work in progress." While growing your purpose is an evolutionary, organic, and natural process, it does not necessarily come easily. Just as exercising a muscle will make you strong, you must work with your purpose to realize its strength.

Greenleaf states that great leaders make "the way to their goal by one action at a time, with a lot of frustrations along the way," and that "Everything begins with the initiative of an individual." One action at a time brings us in sync with our life plan. While we serve "one [person] at a time," we can also embrace the idea of serving many in the future. As our understanding of our greater good expands, so does our ability to enact our purpose.

We must act on our purpose as we know it today. Tapping the power of individual purpose brings a sense of "wholeness." It cultivates an "inner security"—a calmness that allows us to "see oneself in perspective in the context of one's own experience, amid the ever-present dangers, threats, and alarms."

Personal Epilogue

While these steps can lead us to understand purpose in a more holistic and deeper way, there remains the intuitive part—the stuff that is "beyond conscious rationality." We must, as Don Juan advised Carlos Castaneda stop the world, spend time in silent reflection and meditation, and wander in the desert. I encourage you to try these approaches and others to help you find your heart's desire. What you receive may not be earth-shattering or even understandable at first. But as time goes by and you continue to serve your purpose "one action at a time," your passion and personal power will grow. Your purpose will manifest itself with greater clarity.

"Teach the old ways" has given my life a rich purpose. The old ways include bringing back community, which Greenleaf referred to as "the lost knowledge of these times." What I understand today is that communities must be based on equality and partnership. True partnership is only possible between equals. It is critical that Hispanic women and all people have equal opportunity and a place at the table of community partnership.

Until all groups have this sense of identity and wholeness, we will not have a society where people work together in common unity. Common unity is a simple phrase with incredible implication. Common is defined as belonging equally to or shared alike by an entire community, nation, or culture; unity is the state of being combined with others to form a greater whole.

In retrospect, my unifying theme over the years has been to foster a greater sense of community and mutuality within and among all groups. Today as I teach corporate executives, about leadership and diversity, I am finding common ground between diverse people. I share my history as a Hispanic woman and my vision for the future. My vision, rooted in respect for those who have come before us, calls us to become a true community. My purpose is to teach this ancient sense of community and to build mutual respect and unity among all people, particularly between men and women.

18

The New Leadership

Michael Kelley

University of Michigan business school students watched a film of Dr. Martin Luther King Jr.'s "I Have a Dream" speech, boarded a bus for Detroit and spent the day cleaning up abandoned lots or painting dilapidated houses.

At the University of Denver law school, such disciplines as sociology and environmental issues are being integrated into the curriculum.

Teamwork, global perspectives, ethics, humanities—these are the issues being dealt with in the institutions that train people to become leaders these days. The "new paradigm," to use the phrase most favored by industrial soothsayers, focuses on customers rather than profits, long-term satisfaction over immediate gratification, multiculturalism over the country club atmosphere that has dominated corporate hierarchy in the past. Most experts on the subject expect the trend to continue, at least for a while.

"All advanced degrees tend to bounce back and forth between technical skills and human relations skills," said David Ciscel, interim dean of graduate studies in the Fogelman College of Business and Economics at Memphis State University.

"Right now in MBAs (master's in business administration) and in new degrees like master's in health administration," he added, "the emphasis is on liberal arts skills."

The movement got a push last October when Robert Stempel resigned as chairman of General Motors Corp. under pressure from outside directors. Stempel was a typical captain of industry in the United States. He was trained as an engineer, one of the most rigorous and demanding academic foundations in society, the kind of honing that has always produced great leaders in the United States, then rose through the ranks of the country's largest corporation and eventually became its chairman. Ultimately, his lack of contacts outside GM, lack of understanding of the global economy and resistance to change did him in.

Specific skills like engineering or finance are no longer adequate preparation to lead a corporate giant like GM through a crisis, say experts on leadership like Dr. Gerald Graham, a management professor at Wichita State University. Graham says Japanese industry provides a better model for leadership production. "The cultural orientation is quite a bit different," he says. "They emphasize communication skills, participation skills, group decision-making, personal kinds of relationships."

Memphis business consultant Fred Thompson says true leaders of corporations often come through the ranks rather than management training programs and are concerned with issues like moral character, principles, and ethics. "In addition they're going to have to have a global or a world perspective and be able to manage based on fact—to be objective and not get caught up in bias or their subjectiveness—and, of course, group dynamics," he said.

"Money is the oxygen that keeps a business going. We have to breathe to live, but we don't live to breathe," he said. "When managers put that into perspective, they develop long-range vision rather than focusing on the next quarterly report."

The idea was institutionalized by the late Robert K. Greenleaf, director of management research at AT&T and founder of the Center for Applied Ethics (now known as the Robert K. Greenleaf Center, in Indianapolis) and the person who coined the term "servant-leadership."

"Servant-leadership is the values base or underlying philosophy for a number of programs many colleges and universities now offer," said Larry Spears, the center's executive director. "There is a host of people writing about the need for a different paradigm (example) for people to use as far as leadership goes. We have seen a real growth in servant-leadership materials being selected and taught in leadership and management courses at the college and university level."

The concept involves "increased service to others, taking a more holistic approach to work, promoting a sense of community within an organization and between an organization and the greater community, sharing of power and decision-making, and a group-oriented approach to work in contrast to the hierarchical model," said Spears.

Servant-leaders include sales managers who feed their salespeople good leads, home builders who provide their carpenters with the best tools to work with, newspaper editors who patiently unscramble the ramblings of their weary reporters.

They're often also advocates of so-called "total quality management" programs, inspired by Japanese electronics and automobile manufacturers and currently being promoted in service as well as manufacturing industries. Total quality management emphasizes the empowerment of employees, teamwork, and objective measurements of products and services. Take the theory to its extreme and the manager is left with little to do but create a general business mission, hire the right people to carry it out, and help *them* accomplish the company's goals.

Institutions training new leaders for the twenty-first century also are becoming more heavily dependent on experiential education, which increases the use of real-world practical problem-solving in an academic setting.

At Indiana University School of Business, which leapt from fifteenth place to eighth place in *Business Week*'s latest ranking of the nation's business schools, for instance, all business courses have been eliminated for first-year graduate students. Instead, students are divided into four groups; each group works with a team of faculty members, and each student receives one grade for each semester.

The program avoids duplicating standard material being taught to students in standard business courses and allows ethics, the environment, international business, and other courses from outside the standard curriculum to be added.

A similar program for first-year graduate students has been initiated at the University of Tennessee's business school, whose graduate program moved from fifty-fifth to thirty-second place in the nation this year in *U.S. News & World Report*'s annual survey. The independent three-credit hour course taught by a single professor from a single discipline has been abandoned at the University of Tennessee, where, instead, teams of students learn market research, financial planning, cost management, and product development by going into the homes of consumers, grocery stores, and board rooms.

The University of Denver's two-year MBA program underwent a major restructuring recently, including the establishment of the Institute for Professional Excellence within the Graduate School of Business meant to teach students integrity and social responsibility as well as technical business skills.

The school requires students to volunteer 24 hours of community service in such locations as soup kitchens and homeless shelters. Some students have done yard work and painted houses for the Denver Emergency Housing Coalition. Others have traveled to Mexico to paint schools, plant trees, or perform other community services in rural villages.

Graham advises young people who see themselves as future national or state leaders to start at the grass roots level. "You need to get into something—an organization, a hobby group, a club—and work in that club to develop your leadership skills in the minor leagues, so to speak," he said. "That gives you a chance to fail, a chance to learn."

In the future, the traditional sources of leadership—law schools, business schools, the military, engineering schools, divinity schools, and the like—are expected to continue to play a role in the process. They just have to be open to change in the way they teach leadership.

19

Servant-Leadership: A Pathway to the Emerging Territory

Richard W. Smith

As surveyors, Lewis and Clark decided to map out paths to the emerging territories. They were seekers. Their passionate need to make the journey enabled them to stay the course. Many others followed their path—and some surveyed their own path. Over time, the emerging territories became familiar territories.

Like Lewis and Clark, Robert K. Greenleaf was a surveyor. He was a surveyor of paths that led to the emerging territory of organizational structure and leadership. He too was a seeker with a passion that enabled him to stay the course. He had a belief and a dream about how powerful the emerging territory could be for those who accepted his invitation and his challenge to explore this territory. Today, many people are following Greenleaf's path—and others have surveyed and are surveying their own paths—into the emerging territory. More and more organizations, large and small, for-profit and not-for-profit, are leaving the traditional territory and are moving toward the emerging territory.

What does the traditional territory look like, and what does the emerging territory look like? And, what is the pathway that Greenleaf surveyed for others to follow? Simply stated, the traditional territory (the mechanical model) is highly mechanical and contains many pyramids, while the emerging territory (the emerging model) is intensely personal and contains many circles. The paradox is that both territories are necessary; there is an interdependence that must be formed in order to create the most powerful and the most caring organizations possible. The pathway between the two territories that Greenleaf surveyed, and has invited people to develop, is the pathway of relationship embodied in his concept of servant leadership. These concepts are graphically shown in Figure 19.1. The details of each model are listed in Figure 19.2.

The Mechanical Model

Anyone who has ever experienced an organization in our culture has experienced the mechanical model. In fact, this model is so well integrated into our culture that we've assumed it is the correct model for us. We experience it in our homes, our schools, our churches, our businesses, our hospitals, our political systems, and within the nonprofit organizations where we volunteer our time and energy. Even as we move away from this model in our organizations, we move to affirm it in the other systems in which we operate.

There are a number of key areas that contribute to the structure of both the mechanical and emerging models. For our purposes, however, we are only going to briefly examine six of them: Foundation, Values, Beliefs, Puzzle Solutions, Leadership Styles, and Followership Styles.

Foundation

Three of the most influential foundation contributors to the mechanical model were Plato, Isaac Newton, and Frederick Winslow Taylor. Over the centuries, we have combined and integrated their concepts into the foundation upon which the mechanical model was built.

Plato believed that the masses were not able to handle the responsibility and power that went with republican rule, and concluded that one person at the top—a "philosopher-king"—would be needed

Figure 19.1
Territories of servant-leadership.

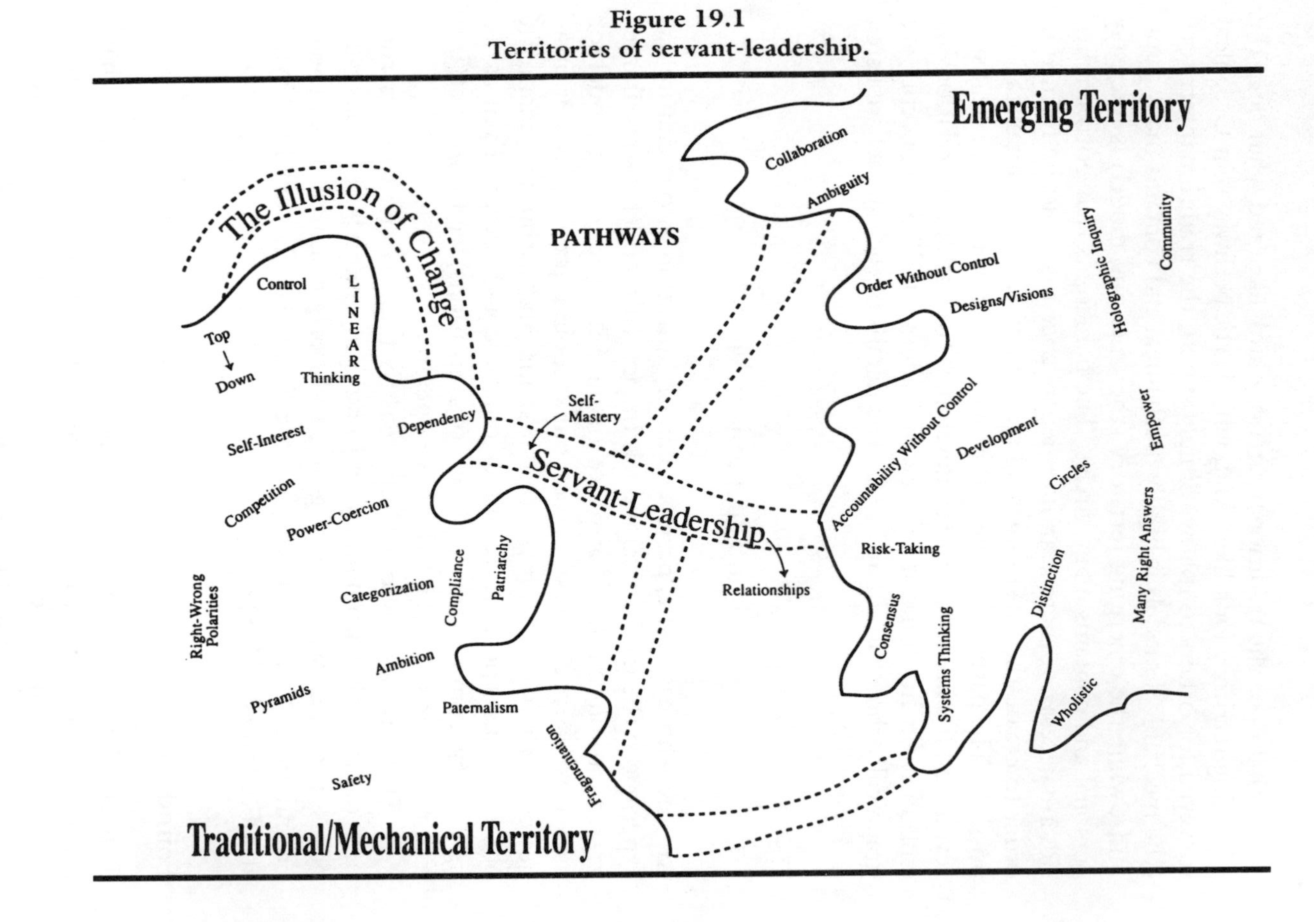

Figure 19.2 Details of servant-leadership territories.

A. THE MECHANICAL MODEL—The Pyramid

1. Foundation:	Plato Descartes Isaac Newton: Newtonian Physics Frederick Winslow Taylor: Scientific Management
2. Values:	Right/Wrong Polarity Objectivism—People Become "Objects" Seeks Equilibrium (Balance)
3. Beliefs:	Control/Dependency are crucial to success Exploitation of Environment is necessary
4. Puzzle Solutions:	Knowing the whole through its parts—reductionism, segmentation, classification, categorization
5. Leadership Styles:	Traditional: Top-Down, Expansive and Controlling, Compliance and Dependency in Followers
6. Follower Styles:	Traditional: Seeks Safety and Dependency, Self-Serving and Ambitious, Compliant and Rebellious

B. THE EMERGING MODEL(S)—The Circles

1. Foundation:	New Sciences: Quantum Physics, Self-Organizing Systems, Chaos Theory (which is rooted in Newtonian Physics), Complexity Theory Peter Senge: Learning Organizations Russell Ackoff: Systems Thinking Hermann Hesse: Journey/Seeking/Serving Robert K. Greenleaf: Servant-Leadership
2. Values:	Developmental Process/Learning Process —Consciousness —Intrinsic Capabilities —Exploration & Discovery Disequilibrium (Chaos Creates Creative Energy) Order vs. Control Accountability without Control Serve Others
3. Beliefs:	Regeneration —Emergence —Whole System Evolution Call-To-Lead by the Followers Complexity—Systems Thinking Observation & No Limits: Quantum Physics Power of Relationship Sharing Information: Whole Picture Thinking Ownership vs. Compliance

Figure 19.2 Continued

4. Puzzle Solutions:	Holographic Inquiry Open Systems Consensus Seeking Many Possible Right Answers
5. Leadership Styles:	Emerging: Collaborative, Council of Equals, Empowerment/Stewardship; Ownership, Trust, Communication are crucial Serving, First
6. Follower Styles:	Emerging: Calls Leaders Forth, Accepts Empowerment, Seeks Ownership, Gives up Dependency and Safety—seeks Inter-Dependency and Risk-Taking (uses Faith and Courage)

The Emerging Model(s) is paradoxical (leading by serving, more from less, many right answers) and needs Trust, Effective Communication Systems, Interdependent Relationships, and Disequilibrium.

Self and Group Discipline are both part of the Emerging Model(s) and there is a need to be highly productive within this model(s).

Some of the negative fall-out that occurs within the Mechanical Model helps breed/foster Cynicism within the organization. Cynicism is perhaps the most difficult barrier to break down within modern organizations.

Finally, a transition from one model to another takes time, energy and commitment. The most challenging transitions occur when moving into the Emerging Model(s) for this transition calls for a grounding within a new foundation—this new foundation is one of the keys to the Emerging Model(s). Without solid grounding, people only experience what I call the Illusion of Change.

in order to guide the republic. This person, generally a male, would be, in effect, a benevolent autocrat. Herein lie the seeds for our patriarchal/paternalistic pyramid.

Isaac Newton contributed concepts and images that we used in designing our organizational pyramids; concepts and images that reinforced Plato's beliefs. We believe that people are influenced by force exerted upon them from a person higher up the pyramid. We believe that we can best manage by breaking things into parts; that indeed, we deal mainly with "things" and not the "relationships." We develop our plans based on the belief that the world is quite predictable, and that we can better manage our world by looking at things (and people) objectively (which is a small step from seeing people as objects).

Frederick Winslow Taylor built upon these two contributions. In the early 1900s he set up a management system called scientific management based on the scientific method. He believed that we can break a person's work down into categories, develop experts in those categories, and then have the experts focus only on those categories. The end product would then be the culmination of a series of efforts by highly trained individuals that could be easily monitored. The assembly line worker was perfected.

Over the years we have refined the contributions of these three men into an integrated system that has become part of our culture, part of our collective myth.

Values

There are many values that have been affirmed as a result of the solid foundation that has been integrated. Three of them bear a brief examination. The first is a value of ***right-wrong***. In our organizations, we have come to treasure this value, trust it, and we teach it religiously, if not dogmatically, to all employees. If one is not right, then one must be wrong; if one is right, then all others must be wrong. We must seek out the one right answer and, when we have it, all others must be wrong. If one listens to what is occurring within our organizations, one hears this polarity being espoused at every level.

The second value is ***objectivism***. We value finding the right answer in an objective way. Objects are valued because they are predictable. If people are treated as objects, and if people's work is seen as objective, then it is easy to find the one right answer. People are still told, "Leave your brain at the door, we are only interested in your body." People, by their nature, are not quite as predictable as objects.

The third value is ***equilibrium***. Organizations value "balance"—equilibrium—and believe that once you achieve balance then all will run smoothly. Balance leaves no room for questioning, for rocking the boat, for taking risks. The ultimate balance is "flatline." When you have a "flatline," you have death. Oddly enough, organizations still seek to live out the equilibrium value even though, if they look around, they will see employees who are "dying" or "dead." One organization I am familiar with even calls 5 P.M. "Lazarus Time" because people come alive again at this hour.

Beliefs

A key belief in many organizations centers around the concepts of control and dependency. The belief is that only by exercising control from above will people actually comply and do their work and not "rip us off." (Perhaps this is rooted in a deeper belief that people are not trustworthy.) This is combined with the belief that, in order to have people give their best, they must be "dependent" upon the organization. This has produced the classical patriarchal system; you give me control over you and depend on me to take care of you and I will give you protection and safety (that is, you will always have a place to work).

Puzzle Solutions

Puzzle solutions have to do with how you approach problems and what methods you employ to solve them. The classic way of solving puzzles within the mechanical model is by reducing the whole into parts, solving the problem, and then restructuring the whole. Commonly, this is done through reductionism (reducing wholes and/or large parts into manageable pieces), segmentation (breaking the whole and/or larger parts into smaller pieces), classification (naming the parts of the whole and then working with these), and categorization (developing ways of putting the pieces into certain categories and then working with them). These problem-solving methods lead to isolation within organizations. That is, one team, area, or division will not talk to and/or cooperate with another. Sometimes they even end up competing with each other.

Leadership Styles

The leadership styles utilized in this model (see Figure 19.3) generally fall into one of two styles: traditional or consultative. The traditional style functions with the leader isolated at the top. It employs the top-down method of leading. As a result, the leader tells those led how to act and controls how much information they need to have in order to perform their jobs. This isolation among those being led because it is not acceptable for them to rely on each other. "Just do as you are told" is the theme of this style. The leader feels pressure because he or she is neither prone to listening, nor able to admit to not knowing (many leaders end up "making up" answers). There is also a fear of being "found out" by or being vulnerable to ambitious ladder climbers as well as peers. The leader expects his or her followers to be compliant and dependent.

The consultative style is closely related to the traditional style in that the flow is still top-down, and the leader is still controlling and

Figure 19.3
Leadership styles.

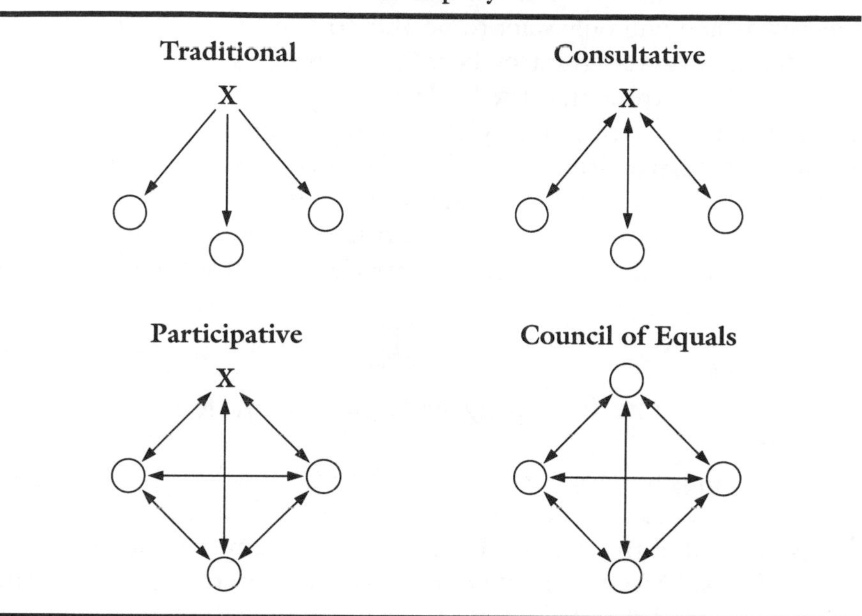

holds the power and expects dependency and compliance from the followers. There is, however, a significant difference: The leader seeks out some followers' ideas and views. Also, the leader has a growing ability to say "I don't know" and "I value your input." Some leaders who use this style simply ask for input; others are open to change via influence and persuasion. Generally, the consultation is one to one and the categorization and fragmentation among those below the leader continues to isolate people, teams, departments, and divisions. For example the marketing and purchasing departments don't communicate effectively with each other.

Follower Styles

Followers in the mechanical model are expected to be compliant, loyal, and dependent. They are trained to perform specific tasks and are told not to think out of their task area. (Some are even told not to think within their task areas.) Those who have integrated these directives say things like, "It's not my job, just tell me what to do and let me do my work, or you can't trust what they tell you." Followers come to see things in simplistic and predictable ways. When they are invited to participate on teams, they will not understand the need for "all those meetings" and will only want to be able to "get my work done."

Some followers react by becoming suspicious, cynical, and rebellious. They know that the leadership style isn't working to their benefit, and they respond by criticizing, complaining, and being passive-aggressive (they come late for meetings, miss work, miss deadlines, and so on). Over time, they experience more and more powerlessness and become more aggressive. They don't believe that they can make a difference, become apathetic, and see work as something to be endured.

The Emerging Model(s)—Circles

The emerging territory contains emerging model(s). (I put an "s" after model because I believe many versions of the emerging model are possible and that we will be discovering them over the next four to five years. "Model" and "models" are used interchangeably in the following text.) The territory and models are called emerging because they are not new; they have been in existence for thousands of years. Another way of looking at this model is as a model that is emerging into our senses and experiences. There are no tried and true blueprints that will definitively show us the way, or show us how to act once we are there. They also are "emerging" because many people are showing us the way to get there and there are many options once we arrive.

Unlike the traditional territory and the mechanical model, there are many right answers, many gray areas, many options and challenges, and many possibilities. Unlike the traditional territory and the mechanical model, we are called to be creators of the territory. We are called to collaborate with one another, we are called to assume authority and responsibility with others for how things go. We are called to take risks and to assume ownership.

There is another side to this, too. We are called into an unfamiliar territory, and that causes a lot of anxiety. We are also asked to examine ourselves individually and in relation to others. Being a loner in this territory only creates more anxiety, because the territory is experienced in its wholeness. On the other hand, if we take the time to examine the emerging model as we know it today then we will discover that we are quite familiar with the model and that we even participate within it.

Foundation

Like the mechanical model, the emerging model has many foundation pieces. One foundation piece comes from what are called the "new sciences"—quantum physics, chaos theory, and self-organizing systems. The contributions of the new sciences will be more directly discussed in the areas of Values, Beliefs, and Puzzle Solutions. Here, I will just briefly state that the new sciences have led us to many possibilities versus the right/wrong polarities of the mechanical model; they have led us to wholeness versus fragmentation, and to systems versus things. In order to truly move into the emerging territory and discover the emerging model, one must be able to have an internal foundation based on these pieces.

Another foundation piece is provided by Robert K. Greenleaf's concept of servant-leadership. This will also be discussed when Greenleaf's contributions are directly addressed. Briefly, a key concept that Greenleaf gave us 30 years ago was the need to move away from the territory of the thing via the Path of Relationship. The ideas of the leader as one who enters into relationship with the followers and that leaders are called to serve first, and "followers who serve are called to lead" are both life and organization changing. Yet without the foundation piece of relationship, the journey into the emerging territory is probably impossible. Greenleaf believed that the key to the success of organizations lies within the individual—the servant-leader—and that all are invited to become servant-leaders. This concept is radically different from the mechanical model's lone leader at the top.

Values

The emerging model values the developmental learning process. This always starts with the individual, then moves to the individual-in-relationship, and finally moves to the relationships-in-the-organization. The organization, then, is a living organism that must develop/learn if it is to flourish. This process is conscious and there is a value that all have the intrinsic capabilities necessary to grow, develop, and contribute to the well-being of the organization. The emerging model also values order versus control; that is, the challenge is, how can a system have order without control? Others raise the question of how you can have accountability without control? These are two challenges that organizations operating within the emerging model must grapple with.

Beliefs

The emerging model believes in continual regeneration; that is, the individual, the relationships, and the organization must actively seek ways of regenerating on a continual basis. This means that all three must have awareness, be committed to growth, and be active learners. It also means that regeneration must be seen and experienced as a whole system evolution and not just as fragmented evolution. Tied to this belief of regeneration is the belief that systems thinking is crucial to the survival of the organization. We all must learn to think systemically and experience the synergy possible in a combination of linear and systemic thought. Another powerful belief is that people within the organization must develop ownership—ownership of ideas, of process, of accountability, of relationships, and so on. This is a radical move away from the idea that ownership is limited to a select few and that the power that goes with ownership must be shared throughout the organization. What this will look like, and how it will be accomplished is the challenge facing each person and each organization—there are no blueprints for this.

Puzzle Solutions

Puzzles are seen holistically and solved by a number of methods. Consensus decision-making and holographic inquiry are two powerful methods for solving puzzles. Consensus decision-making is a skill that must be practiced and learned by all in order for ownership to occur. Not all decisions can—or should—be made by consensus. However, the decisions that will have the most impact on the organization should be made by consensus in organizations that operate within the emerging model. Learning the skill of consensus decision-making takes time, energy, and a commitment to practice. It is not just a skill to be learned; one must have the deep belief that consensus is the method that must be used in key situations. Without this commitment, one will have difficulty learning the skill and be prone to sabotage the efforts of the group to reach consensus.

Holographic inquiry is another skill that will take time and effort to learn. Simply stated, it is the skill of seeing the issues from all sides and perspectives. It means accepting the perceptions of others as valid and that all opinions are valid. This is not an easy challenge to meet; we all bring our own prejudices, judgments, stereotypes, perceptions, and life experiences to a problem, and we want to be supported in how we view the world. Being open to viewing the world from another point of view tends to threaten us because we might have to admit that a view we have held for years is not right. Finding a way to enter into holographic inquiry and not be paralyzed by our anxiety is another challenge for individuals and organizations.

Leadership Styles

Within the emerging model, leadership is expanded from a designated role to a territory (see Figure 19.4). This means that virtually anyone

Figure 19.4
Leadership styles.

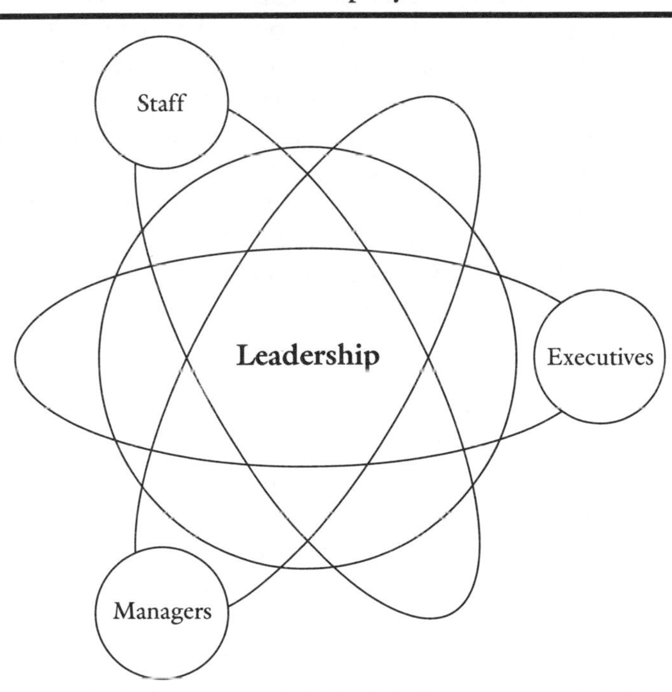

in the organization may be called to lead, even though not all of them will accept the call. We can look at it this way: Each organization has three main roles—executive, manager, and staff. At any given time, any of them will be involved in leadership.

In order for this combination of designated leader and leadership territory to work well, the emerging model calls for two leadership styles. One is participatory; the other is based on Greenleaf's Council of Equals.

The participative style is a both-and style; that is, it is connected to the mechanical model and the emerging model at the same time. The style is inclusive, based on a strong trust-communication cycle that actively involves both leader and follower. It requires buy-in by all involved, and calls for all to actively participate in the decision-making process. When it works well, this style is effective and exciting. People love to be in situations where it is working well. When it is not working, though, it goes something like this: The designated leader calls the team together and invites them to help solve a problem. The leader is genuinely interested in having the others help, and approaches the group with openness and sincerity. The group wants to help and may actually look forward to participating in the process. The leader explains the problem and asks the group to take a few days, reflect on the problem, talk with others, and come back together with possible solutions. The group reconvenes a few days later, and the leader wants to hear what they have to say first so they won't be influenced by the leader's comments. The members state what they believe to be the solution. For brevity's sake we'll say that there are four members and they each want a solution called A < > B. After listening to their suggestions, the leader offers G < > H as a solution. There is silence. The leader waits. Finally, someone says that he or she has been thinking about G < > H all along and that this is the best solution. After some discussion, everyone ends up supporting G < > H. After the meeting, you hear one person telling another, "We made a decision of G < > H, and I want you to know I was forced into it by X and the others." (The words may change from person to person but the idea is the same—the group capitulated.) This scenario is played out quite often and helps breed cynicism and inaction within teams/organizations.

The other leadership style involves what Greenleaf calls a Council of Equals. In current business jargon, these are referred to as "self-directed work teams." This style is paradoxical in that there are no Xs, and yet all are Xs at the same time. Generally, the first response to this style is that "it will create chaos" and "you can't make decisions this way." People seem to grasp quickly that, in order for this style to work, some beliefs must change. For example, power must be shared and all must step up and accept the power; ownership is a must, buy-in is not powerful enough. "We are all accountable" and "we won't control" are two crucial positions for the members.

Interdependent relationships help create collaboration and help minimize internal competition. We know how difficult it is to embrace these beliefs, especially since most of us don't know how to play them out in reality. On the other hand, without these and other beliefs in place, this emerging territory of "equals" can't be experienced. This is not to say that people should not commit themselves to grow into this style, quite the contrary. Greenleaf extends us all an invitation to grow into this style both personally and as councils (or teams). Here's an example of how this works: A council comes together and the organization's mission is read. The first question asked is: "How can I help you?" This indicates the desire to serve first and to lead from the position of serving. The council approaches the problem with the belief that together they can find a workable solution. This solution might be delegating the problem and its solution to a council member or to someone outside of the council. Alternatively, the council may decide that the solution must come from a consensus. This means that all must participate and that the council must invite those who are quiet to actively join the dialogue. There is a belief among the members that a consensus will be reached through dialogue (asking effective questions, listening intently, offering reflective insights, and relying on each other's strengths) and time.

Consensus does not mean total agreement, however. It does mean that everyone has had a say, been listened to, and can support the wisdom of the group ("I believe that the wisdom of the group is greater than my wisdom alone"). The implications of this style in terms of trust, communication, shared information, ownership, and empowerment are quite clear, and those wishing to enter this territory must enter the arena of self-development and dialogue.

Follower Styles

Within this model, the followers call forth the leaders, and they demand effective leadership. They give up being dependent and compliant and move toward being empowered and to accepting ownership and accountability for the decisions that are made. They seek interdependency and take risks. They enhance the trust-communication cycle, and they develop their own faith and courage to act. They commit themselves to becoming learners and accept the invitation to enter into the leadership territory as servant-leaders.

Some followers do not accept the invitation. These followers respond with the old responses from the traditional, mechanical model. The power of these responses indicates two things: how much we've integrated the mechanical model into our lives, and how much anxiety comes with change. When we were toddlers we welcomed change; we sought it out; we thrived on it. As we grow older we believe what the mechanical model taught us—change is bad; balance is good; find your niche and stick with it. If you stay in the role you have, the system will be stable and you will be rewarded with a place to work for the rest of your life.

Things are changing, though. People are finding out that this quid pro quo is no longer valid. Today, change may very well be the norm; the stability promised by the mechanical model is no longer there for many of us. Today, more than ever before, followers must discover what it means not to be a follower.

The emerging model is paradoxical because it calls us to lead by serving, tells us that we must learn how to get more from less and use our current resources more fully, and acknowledges many right answers. This model is built on relationships and a strong trust-communication cycle. Both self and team are crucial to success. This model calls for an examination of our deepest beliefs and a discipline that is more demanding than we were used to in the mechanical model. It calls for a purpose that will help us stay the course, especially in the face of the ever-present cynicism that is currently being bred and nurtured within organizations.

The transition from the mechanical model to the emerging model takes time, energy, and commitment. It calls for a grounding in a new foundation, the foundation of relationship rather than things. Without this grounding, organizations will only experience what I call the "illusion of change." Organizations will spend money and time learning a model, and the model will not be integrated. In fact, what will happen is that within a brief period of time—a few months to a few years—people will be doing what they've always done before. Learning the skills without the grounding in relationship will only guarantee that the mechanical model will prevail.

Greenleaf's Contribution

As a surveyor, Robert K. Greenleaf's contribution to the path from the traditional territory to the emerging territory is one that calls us to change. The change involves seeing and embracing the power of relationships, that the key foundation piece is one of relationships, which include the relationship one has with oneself; that one has with others; that occur between teams, areas, departments, and divisions within organizations; and that occur among organizations within society. Science has taught us that the root is not a thing, like the atom, but the root is relationship between and among in such a way that the building blocks are relationships. Our challenge from Greenleaf is to figure out what this means for us and for our organizations and to develop ways of playing out the power of relationships. The path that he invites us to follow is somewhat mapped out for us; however, as we progress along the path it becomes clearer and clearer that we need to become our own surveyors—we need to take ownership of our individual and organizational journeys and take the risk to develop our own maps. And we must do this in relationship; the single leader is not able to lead us to the emerging territory. Greenleaf says that the servant-leader can help us by making sure we are served well as we make our journey; the servant-leader is crucial to this journey. And, Greenleaf asks, do those served on this journey "grow as persons; do they, while being served, become healthier, wiser, freer, more autonomous, and more likely themselves to become servants?" This is one of the tests that must be applied as the journey is made.

We will only know if this journey is worthwhile after we take it; we have no guarantee that it is the "right" journey, and so we must decide ahead of time—and reaffirm along the way—that the journey itself is worth it. The journey is the end; another paradox. Only if we see it this way will we be able to echo what Robert Frost meant when he wrote:

> Two Roads Diverged in a Wood, and I—
> I Took the One Less Traveled by,
> And that has Made All the Difference.

PART FOUR

Greenleaf's Legacy

20

Robert Greenleaf's Legacy: A New Foundation for Twenty-First Century Institutions*

Peter M. Senge

I believe that the book *Servant Leadership,* and in particular the essay, "The Servant as Leader," which starts the book off, is the most singular and useful statement on leadership that I have read in the last 20 years. Despite a virtual tidal wave of books on leadership during the last few years, there is something different about Bob Greenleaf's essay, something both simpler and more profound. This one essay penetrates to such a depth that it resonates in us, like the aftertones of a Buddhist meditation gong, calling us to quiet.

---

*Based on a talk at the Annual Conference of the Robert K. Greenleaf Center, October, 1992.

Rereading the essay, I found myself stopped, repeatedly, by a single sentence or phrase. For many years, I simply told people not to waste their time reading all the other managerial leadership books. "If you are really serious about the deeper territory of true leadership," I would say, "read Greenleaf." Today, there are now a few other books of comparable eloquence and insight, which is a hopeful sign that the message is spreading.

This is an opportunity for me to salute a body of work that has had an enormous personal impact on me. I suggest that Greenleaf opened up a pathway, and that the territory into which it leads is bigger than the pathway itself. What he did is part of something larger. I'd like to consider what that something larger is. My hope is that this will give us all a deeper appreciation of what it means to carry on with the work Greenleaf started.

But, before we can go too far, all of us must have some idea of what the pathway is. I would like to start with a question for those of you who, like myself, have been living with this book for awhile. What has it meant to you? What has the idea of the leader as servant meant to you? Some audience responses:

- "It's a way to change life. First, you change yourself, and then you change institutions."
- "It made me aware that there were others out there who thought similarly, whereas before I might have thought I was alone, or just had a hard time finding people who were thinking the same way. That was pretty important."
- "It has given me more of an openness. Once, the question 'where am I getting this wrong?' made me feel there was a problem with me. Now I feel that this question is probably more of a strength than a weakness."
- "It has given me more meaning and purpose for my position in corporate America. At times I think that I was questioning whether or not that was the right place for me to be. But, now I see a real value in terms of servant-leadership and having an impact on corporate America as well."
- "Greenleaf's book has a sense about moral authority and the whole idea of leadership. It restores hope that leadership can be a source for the good of society."

- "It helps me integrate the concept of collaboration, rather than competition. I'm finding that I have a vocabulary to be a team member, and not the 'I' that I used to feel."
- "I don't know quite how to say this but, in the best sense, it has given me a way to think about using the strength of my ego, while keeping it in check."
- "It's given me the courage to talk to people from the heart and actually feel their heart talk back to me."

Well, for any of you who walked into this room this evening not knowing servant-leadership, you now know a little bit.

My History with Servant-Leadership

About 10 years ago, a man named Joe Jaworski was embarking on a very interesting new enterprise. Joe is the son of Leon Jaworski, who was the chief Watergate prosecutor. Joe was, himself, a very successful trial lawyer. He was a senior partner in a large international firm. During the period of the Watergate trials, and for a year or so after, Joe and his father had many conversations about leadership in this country. Based on those conversations, Joe ultimately decided to quit his career and start a new venture, which he called the American Leadership Forum (ALF), which now operates to develop local leadership networks in many cities around the country.

Joe was the first person who told me about Greenleaf's work. In his own wonderful way, Joe had approached the founding of ALF as a quest, immersing himself in meeting anybody who had done anything important on leadership. John Gardner had told Joe to read this book by Robert Greenleaf.

I will never forget a particular evening plane flight to Houston. I was going to do the three-day "Leadership and Mastery" program for that first group of American Leadership Forum fellows. On the plane, I started reading the book Joe had sent to me, *Servant Leadership*. I rarely read a book page-by-page, but I read this book that way. I'll give you a brief recap, so you can understand the quote that follows. Greenleaf based "The Servant as Leader," on Hermann Hesse's *Journey to the East,* which is the story of a party of "seekers" searching for enlightenment in the form of a particular secret spiritual order. They are attended to by a servant, Leo, who does their menial chores. Throughout the journey, the party is sustained by Leo's "spirit and his song." Eventually, Leo disappears. The party gets completely lost and abandons its search. The narrator carries on but suffers immense emotional and physical stress. Eventually, he comes to realize that it was his servant, Leo, who held him and his party together. After many years of wandering, the narrator finds Leo again, who, as it turns out, is the head of the spiritual community that the narrator was seeking all along.

Greenleaf summarizes that story in the first three pages of his essay. At the end of the essay, he quotes from Hesse's story. It is this passage, more than anything else, that has prompted me to say for many years that there is nothing you should read about leadership until you first read *Servant Leadership*. By the end of Hesse's story, it has become more and more clear that the narrator is an autobiographical character. At the end, after the narrator's initiation into the Order, he and Leo are talking and they are holding a small transparent sculpture of two figures joined together. One is Leo and the other, the narrator (Hesse). The narrator notes that there is a movement, apparently a movement in substance within this transparent sculpture, and then Hesse writes:

> I perceived that my image was in the process of adding to and flowing into Leo's, nourishing and strengthening it. It seemed that, in time . . . only one would remain, Leo. As I stood there and looked and tried to understand what I saw, I recalled a short conversation that I had once had with Leo during the festive day in Bremgarten. We had talked about the creations of poetry being more vivid and real than the poets themselves.

As I read that passage on the airplane that evening, I cried. I knew that this man understood something, something we have lost in our modern "transactional" society, where "what's in it for me" is the assumed bedrock of all actions. We have lost the joy of "creating," of working for something just because it needs to be done. In our frenzy to get something for ourselves, we have lost ourselves. We have doomed ourselves to a sullen, dull sort of life, full of the things we acquire and empty of any deeper happiness. We have forgotten that, as Robert Frost said, "All great things are done for their own sake." To think that this reorientation of spirit might be a foundation for true leadership stunned me. Bob Greenleaf put a stake in the ground. He took a stand that resonates very deeply in many of us—I suspect in ways that we don't even consciously understand.

A New World and a New Worldview

Servant-leadership is an interesting phrase, a juxtaposition of apparent opposites, which immediately causes us to think freshly. But I actually think that the phrase is a sort of gateway. With this phrase, Greenleaf takes us by the hand and leads us into a different universe. It's a universe in which most of us, I believe, have a deep hunger to participate. In fact, it's what the ancients called "the great hunger." It's a universe where our sense of self is very different. It's a universe toward which, in some way or other, all the great esoteric and spiritual traditions point. I believe one of the things Greenleaf was trying to do was provide a pathway that was not based exclusively on any of their ancient traditions, but was more congruent and meaningful for us in our present-day world. He was seeking a way we could live our lives productively in contemporary institutions so as to be connected with our own spiritual journey. But even the phrase, "spiritual journey," is problematic today. The subtle distinctions required for its meaning to be evident have been lost.

So, I'd like to talk about this "alternative universe" in some different ways. I would like to explore with you several ways into this "alternative universe," which includes what Greenleaf said, but also some ways that he didn't articulate. Today, there is actually quite a bit that connects with and is implied by his work, but actually goes a bit further.

Something very dramatic is happening in this century. But like most important changes, almost nobody is noticing. There are two particular developments I'd like to ponder together—one of which we all sort of know on a gut level, and the other of which relatively few recognize.

The one that we all know on a gut level, but rarely talk about (although much that we talk about comes from this awareness), is illustrated by a story Greenleaf tells about how he got into his career even though he was not particularly interested in business. He ended up spending his career at AT&T because he had a professor in his last year in college who told him, "Big institutions are becoming more and more dominating of society, and they don't seem to be serving very well. Maybe that's a good place to go and apply yourself."

I'd like to say this a little bit differently and a little bit more broadly. Over the course of the past 150 years or so, we have witnessed an unprecedented increase in our collective "power," our ability to influence our world. There are three primary driving forces: economic growth, technological growth, and the growth of global business institutions. Together, these changes have brought us to a point of extraordinary ability to affect life on planet earth. We are altering global ecosystems. We are intervening in the evolutionary dynamics of the gene pool. We are reshaping the future in ways that would have been unimaginable 100 years ago. And, we have almost no ability to predict the long-term consequences of these changes. We have developed extraordinary power but have little ability to control the application of that power.

If you ask how many people consider the world today to be more dangerous than the world of 100 years ago, about 75 percent will say it is. What's going on? We all know enough about the changes in the last 100 years to know that life expectancy today is somewhere around 75 to 80 years, or roughly twice what it was 100 years ago. So how is it that the world today is more dangerous than the world of 100 years ago? What's changed? Again, if you ask people, here are some of the responses you're likely to hear:

- "Violence."
- "Stress."
- "Acid rain."
- "Nuclear weapons."
- "Drugs."
- "AIDS."
- "The obliteration of indigenous cultures."
- "Things are more impersonal."
- "Destruction of community."
- "Global warming."
- "Things that go bump in the night."

From an evolutionary standpoint, such threats represent a profound shift in the conditions for survival for our species.

For most of our history as a species, the primary threats to our survival came in the form of sudden dramatic changes in our environment. You want to know where "crisis management" comes from? It's not because we're bad managers. It's because of *us*. If you were designing the optimal cave person, that person had better be able to recognize a saber tooth tiger creeping up from behind, and react. Take the Gulf War for example. I don't think there are many people in this country who would feel that going off to Saudi Arabia to fight Saddam Hussein was at the top of the nation's priority list. It was important, don't get me wrong. But by comparison to the decline of the education system, the decline of our national productivity and our economic base, the loss of jobs, the loss of industry, few would say that the Gulf War was more important than those problems. Yet, notice what got our attention. Notice how our whole system of public awareness and concern orients itself to deal with a crisis. That's the way we are designed.

Here's the basic problem: Today, virtually all the primary threats to our survival are slow, gradual processes, not sudden events. We're not geared to deal with gradually developing crises. We want to wait until a dramatic crisis occurs. Then we'll do something. But, guess what? By the time such a crisis occurs, it may be too late to do something.

Another, equally important problem is that, for almost all of our history, the threats to our survival were external in nature. They came from outside of ourselves. Today, all the primary threats to our survival are of our own making. There is no enemy to fight, no beast to slay, no one individual or group to blame. Even though we might seek to establish a villain, for the really big issues, we know the causes are more complex. The causes stem from our collective actions. Usually, they do not arise from an individual's actions. The primary threats to our survival today represent a new class of systemic threats for which we are more poorly prepared than we are for sudden crises.

This is the larger concern behind our big institutions, which are not serving us. We have developed an extraordinary capacity to influence our world through our institutions. But I think it would be fair to say that our wisdom, our understanding of ourselves and how we are influencing our world hasn't advanced to keep pace with our power. Therein lies our real crisis. That's the change that we all feel in our gut. There are very few people walking around (those who don't have their heads deeply buried in the sand) who don't feel uneasy these days.

There is another change that even fewer people are aware of. The real issue, I think, is whether these two changes can possibly result in some positive interaction. This change concerns an unfolding revolution in our scientific worldview. Interestingly, although Greenleaf wrote only briefly about this, I believe the emerging "systemic" worldview reflects his ideas in a central way.

The world that our culture teaches us to see is profoundly inaccurate in ways that we are just now beginning to understand. In our culture, *things* seem to us more real than *processes*. Think about this: What can be more real than this table? Well, guess what. A table is more than 99 percent empty space. It's an illusion of our senses that it appears solid. We now know that scientifically.

What happens when my fist opens? Where did the fist go? A good friend and colleague at MIT, Fred Kofman, says that this is a koan that will be the disintegration of Western culture. What happens to the waves when they hit the shore? Where do the waves go?

We think of our bodies as the most substantial, the most "real," aspect of who we are. But do you have any idea what the average lifetime of a cell in the human body is? There's all kinds of cells—liver cells, bone cells, skin cells, brain cells. Some only live a few days; some, like bone cells, live longer. The rate at which they regenerate changes as we get older. But virtually none of the cells in your body today were there three years ago. Simply put, you're not the person you used to be. I'm beginning at this very mundane level, at this physical level, in saying that this "body thing" is not what we think it is.

Buckminster Fuller used to run a little experiment, pointing out the average lifetime of a cell of the human; then he would say, "You're not a thing, you are patterned integrity." That was the phrase Bucky used to like to use—"a patterned integrity." Even at the physical level, if you want to ask, "What am I?" I am the capability to keep regenerating this "thingness."

For a long time the holy grail of our Western scientific quest was the idea that, eventually, if we kept going deeper and deeper, if we could design really sophisticated instruments and look at smaller and smaller things, we'd finally find the fundamental reality. What is this fundamental reality? The *atom*—the essential "thing." Deep in our culture, we believe that "things" are the bedrock of reality. Ironically, we've now gotten good enough at this game of probing deeper and deeper that we can't find any more "things." This was the profound philosophical crisis for the early twentieth-century physicists. It's not yet our philosophical crisis, but it should be.

Here's the way people in physics are starting to think about it. It appears that "things" are not the most fundamental aspect of reality. What is more fundamental than "things" are "relationships." What characterizes reality, "substance," at a very basic level, are patterns of interrelationship, Fuller's "patterned integrity."

Greenleaf suggested that we might actually build institutions predicated fundamentally on interrelationships, not things. He suggested that the fundamental foundation of the institution might be interrelationships, not things. If we could accept this, our institutions might be in deeper harmony with our emerging understanding of the physical universe and a more positive force in our increasingly interdependent world.

Institutions Based on Conversation and Community

How might this new scientific worldview penetrate more broadly into society? We know from history that it typically takes hundreds of years for a new scientific worldview to permeate broadly into the mainstream of society. The industrial revolution lagged by several hundred years the birth of the "objective, rationalistic" scientific paradigm, which began with the early scientists of the Renaissance and eventually gave rise to Bacon, Newton, and Descartes.

Unfortunately, we may not have the luxury of waiting a few hundred years for the new worldview of the primacy of interrelatedness to permeate through society. We can accelerate this process by recognizing, tapping, and extending two very old ideas that echo from an early age during which our societies incorporated an awareness of interdependency, not because of their understanding of quantum reality, but because they were more embedded in the natural world. These ideas concern conversation and community.

It is worth pondering this seemingly mundane word, "conversation." Buddha is said to have spent a good deal of his life contemplating and writing about conversation. He said that it is the single most valued aspect of human existence. Emerson wrote at great length about what he called "dialogue." Goethe called conversation "the most sublime of human experiences." The phrase "the art of conversation" used to mean something in our culture as recently as one hundred years ago. People considered the capacity for conversation to be one of the most important aspects of a person's growth throughout their life. I do not think the phrase has much meaning anymore.

There is an old distinction in our culture that it is time to reexamine. It has to do with the words "dialogue" and "discussion." The word "dialogue" comes from the Greek *dia-logos.* Logos means *meaning* or *word.* Dia means *through.* The original meaning of the word "dia-logos" was *meaning moves through* or *flow of meaning.* When a group of people talk with one another so that there is a flow of meaning, this is a very special type of conversation. We become unconcerned about who says what, about whose view prevails, or who saves face. We enter the domain of truly thinking together. By contrast, the word "discussion" comes from the same roots as "percussion" and "concussion." It literally means to "break apart." A discussion involves heaving one's views at one other. Who wins and who loses is often all that matters. Quite an interesting contrast in images. Meaning moving through versus heaving one's views at the other.

One facet of the research at MIT is studying the work of management teams. Often, this involves tape recording meetings and then, with the team, analyzing the character of the conversations. Here is some data that is worth reflecting on: A three-hour meeting with a senior management team, during which they were dealing with what they regarded as critical issues, there was no lack of motivation, no lack of knowledge. But in three hours not one question was asked. What was going on?

The distinction between dialogue and discussion was first pointed out to us by David Bohm, one of the leading quantum physicists of this generation. For the past 10 years, Bohm has been studying the nature of thought. His view is that thought is far more collective than we realize, especially generative thought, where new ways of thinking are emerging. Another famous physicist, Werner Heisenberg once said, "Science is rooted in conversation." I remember reading Heisenberg's autobiography when I was in graduate school. It is nothing but a retelling of conversations he had had during his life with other famous physicists, such as Schroedinger, Pauli, and Bohr. Again and again he shows how, as these conversations evolved, people began to think in ways they had never thought before.

Bohm believes that the Greeks were the last Western society to remember what dialogue was all about, and to hold it as a central element in their culture. His view is that, from the beginning of the agricultural revolution, there has been a progressive fragmentation in the social order and a progressive "fragmentation in thought," and that the two have interacted and reinforced each other. It is interesting that so many "primitive," that is preagricultural, cultures seem to engage in the practice of sitting in a circle and talking and talking until, as many Native Americans used to say, "the talk starts." It is clear that many such cultures do not hold the view that is so common in the West today, that thought is a purely individual phenomenon, occurring within our own heads. I remember talking with a man who had spent many years with a particular bush tribe, and he recalled an elder telling him about a particular dream he had been having for many years. "I no longer have the dream," the elder said, "because the man in the neighboring tribe has it now."

I think we have some dim recollection of what we have lost, a deep hunger for something that is missing in our lives today. The movie, *Dances with Wolves* struck a deep chord in many people's hearts because at some level we are aware of the monumental consequences of the steady destruction of indigenous cultures. We have not just "lost a few Indians"; we have destroyed a strand in the web of our cultural heritage. We have lost a particular sensibility of what it means to live together as part of a larger natural order. The depth and consequences of this loss are unknown and unknowable to us today. But we still have some idea of what it means to live with a different sense of community. Midway through the movie, as the Kevin Costner character is gradually being drawn into the tribal community, he returns for the last time to his outpost fort, where he has lived alone for many months. He contemplates the two worlds pulling on him, his own culture and the Sioux culture, and thinks of his new friends. He writes in his journal, "There have been many times in my life when I have been alone, but this was the first time I was lonely."

Although the indigenous cultures are all but lost in the world, we still carry within us some of their knowledge of conversation and community. How many of you have had a conversation where time "seemed to stand still," where you looked down at your watch and suddenly realized that three or four hours had gone by? Or, how many of you have had a conversation, perhaps in a work setting, where, when it was over, people walked out energized and excited, and someone said, "That was a terrific conversation, who said what?" People can become so caught up in what they are talking about that who takes what position becomes irrelevant. These are the conversations that seem to "come alive," where the flow of meaning becomes strong, and we all get caught up in the current. These are small tastes of genuine dialogue. We have not totally forgotten.

Apparently, one reason the Greeks considered *dia-logos* so important was their view that it was vital to self-governance. Once a society loses this capacity, all that is left is *discussion,* a cacophony of voices battling it out to see who wins and who loses. There is no capacity to go deeper, to find a deeper meaning that transcends individual views and self-interest. It seems reasonable to ask whether many of our deeper problems in governing ourselves today, the so-called "gridlock" and loss of mutual respect and caring in government, might not stem from this lost capacity to talk with one another, to think together as part of a larger community.

Interestingly, the contemporary metaphor of "organization development" is gradually giving way in our work to an older metaphor, "community building." I do not think this is merely a matter of substituting one term for another. An organization, for most of us, is a *thing,* whereas a community is not. A community is comprised of people and how they interrelate. As we continue to pursue basic questions like "How do shared visions develop?" and "How can widely shared mental models change?" the organization metaphor is becoming increasingly inappropriate. Can an organization "have a vision," or "hold a shared mental model," or "learn?" Surely this is a classic case of reification, of treating an abstraction as if it actually existed. But communities *can* hold visions, share assumptions, and enhance collective capabilities; that is, learn. So perhaps we have been misleading ourselves for many years when we have spoken of "building a shared vision for an organization."

A New View of Institutional Leadership

It is not possible to talk of a new type of institution without talking about a new type of leadership. Above all else, leaders build organizations. So, any shift in the predominant character of institutions like business will be inseparable from a shift in the predominant theory and practice of leadership. Greenleaf understood this very well.

The traditional leadership model in Western culture suggests a one-way link. The leader acts on the followers. The leader sets the vision and then works to get people to buy in. The leader creates the organizational policies and structures that determine how things get done. The leader motivates people.

Greenleaf had another notion. He questioned whether we should reject the notion of leader altogether. Perhaps there's no room for the word "leader" in a system of management fundamentally predicated on interrelationship. It's a very good question. My hunch is that Greenleaf was probably still open on this question. Nonetheless, he suggested that perhaps we can salvage this notion of leader as long as we give up the notion of the one-way effect on follower, and begin to see leaders and followers interacting in a continuous process of mutual influence. For example, he talked about the "first impulse" of servant-leaders always to "listen first"—not to talk. Larry Spears has said that this will be the ultimate accomplishment in the discipline of servant-leadership—to listen first. Bob Galvin, retired chairman of Motorola, once said this very eloquently, "My job is to listen to what the organization is trying to say, and then make sure that it gets forcefully articulated."

There are certain basic functions common to leadership in all institutional settings. First, there is the question, "How do we establish a direction?" How do we establish an aim? Probably the oldest idea associated with leadership is vision. It's interesting that it has now come back into popularity and has become a bit of a fad, but it actually has a very rich history, as exemplified by the Biblical phrase, "Where there is no vision, the people perish."

In our conventional one-way leadership model, this phrase is interpreted to suggest a strong leader who sets a direction and gets people to "buy in." It doesn't matter, by the way, whether it's called "strategic objectives," "goals," or "vision"; it's the same old wine in new bottles. The people in organizations know this. They've seen that strategic objective statement, the strategic mission statements. And they are now seeing the "vision statements." People know it's the same old wine; they're not easily fooled. The leader, or perhaps the leadership team, comes up with the vision and then lays it on the others.

But there is an alternative interpretation of the Biblical warning: that people's lives flourish when they have a sense of purpose. In this view, what matters is whether a *shared* vision exists, which is quite different from people following someone else's vision. New visions can emerge from many different sources, not just from "the top." The job of people in leadership positions is to make sure that good ideas are brought into the open, are considered seriously and, where possible, tested, so that eventually shared visions develop.

A question that has long been at the heart of our work is, "How do shared visions develop?" "How do you go from the vision of a few people to larger numbers of people operating with a common conviction and with shared images of the future?" As we reflect on such questions, we begin to see how valuing dialogue and generative conversation might shift our thinking. Today, we tend to think of vision as a "thing." We even speak of "the vision thing." Thinking in terms of things, we attempt to establish a shared vision as if it were a car we could build. Along with this is the equally crazy notion that everybody has to share the same vision. Thinking of vision as a thing, we naturally gravitate toward simple agreement as our measure of whether a shared vision exists. If we can measure people's agreement, then we consider a shared vision real.

The idea that everybody has to be in agreement about "the vision" is complete nonsense. If you, as a manager, push for such agreement, you probably will get it, but it probably will be superficial. What really matters is not superficial, "intellectual" agreement but what is in people's hearts and minds. In a 1,000-person organization there had better be 1,000 visions. Otherwise, you won't have anybody committed to anything. You will have only superficial compliance to the official vision. For each of us, only when we touch that about which we care most deeply does our genuine commitment come foreward. Our commitment comes from what we care about. You don't have to get people committed to their children; they are naturally committed. When I work to bring into being something that I deeply care about, my life energy moves naturally in that direction.

Building shared vision is not about people surrendering their individual visions. It is about deepening each person's unique sense of vision and establishing harmony among the diverse visions so that we can move forward together. It does not require surrendering our uniqueness. If anything, it requires more, not less, of our uniqueness.

A second basic function of leadership is to answer the question: "How do you build the capacity of a group of people to move toward their visions?" One facet of this challenge concerns individual growth. "The best test of the servant-leader," says Greenleaf, is to determine "do those served grow as persons? Do they, while being served, become healthier, wiser, freer, more autonomous, more likely themselves to become servants?" From my experience, I, too have found this to be a very discriminating criterion. Many who aspire to servant-leadership or who espouse its ideals fail this test. It may not indicate that they are insincere in their beliefs about serving. More often it indicates that they are simply not yet able, at this stage in their lives, to operate consistently as servant-leaders. The breadth and depth of the servant-leader's commitment to people's growth is distinctive. For example, retired

Hanover Insurance CEO Bill O'Brien wrote extensively about "advanced maturity," his vision of people developing their capacity for personal vision, delayed gratification, objective self-assessment, and the capacity to commit to something larger than yourself.

A second facet of the capacity-building challenge concerns collective capability. How do groups of people form into effective communities of action? How is collective action coordinated and guided? And, how is the community's capabilities for coordinated, effective action enhanced over time—that is, how does the community learn?

The Western system of management is based on a particular mental model of how we move from individual views to collective coordinated action. Like most mental models, it is highly tacit, its assumptions rarely questioned. It is based on the following linear progression. First, it is necessary to establish a shared view of the goals. We all know that people have differing views, so there must be some process whereby the diversity of individual views are reconciled to a shared view. The humanists argue for open exchange of views based on mutual respect, good listening skills, and the building of a consensus or a synthesis of alternative views. We all know that a more political model often dominates in real organizations. The boss's view prevails. If I am not the boss, I have to find some way to influence him or her. This is a root source of much of the "gamesplaying" and internal politics that so permeate most organizations. The second basic step in our prevailing model of coordination is to convert the shared goals into an action plan, including roles, interim objectives, and reporting, relationships that provide an organizational foundation. Third, there must be some control mechanisms to assess where we are today relative to our goals, and adjust accordingly. This essentially linear sequence represents the holy trinity of Western management: planning, organizing, controlling.

This traditional view of how to achieve coordinated action is breaking down because the world in which we live is changing. The world often doesn't stay put long enough for our plans to be implemented. No sooner have we set a goal and figured out an action plan than everything seems to change. Consequently, tight control from the center just doesn't work like it used to in large organizations. Those organizations that were unwilling to surrender centralized control—be they IBM, General Motors, or the government of the former Soviet Union—have suffered what O'Brien calls a "breakdown of the central nervous system."

The most common response to the breakdown of centralized management has been to distribute decision-making more broadly, "empowering" front line people to make more decisions on their own. But distributing responsibilities for planning, organizing, and controlling may only increase problems. If local people in their functional silos make more decisions, they need to *understand* how their decisions might influence those in other silos. Such systemic understanding was never needed in traditional organizations. We used to be able to translate the overall corporate plan into separate plans and policies for marketing, manufacturing, and research. Thus, people never had to develop the capability to think across functional boundaries and to understand larger systems. So, there is no guarantee that empowerment improves the quality of decision-making. Historically, most organizational efforts to decentralize fail, leading eventually to recentralization.

The emerging theory of dialogue suggests a completely different process whereby coordinated action can arise. In effect, it suggests a different mediating process between individual thought and collective action. Instead of the linear sequential view of "planning, organizing, and controlling," it suggests that as people increasingly "participate in a pool of common thought," as Bohm puts it, their actions will naturally fall into increasing alignment. As they begin to think together, they will more and more tend to act together. While such notions might seem horribly naive from our traditional managerial perspective, they don't to the jazz musician or member of a championship sports team. In such domains, people come to appreciate in very concrete ways what it means to think and act together.

This alternative theory of coordinated action is actually illustrated beautifully in the movie *Dances with Wolves*. There is a sequence of scenes in which the tribal council meets. (We often show these scenes to give people a concrete feel for how dialogue can operate.) These scenes are quite interesting: They are full of conflict, with different members of the council voicing strong and differing views. But deep listening is also taking place. After each person talks, there are visible and audible signs of acknowledgment. There are frequent pauses, as others consider the views expressed and their own thoughts. Interestingly, there is typically no convergence on critical issues. Apparently, there is no need for superficial signs of agreement. People are pondering complicated and puzzling issues. Typically, the tribal elder concludes a session by saying, "These are complex issues. It is easy to become confused. We will have to talk some more." Western managers watching these scenes generally report strongly mixed emotions. On one hand, they appreciate the careful listening, the acknowledgment of one another; on the other hand, no decisions are made, no action plans are drawn up. It is unclear what, if anything, will come of the conversation. "All they do is talk," said one manager. To impatient Westerners, such conversations often seem useless.

Interestingly, however, in a scene in the movie that follows shortly after the series of council meetings, we see the tribe participating together in the buffalo hunt. Rarely has a movie recorded such a moving mosaic of coordinated action. In a context where no simple action plan could ever suffice, where each actor must be acutely aware of one another, and where they ultimately must share responsibility for the overall results and for one another's safety, the tribe operates with a fluid collective grace which is stunning. Perhaps there is a larger process here. Perhaps the capacity for the council to sit and think together is inseparable from their capacity to act together. Perhaps there is a larger coordinating process beyond what could possibly be achieved through a linear plan.

Much remains to be done to develop this new theory of coordinated action. My hunch is that, as we better understand it, it will appear less as a stark alternative to planning, organizing, and controlling and more as a complement to the traditional model. There is no reason that groups participating in a larger "dialogic change process" should not also set goals, define roles, and organize as best they can, and monitor how they are doing. They just would not see these activities as the be all and end all. They would have more flexibility and adaptiveness, more capacity to disregard the plan and do what is needed in the moment—and to act in the moment in a fashion that spontaneously coordinates across their organizational boundaries.

A third basic function of leadership answers not only how we develop people's ability to think and act together, but "How do we improve the quality of thinking—especially regarding people's abilities to understand increasingly complex, interrelated realities?" This relates to what Greenleaf called "conceptual leadership." In particular, he talked about the fundamental evil of "fuzzy thinking." "Who is the enemy?" he asks. "Not evil people. Not stupid people. Not apathetic people. Not the 'system' . . . The better society will come, if it comes, with plenty of evil, stupid, apathetic people around and with an imperfect, ponderous, inertia-charged system as the vehicle for change. Liquidate the offending people, radically alter or destroy the system, and in less than a generation they all will be back. . . . The healthy society, like the healthy body, is not the one that has taken the most medicine. It is the one in which the internal health building forces are in the best shape."

In this statement Greenleaf offers an eloquent rendering of the need for a different type of thinking, a new basis for "health." Rather than just correcting problems, we need to understand the deeper forces that shape reality and make enduring change difficult. We call this type of thinking "systems thinking" because it is about understanding the underlying structures that generate forces that give rise to the problem symptoms we, as managers, spend so much time attempting to ameliorate.

There is a cartoon that shows a man pushing a huge domino out of his way. Unfortunately, he doesn't notice that he is sitting in the midst of a circle of these dominoes, and has set off a chain reaction of falling dominoes which will eventually come back around to crush him. He has taken a decisive action but, after a while, he's going to have a new, larger problem crashing down upon him. Of course, if it takes three or four years for the dominoes to go around that circle, the person who took the original decisive action probably will have been promoted, and some other poor sucker is in his place. This illustrates the classic dilemma of problem solving in complex systems. We don't see the larger structures within which we are operating. Consequently, our solutions eventually come back to haunt us—or to haunt someone else, someone in another part of the larger system, or in the future.

This phenomenon has become so pervasive in modern medicine there is now a term for it. "Iatrogenic" pathologies are medical problems that have been created as a result of an earlier solution to a previous problem. No one knows how large a part of our runaway health care costs are, in this sense, self-inflicted. I have heard some estimates that as many as one-third of the people currently in hospitals are there as a result of adverse reactions to drugs *administered by their physicians.* Needless to say, attempting to change such a situation through massive system-wide cost controls, as undoubtedly are coming in healthcare, is a "crude bludgeon" for very deep problems, problems that have their roots in pervasive elements of modern medical practice, medical education, the power of drug companies, and ultimately deeply entrenched patterns of reductionistic thinking throughout society.

As a further example of this new way of thinking, consider a systems principle called "shifting the burden." Whenever we face difficult problems, there typically are many ways to make the symptoms of the problem go away, at least for a little while. Conversely, there are usually far fewer "fundamental solutions," which, if pursued, might get at deeper causes and result in a lasting solution to the problem. Such fundamental solutions are often more difficult to identify, take time to either implement or to achieve their full consequences, or entail considerable uncertainty as to their effectiveness. Consequently, there are usually a lot of good reasons to apply symptomatic solutions or quick fixes. The problem is that, not only are their benefits often short-lived, they have a way of becoming more and more necessary over time, during which we "shift the burden" to depending on what was originally seen as a one-time quick fix.

For example, consider the number of state lotteries there are in America right now—about 40. Ten years ago, there were only two or three. The problem symptom we're dealing with here is fiscal stress at the state level—budget deficits, shortages of revenues relative to outflows. The fundamental response is to find a way to live within our means, right? Reduce spending or raise taxes in a sustainable manner. A lottery is a politician's heaven. It brings in money quickly. No tough decisions need to get made. Almost no one complains. The problem symptom of a budget shortfall is improved quickly. But, since the underlying cause of the problem, the absence of fiscal discipline, hasn't been affected at all, the problem symptoms eventually return. We get a short-term improvement in the state budget balance, but after two or three years, spending has continued to creep up, tax revenues have either flattened out or not kept pace, and we're back in the soup. What do we then do? Recognize the folly of our ways? Become seriously committed to fiscal discipline? Do we say, "Oh, we made a mistake. Clearly, this lottery stuff is no real solution to our problems." No, we expand the lottery. We look for some other ways to use gambling to add to the state coffers.

Over time, we "shift the burden." What was a one-time quick fix becomes a way of life; it becomes institutionalized. And, of course, the real tragedy is that the more the short-term fix works, the more it will continue to undermine our capability for long term improvement. Herein lies the insidiousness of shifting the burden—the more effective the quick fix, the more dangerous it is.

This example has the classic dynamics of dependency associated with addiction. Shifting the burden is the most common systemic cause of addiction to drugs, alcohol, and food. People do not seek to become addicts, so why are addictions so common? Addiction develops as a byproduct of being unable or unwilling to face difficult problems *and* having alternative quick fixes at one's disposal. In this sense, you can see why addiction is a common phenomenon in social systems. In fact, it is not just an individual phenomenon; corporations and societies also become addicted.

Hopefully, this illustrates why the quality of thinking is so important as we confront complex, highly interrelated issues. Given the typical ways of focusing on symptoms and "fixing" them, not only will we tend to take low-leverage actions that will ameliorate without curing, over time real cures will become harder to identify and implement. This is the classic long-term consequence of nonsystemic thinking—the problems get worse and our ability to confront them weakens.

It is difficult in our present institutions to find good examples of systems thinking. Here and there we find people in corporate life who have started and grown organizations over an extended period time and who have a rich intuitive grasp of what will make their enterprise healthy. Unfortunately, these people often find it almost impossible to explain their insights. Ironically, this may lead them to practice highly authoritarian styles of leadership.

Today, systems thinking is almost completely absent from public life. This is an especially great tragedy because authoritarian leadership by a "philosopher king" is no longer an option in public life. As a result, even more so than in corporations, we are thrown back on the collective intelligence of the society as a whole. This, undoubtedly, is at the root of Jefferson's fervent conviction that the quality of a democracy will never be greater than the quality of its public education, and why much of his later years were devoted to establishing the University of Virginia. It is not just the quality of our public education institutions that is at issue here, but the public's ability to understand what is going on in our world. To me, the saddest thing that I have seen in American politics in recent years is our tendency to elect people as cheerleaders. It seems that our recent presidents have been more interested in telling us that everything is okay than in helping people understand the issues and the choices we face. People know that things are not okay. So, when politicians try to convince people otherwise, the credibility of the whole political process sinks still further.

I'm suggesting that leadership's responsibility is to help people understand a complex world. Without such understanding, all the vision in the world may be of little value, and efforts to sustain effective coordinated action will be continually thwarted by actions that prevent enduring improvement.

Education and Evolution

Developing capabilities for recognizing our own mental models and for dialogue, for building shared vision, and for systems thinking is a long-term undertaking. Tools and methods such as those being developed through our Learning Center at MIT can help. But, it is also important to realize that it will not be enough to focus only on our business institutions. We must move "upstream." It is foolish to think we will make 25-year-old adults into systems thinkers and "lifelong learners" when the preceding 20 years of their lives have been spent breaking problems apart into pieces and convincing one another how much they know. It is impossible to conceive of the profound changes needed in learning capabilities within business without recognizing the need for comparable changes in the entire educational process.

Once we begin to grasp the whole of what is required, we also discover how much we have to work with. One powerful indication of this comes from efforts to teach systems thinking to children, from about grade 5 on up through high school and into universities. Children, typically younger ones, seem to love it. They seem to be natural systems thinkers. They grow up within a world of interrelatedness, and their capacities to grasp the systems of their everyday lives are vital to their success. If this weren't the case, how else could these little people be in such control? Find me a four-year-old, for example, who doesn't know that if they don't clean up their room, mommy or daddy will. It takes a systematic, (not to be confused with "systemic") 15-year effort to make over these natural systems thinkers into reductionists.

This effort starts out the first day of school, and continues with virtually every exam you take. I remember reading an article by an educator, many years ago, who said, "We have no idea the trauma the young child suffers in school." I've never forgotten that sentence. What's that educator talking about?

Children are masters of learning. You want to learn about learning? Hang out with a two-year-old. I'm not being facetious now. Did anybody teach us how to walk? How did that process work? Through observation and practice. A one-year-old who falls down after two or three steps doesn't suffer a psychological trauma. The child may have a bruised knee, but he or she will get up and fall down again, get up and fall down again. After a while, he or she is walking. And, a year or two later, that same little person will master natural language, using the same learning-by-doing process. Many psychologists would argue that the most profound learning experience that any human being goes through in life is the mastery of natural language. And almost all of us succeed in this profound learning by the age of three, some with even two or more languages. And we master this incredibly complex new capacity with nobody actively "teaching." This is what I mean by master learners.

Put that same human being in a classroom five years later, and give him or her a test back with a big red circle that says "wrong." Do they suffer a profound psychological trauma? The fundamental drive of his or her life is learning, and that child's love of learning is now being replaced by a fear of making mistakes. He or she has now been told to forget learning, that education is about knowing, not learning. It is about studying what someone else says you need to know, not pursuing your intrinsic motivation. It is about performing for someone else's approval, not setting one's own goals and assessing one's own progress.

You can begin to see the types of changes that would be needed in our educational process if it were to actually prepare people for a lifetime of continual learning. To develop people who were intrinsically motivated to learn, able to reflect on their own assumptions, able to learn together, able to objectively assess their own learning, able to think systemically—this would take some major changes in the content and process of education.

If our education process is to succeed, it would have to prepare people for a twenty-first century that would differ dramatically from the nineteenth and twentieth centuries. This would include not only new skills and capabilities, but new attitudes and awarenesses. Paramount among these new awarenesses would be a deeper understanding of the evolutionary process and how the human community might contribute to it. Without such understanding, there is little hope of bringing the global industrial system into harmony with the larger natural world upon which we all ultimately depend.

Our prevailing view of evolution is dominated by the idea of competition, not by the idea of interdependency. We think that the essence of evolution is competition, "survival of the fittest." This was a very convenient interpretation when the theory of evolution was first articulated, because it fit beautifully with the needs of the industrial era of the time. Surely, if nature were "red in tooth and claw," the same could be expected within the marketplace. In the "industrial jungle," businesses compete for survival just as we imagine species competing for survival. Eventually, the internal environment within institutions, be they in education, business, or government, began to resemble the jungle (or more precisely our mental model of the jungle) as well—with students, managers, and politicians pitted against one another to see who would "survive."

It is beginning to appear that our prevailing view of evolution is a very simplistic, inaccurate, and incomplete picture of how this theory works in nature. There is competition, but it turns out that there is also collaboration in evolution. Species form symbiotic relationships that help them to mutually survive. Many scientists are also wondering about the pure randomness of the mutation process. Some are claiming that the rate by which new forms evolve is much faster than could ever be accounted for by random mutation alone. Some even claim that there must be other processes subtly guiding the mutation process toward more complex and appropriate forms.

There may even be a larger collaborative process at work within evolution, at the level of life on earth in its totality. There is a wonderful writer on evolution who is an appropriate complement to Greenleaf's work. His name is Thomas Berry, and he has been for many years the president of the American Teilhard de Chardin Society.

Chardin, an eminent biologist who was also a Jesuit priest, was perhaps the first prominent Western scientist to articulate the notion that the planet Earth, and all life on earth, might actually be a form of life at a higher order. Today it is known as the "Gaia Hypothesis," and has some illustrious supporters, including Boston University biologist Lynn Margulis. To this idea, Chardin added the notion that, with increasingly complex species like humans, the biosphere is being extended to include a *noosphere,* the pool of collective thought on the planet. Chardin felt that the noosphere represented a significant new chapter in evolution on earth, life becoming aware of itself.

Like Chardin, Tom Berry is a Jesuit. Building on Chardin, he has said that what we need today, more than anything else, is a *new story.* Without a new story, the noosphere is not in harmony with the biosphere. The old story by which our culture guided itself was dominated by redemptive Christian theology on the one hand, and reductionist science on the other. As time has passed, these two have become increasingly irreconcilable, leading to a deep fragmentation in our culture and in ourselves. The new story that is needed, according to Berry, must draw together all facets of the human community.

Berry says that one way to approach the new story is to appreciate evolution. Evolution, he says, has three fundamental dynamics. One is increasing differentiation. As evolution proceeds, there is richer and richer variety among and within species. One of the functions of evolution is to produce variety. The second dynamic is what he calls increasing "interiority." With the evolution of species, there is a richer sense of what it means to be a *self.* He called that "interiority." We could call it "consciousness." Berry said there's a third element of evolution, which is a richer capacity for "intercommunion." As variety and interiority increase, there is a greater possibility for awareness of one another, both within species and between species. "It is the destiny," he says, "of our present and all future generations to develop this capacity for communion on new and more comprehensive levels."

I think Bob Greenleaf would have liked Tom Berry. Berry argues that evolution is bringing us to increasing awareness of "the Earth process" of which we are an integral element. To this, Greenleaf would surely have added that this requires institutions fundamentally based on interrelatedness, not on "thingness." Robert Greenleaf was onto something very important. He pointed us toward a territory that is bigger than any of us can see, perhaps bigger than he could see.

While he might not have given us a complete map of the territory, Greenleaf did provide a sort of compass. He said nothing will change until *we* are ready to change. "The servant," he said, "views any problem in the world as *in here,* inside oneself, not *out there.*" There are lots of changes that need to happen in our world, but they won't happen there unless we are committed to something changing inside ourselves.

Above all else, this is the stand Greenleaf took. Everything he wrote, he wrote from that viewpoint. It's the music you can hear behind the words. It's where the deep resonance we feel comes from. The changes needed in our world require a shift in our way of thinking, a shift in our way of interacting. Greenleaf recognized that what is actually called for is a shift in our way of being. We owe it to him to continue exploring this territory boldly, or as he quoted Camus, to "create dangerously."

21

Chaos, Complexity, and Servant-Leadership

Jeff McCollum

Robert Greenleaf, a self-described "student of organizations," both for-profit and eleemosynary, wrote about them at a time when the "American" model of management and organization was experiencing the first, disorienting effects of the scientific, cultural and competitive shock waves with which today's leaders, taking their organizations into the next millennium, struggle. He worked for AT&T at a time when the American model, described by Henry Mintzberg as the "machine bureaucracy," was being exported to other parts of the world in the belief that the American model was the reason for the enormous economic success of U.S. companies. The machine bureaucracy consists of five organizational elements: the strategic apex, usually a team of senior managers responsible for organizational strategy, control and direction; core workers who perform the essential work of the organization; middle line managers whose principal role is communication; a technical staff that develops the expertise required by the core work; and a support staff.

In "The Institution as Servant," Greenleaf describes the tension that he experienced between the mechanical, impersonal, and dispassionate style of AT&T and other bureaucratic institutions that had mastered the machine bureaucracy and the ferment of the college campuses he visited in the 1960s. That tension colored much of his thinking about leadership and led him to describe the concentration of power in a single person, atop a hierarchy, as abnormal and corrupt.

During Greenleaf's years at AT&T, organization development (OD), the field that emerged to deal with the employee alienation and disaffection bred by the machine bureaucracy, developed rapidly. Greenleaf was an active OD practitioner and part of the movement that brought language like "leadership style," "task versus relationship behavior," and "team building" into the managerial lexicon.

These were powerful, temporal impacts on Greenleaf. Therefore, 30 years after the founding of the Center for Applied Ethics, now known as the Robert K. Greenleaf Center, and 25 years after the publication of *The Servant as Leader,* it is useful to test Greenleaf's ideas against emerging theories of organization and leadership which, in turn, derive from emerging discoveries in science. That examination leads to the conclusion that Greenleaf's concept of leadership is as relevant and timely today as it was when written.

The idea of servant-leadership flows from a spiritual tradition. It appears in Christian scripture. It also appears in the writing of Lao Tzu:

> A leader is best
> When people barely know that he exists,
> Not so good when people obey and acclaim him,
> Worst when they despise him.
> "Fail to honor people, they fail to honor you":
> But of a good leader, who talks little,
> When his work is done, his aim fulfilled,
> They will all say, "We did this ourselves."

Leading-edge scientific exploration is generating new support for the concept of servant-leadership. This research reveals that the most successful organizations (plant and biological) found in nature are "self-organizing." Servant-leadership appears to be an appropriate philosophy for their governance.

As we head into the next century, we find contemporary scientific thought and longstanding spiritual thought converging. In that convergence, servant-leadership takes on more profound importance since leadership is about both the relationship of an organization to its environment and about the way in which elements of the organization relate to each other. As we near the end of the information age and the advent of its successor, we will be confronted with the new technologies and the concomitant requirement to build new kinds of organizations.

The Changing Organization Context

In the belief that the form of our organizations will change as technologies change, it is worth stepping back and taking a look at the current context in which our institutions operate because it will—and for that matter must—influence them.

All around us, we see the shattered remains of Newtonian assumptions about the world and about organizations. Throughout the industrial age, we wanted to believe in a benevolent and omniscient leader who could organize work and promise us long careers. Politically, we look for leadership that promises us no pain and much gain. Instead, we have seen a steady stream of corporate dislocations in the form of "downsizing," "right-sizing," "delayering," and "streamlining." Factories close and social programs go broke.

We want to believe that for every effect there is a single cause. Instead, we face the growing realization that our problems are interrelated and cannot be laid at the feet of the Japanese, the unions, greedy management and stockholders, or any other single cause.

We want to believe that we can bring nature under our control. Yet we are constantly reminded about how fierce the universe really is. In 1993 alone, the East Coast experienced a "white hurricane," the Midwest experienced devastating floods, and the West Coast had drought and fires which were followed, in early 1994, by an earthquake and mudslides.

We practiced "scientific management" believing that if we could only isolate the "correct" variables and work on them we could assure ourselves of successful outcomes. Despite elaborate planning systems and econometric models, surprise, not certainty, is the order of the day.

Events of the 1980s and 1990s have taught us that the global economy is volatile and not equally benevolent to all players. We look to our leaders as embodiment of our aspirations and then grow cynical when they fall short. We keep looking for the answer in the "back of the book"—where it always was for those trained in technical disciplines—and can't find it. The inherent messiness of organizational life betrays our desire for simple cause-and-effect analysis and problem solving.

We are struggling to run our information-age institutions with industrial-age models that are based on Newtonian science. It is no coincidence that Mintzberg described the prevalent organizations model of the late twentieth century as the "machine bureaucracy." Enmeshed in the machine era, we could think of organizations as machines and the leader as the "servo-mechanism" that drove them. Unfortunately, people became "piece parts" in the mechanism and had to surrender much of their individuality to meet the requirements of their work.

The machine bureaucracy also generated a style of management that Peter Block has described as patriarchal. (Since virtually all CEO and senior managers during this period were men, the masculine form seems appropriate.) Senior managers, those near the strategic apex, were in charge. They were deferred to. They were *responsible.* They were the parent, and the organization was the child.

The "single CEO" concept was nettlesome to Greenleaf. He advocated the old Roman concept of *primus inter pares* as a way of dealing with his belief that the single chief, sitting atop the hierarchy, was obsolete. The lone chief was also "abnormal and corrupt." The role can be seen as an extension of believing in single causes and effects.

Running Information Age Businesses with Industrial Models

In his book *Future Perfect,* Stanley Davis offers a compelling explanation for why our institutions seem to be foundering as we move through the information age. There is a predictable sequence of events that emerges from scientific inquiry: First, scientists investigate the universe, identify and create new "sciences"; then, when the new sciences offer solutions to human wants or needs, they become technologies—tools that can be applied. Third, when technologies find markets, businesses are created. Finally, once the business has been created, organizations are developed to manage the business.

Organization, Davis argues, is the last phase. As a result, those who discover the new technologies and create new businesses manage themselves with models from the previous age. Therefore, the AT&T in which Bob Greenleaf worked simultaneously mastered the "machine bureaucracy" and helped to create the information age. Taken in the context of broad systemic change, "downsizing," "delayering," "high-participation management," and other efforts to create organizational change reveal the challenge of creating an organizational model that fits the information age. (On another level, the actions may also be the "death rattle" of the patriarchal style. They are causes intended to create the effects of increased competitiveness and profit. The fact that they are so often made in a top-down style indicates that they may flow as much from the leaders self-interest (power, income) as they do from need for competitiveness.)

Past technological ages were long-running affairs. There was time to work out the organizational problem in the context of the age. As technological ages come and go with increasing velocity, we face the prospect of organization being out of phase with the prevalent technologies, unless we develop a concept of organization that transcends those technologies. The frontiers of the "new science" are a source of hope.

Lessons from the New Science

The Davis model (Universe → Science → Technology → Business → Organization) suggests that we should look to science for clues about organization. If Newtonian science and assumptions influenced the creation of the machine bureaucracy, how does the new science influence information age organization? In exploring the question of organization, we will come, in turn, to the question of institutional leadership. That examination will help us determine whether Greenleaf's ideas about institutional leadership sit as time-warped anomalies of the 1960s and 1970s or whether they represent something more than that.

A growing body of scientific research suggests that successful organizations (natural and social ones) in rapidly changing environments have a set of properties that allow them to adapt, through autonomous action at every level, to apparently chaotic changes in their environment. That scientific research is being complemented by social systems (economies, organizations, teams) researchers, and writers. One of them, Margaret Wheatley has been a pioneer in probing the leadership implications of the new science. Another, M. Mitchell Waldrop, describes the work of scientists at the Santa Fe Institute who have created the new science of complexity. By generating dialogue across scientific disciplines, they are discovering that there is more in common among biology, economics, physics, and brain chemistry than any would have previously imagined. Still another writer, Gary Zukav, outlines how modern subatomic physicists were discovering what Oriental philosophers seem to already have known—that, at some level, all matter (and all people) are connected.

Taken together, new discoveries in subatomic physics, nonlinear science (chaos), and complexity seem to hold clues about which types of organizations will emerge and what kind of leadership will be required in them. All of this work seems to move away from Newtonian characteristics of cause-and-effect and reductionist thinking (if we reduce something to its most finite element, we can understand it), and toward looking for connections, patterns, and systemic relationships. Some of their lessons are astonishing. Science becomes art, philosophy, and poetry. Science leads to faith. Subatomic physicists deal with properties they *believe* exist but which they cannot see.

Zukav's book is entitled, *The Dancing Wu Li Masters.* The Chinese ideogram, *Wu Li* can have a variety of meanings determined solely by the speaker's intonation. It can mean physics; it also can mean, "patterns of organic energy," "nonsense," "I clutch my ideas," "my way," and "enlightenment." According to Zukav, a master teaches essence. Therefore, the Wu Li master teaches both physics *and* enlightenment.

By extension, the organizational counterpart of the Wu Li master, the leader, teaches about the organization *and* enlightenment. This thought evokes Greenleaf's test of leadership, ". . . do those served grow as persons; do they, while being served, become healthier, wiser, freer, more autonomous, more likely themselves to become servants?" To Zukav, a master is simply someone who has entered the path before us. Certainly, that seems to be the case with Leo in *The Journey to the East,* the book by Herman Hesse that so influenced Greenleaf, which seems to inspire Greenleaf's "test."

Subatomic physicists now believe that all matter is connected. In taking his journey, Hesse's narrator (whom Greenleaf believed to be Hesse, himself) made several discoveries. First, he learned he had to take his or her own journey. Second, he learned that there were other travelers—independent yet connected. Third, he learned not to confuse role with mastery. Leo had a menial role, yet Leo was a master.

Perhaps the essence of human experience is to discover connection. In that case, the leader's role is to help others discover the paradox that they must take their own journey and that they are not alone.

This ineffable quality of connection that exists in some social organizations has been described as "spirit" or "community." In *Leadership and the New Science,* Margaret Wheatley discusses "fields" as unseen structures which affect behavior. Drawing on Zukav and biologist Rupert Sheldrake's descriptions of "morphogenic fields" that govern species behavior, Wheatley extends the field metaphor to organizations.

> Field images, when applied to organizations and employees, become quite provocative. We can imagine organizational space in terms of fields, with employees as waves of energy, spreading out in regions of the organization, growing in potential. How do we tap into that energy? How do we turn the employees' energy into behavior for the organization, into something observable and probable?

The Newtonian answer, modeled into the machine bureaucracy, was to create rigid, confining, and stultifying behavioral controls. The servant-leader's answer is in creating ways to help people grow. It seems to start with the core assumptions of the leader. Greenleaf writes,

> The servant-leader is servant first . . . It begins with a natural feeling that one wants to serve, to serve first. Then conscious choice brings one to aspire to lead.

Relating Greenleaf's "natural feeling" to the concept of morphogenic fields leads to the conclusion that the desire to serve, by itself, creates a field in which people grow and develop. That field, rather than explicit behavioral controls, inspires organizational members to serve customer-clients, and each other. AT&T's long distance business provides a case in point. Long distance operators are apparently instructed to say, "Thank you for using AT&T." Some sound like they mean it; some don't, and have the personal authenticity of a computer chip. It can be surmised that some leaders create a "field" for courteous service and some create a "field" of behavioral consistency. The leader's assumptions show up in the customer's experience.

Vision, perhaps the most discussed aspect of leadership in the 1980s and 1990s, illustrates how scientific assumptions and beliefs can influence our thinking about leader behavior. As commonly presented, "the vision thing" appears to be rooted in Newtonian assumptions. It has a linear cause and effect quality to it. According to one school of thought, if the leader is clear about his or her vision, and communicates it in a compelling way, that vision will apply force to the present and pull the organization toward the desired future articulated by the leader. Moreover, good leaders "enroll" their organizations in the leader's vision.

Taking a somewhat different position, Greenleaf, Wheatley, Peter Block, and Peter Senge speak to the "field" properties of vision. They view vision as an individual responsibility, not as a top-driven phenomenon. To them, vision takes on an aspirational quality.

Wheatley writes, "If vision is a field . . . , we would do our best to get it permeating through the entire organization so that we could take advantage of its formative properties." To Senge, "shared vision," one of the five disciplines, flows from individual vision. Block encourages managers to develop a clear, values-based picture of how customers are to be served and how organizational members will relate. This "vision of greatness" is not, to Block, an end. It is a powerful influence that informs our actions. Greenleaf talks about the importance of dreamers of great dreams. Service to others can be a field that has formative properties. Therefore, Greenleaf, Block, Senge, and Wheatley all seem to agree that vision (field creation) is not the sole province of managers. It is a byproduct of individual visions.

This idea is expressed in the Book of Proverbs as, "Without vision, the people perish." The new science of "self-organizing" systems identifies how autonomous, individual elements of a system, those closest to the boundary between the system and its environment, are somehow encrypted to operate in a way that supports adaptation and success. Individual vision creates the field for action. Individuals create the action and, in acting, create the best possibility that the organization will survive over time. Greenleaf, Block, Wheatley, and Waldrop all come to this point.

Greenleaf's test of leadership is whether individuals are wiser, freer, and more autonomous. Block includes personal autonomy as one of the requirements for empowered employees and empowered organizations. Wheatley writes about the participative nature of the universe. This autonomy, they argue, leads to organizational success.

Their conclusions are supported by the discoveries of scientists researching complex, adaptive systems. John Holland of the Santa Fe Institute and the University of Michigan has led the way in defining the properties of such systems.

In a curious coincidence, Holland, like Greenleaf, was influenced by reading Herman Hesse. *Das Glasperlenspiel*, literally translated as *The Glass Bead Game* but most often translated as *The Master of the*

Game, led Holland to the conclusion that the "game" for all—natural organizations, human institutions, and individuals alike—is adaptation, evolution, and learning. Successful organizations have the properties shown in the following list:

- They are comprised of a network of individual agents.
- Each agent finds itself in an environment created by its interaction with the other agents.
- Control is highly dispersed.
- Coherent behavior arises from competition and cooperation among agents.
- Control is learned from the "bottom up."
- There are hierarchical levels to the system.
- The organization is constantly revising and rearranging itself with experience.
- The organism can anticipate the future using an implicit encryption that is beyond consciousness.
- The system creates many niches and opportunities.

If, as Stanley Davis argues, organizational models have their origin in science, Holland's work points toward a very different kind of organization than the machine bureaucracy which mirrors the science of Newton and the industrial age.

The industrial model assumes that control is exercised from the top. Boards of directors, CEOs, and senior hierarchical levels usually find "control" somewhere in their job description. If the descriptors of complex adaptive systems are correct, control will come from the "bottom up" and will be highly dispersed. Greenleaf's test of a leader becomes inextricably bound with long-term organizational success. Is he or she developing people who are freer, wiser, and more autonomous?

The machine bureaucracy has tended to breed a management style which is called "command and control." Sometimes condemned by social scientists, command and control has frequently been extolled by others. It is valued for the consistency it creates. However, if organizations become less mechanistic, more complex and more adaptive, top-driven consistency, like top-driven control, will prove to be a chimera.

The industrial model imposes a formal hierarchy. In complex adaptive systems, a more organic hierarchy emerges as the organization adapts to and learns from its environment. *Primus inter pares* takes on a new importance. The industrial model operates on the assumption that all people are pretty much alike and are interchangeable. Complex adaptive systems survive based on the ability of their members to act autonomously and congruently. This diversity in thought and action creates strength. The industrial model vests the strategic apex with responsibility for planning the future. Complex adaptive systems rely on the ability of each element to anticipate and create the future.

The industrial model relies on top-down conflict resolution. Complex adaptive systems assume that conflict and cooperation are two sides of the same coin. Holland flatly asserts that top-down conflict resolution is wrong.

Industrial planning models rest on the assumption that an optimal equilibrium point can be found. Managers, growing up in mechanistic organizations, have been taught that organizations go from "steady state," through change, and then return to steady state. According to Waldrop, in complex adaptive systems, "An agent can learn to play the game better—that's what adaptation is after all. But it has just about as much chance of finding the optimum, stable equilibrium point of the game as you or I do of solving chess (1 in 10^{120})."

Much organizational theory talks about equilibrium. The work with complex adaptive systems suggests that equilibrium will be a virtually impossible goal. Holland talks about evolution (which would include the evolution of human institutions) as a "journey of constantly unfolding surprises." Surprise seems to be anathema to managers in the machine bureaucracy. During my 20-year career, working for and selling to managers in such organizations, I encountered frequent "No surprises!" admonitions on desk accessories and wall plaques.

As science, technology, and the people who use our services (whether our institutions are for-profit or not-for-profit) continue to change rapidly, the organizations in which we find ourselves will be constantly changing and riding along the bumpy boundary between order and chaos, which, Waldrop observes, is where "life has enough stability to sustain itself and enough creativity to deserve the name of life."

According to the scientists at the Santa Fe Institute, that boundary is "complexity." There are no neat, simple cause-and-effect relationships. There is only the messiness of life. In that realm, organizational success relies on the competent action of autonomous agents somehow being able to create the future, somehow connected in a communications field and operating in harmony with its environment.

When we are far enough into the next century to gain a good perspective on the industrial age, I believe that we will come to understand it as an aberration on the path of human development. In that period, we separated "heart" from "head" in our pursuit of science and logic. In that period, we severely damaged the planet on which we live. In that period, we created work environments that were crushing to the human spirit. We lost touch with our natural surroundings. The scientists of chaos and complexity seem to be returning us to that standard.

Joseph Campbell says that, "Nature is the bouquet of the spirit." Creating technologies and institutions that harmonize with nature may lead to a more spiritual experience for those who work in those institutions. The promise of the new science is that it will lead to a new concept of organization that leads to fuller spiritual fulfillment for its members.

The Santa Fe Institute

As described by Waldrop, the Santa Fe Institute was initially conceived by George Cowan of the Los Alamos Laboratories. Cowan, who was concerned by the intellectual fragmentism in science, sought to create something more like Medieval scholarship. The Institute seems remarkable as much for the process by which it operates as for the science it has discovered.

The Institute can best be described as a "floating seminar." Eminent economists, biologists, and physicists (including many Nobel laureates) are invited to become "fellows" of the Institute and, while on site, engage in an ongoing dialogue. This dialogue is used in the way described by Edward Boehm and Peter Senge. It is a deep discourse into underlying assumptions and beliefs in which each participant is "open" to the ideas of others and "opens up" his or her assumptions to the scrutiny of others. What has emerged from that dialogue is a science of complexity that was produced by looking for what is shared by these disparate scientific disciplines.

For example, Stanford economist Brian Arthur postulated a "new economics" based on the discoveries from the dialogue of the scientists of complexity. This new economics is viewed as high-complexity science, based on biological concepts like structure, pattern, self-organization, and life cycle; and recognizes people as individual and different and characterized by "increasing returns." By comparison, the old economics, viewed as "soft" physics with heavy emphasis on quantitative modeling, was based on nineteenth century physics, and assumed all people were identical and operated with diminishing returns. Arthur's view is that an economy is constantly on the edge of time with changing structures. In "classical" economics, the economy was stable.

It's only supposition, but I can imagine that Greenleaf would have been interested in how the Santa Fe Institute operates. He spoke and wrote about being open to and listening carefully to others. The scientists in Santa Fe have put these principles into practice. From Greenleaf's writing, it can be inferred that he valued interdisciplinary dialogue. Early members of the Center for Applied Ethics, which Greenleaf founded and from which the Robert K. Greenleaf Center has evolved, describe it, too, as a "floating seminar."

Thoughts on Power

No discussion of institutions and organizations would be complete without raising the subject of power. On the assumption that our organizations will be operating in the realm of complexity—the place between order and chaos—we have to face the reality that our personal inclinations could create the kind of power and leadership that is neither in our own long-term interest or that of our organization.

Jeffrey Pfeffer observes that, in times of instability, organizations have a tendency to go toward central power which, in turn, institutionalizes it at or near the top. Institutional power has several consequences. It leaves the organization with decreased ability to react. It constricts the participants' freedom of action. It provides certainty in social interactions and creates an emotional sense of certainty and control.

As discussed earlier, institutionalized power, especially in the form of a single CEO, concerned Greenleaf. Therefore he wrote about "countervailing power" as a "necessary condition of all human relations. *No one should be powerless* (Greenleaf's emphasis)."

These tendencies described by Pfeffer and loathed by Greenleaf, lead to what Block described as the "patriarchal contract." Organizational members, seeking emotional security, turn their personal power over to those in whom power is institutionalized. Those who seek the power—either from a desire to be benevolent caretakers or from a desire to amass more power—readily concur. The deal is made. Unfortunately, none of these choices builds the capability of the organization to adapt and so to survive.

Benevolent caretakers may be confused with servant-leaders. The kind of servant Greenleaf describes is one who stands up for and insists that those around her or him grow and develop—become autonomous agents. It is a tough-minded and open-hearted stance. It is frequently misunderstood, and it is not always appreciated.

Leo's "role" to the travelers in the *Journey to the East* was as a servant. His act of service was recognizing and insisting that each traveler make the journey on his or her own. Leo was, in Campbell's metaphor of the *Hero's Journey,* the quest companion who knows the path and also knows that we must take it ourselves.

Once we take our own path, we find community. This was the lesson of *The Journey to the East.* The scientists of complexity talk about the behavior of "networks" being determined by the quality of the connections. They talk about individual agents, each seeking self-consistency, being able to transcend themselves. Power becomes infinite, widely dispersed and connective. Leadership becomes broadly distributed and flows from personal authenticity.

Leader Development

Greenleaf was a pioneer in the development of assessment centers. As it has evolved, the practice of assessment sometimes has the mechanistic, linear qualities of the industrial-type organization. The practice usually goes something like this:

- Watch what successful leaders do.
- Document their behaviors.
- Develop an instrument.
- Ask people to provide perceptual feedback on how frequently an individual practices those behaviors.
- Copy the behaviors of those who are successful.

The process seems to confuse replication with development.

The core of Greenleaf's test of leadership is whether the leader develops those around him or her into independent agents. It assumes a level of personal development and enlightenment. The type of leadership that Greenleaf argues for in his test seems to be what is demanded by the model of organization that is emerging from the sciences of complexity and chaos.

Speaking through Ian Malcolm, the voice for ethical behavior among the scientists in *Jurassic Park,* Michael Crichton writes:

> Most kinds of power required substantial sacrifice by whoever wants the power. There is an apprenticeship, a discipline lasting many years. Whatever kind of power you want. President of a company. Black belt in karate. Spiritual guru. Whatever it is you seek, you have to put in the time, the practice, the effort. You must give up a lot to get it. It has to be very important to you. And once you have attained it, it is your power. It can't be given away: it resides in you. It is literally the result of your discipline.
>
> Now, what is interesting about this process is that, by the time someone has acquired the power to kill with his bare hands, he has also matured to the point that he won't use it unwisely. So that kind of power has a built-in control. The discipline of getting the power changes you so that you won't abuse it.

Malcolm later goes on to conclude, "Ever since Newton and Descartes, science has explicitly offered us the vision of total control. Science has claimed the power to eventually control everything."

Returning to Stanley Davis's argument that science ultimately drives organization, we can see why Newtonian physics gave us an organizational model that institutionalized the belief that managers with formal power were responsible for controlling the entire organization.

Crichton's implicit argument is for leader development that includes personal discipline and leadership by example, rather than through the institutionalization of power. It's an argument supported by the new sciences of chaos and complexity, and it's an argument supported by Greenleaf's ideas.

In his address to the 1966 graduates of Redlands College, which he entitled "Servant Responsibility in a Bureaucratic Society," Greenleaf advocated a "lifestyle" or discipline that included beauty, momentaneity, openness, humor, and tolerance. Beauty keeps one in touch with the unsearchable and secret aims of nature. (The scientists of complexity might argue with Greenleaf's notion of unsearchable. Physicist Doyne Farmer, quoted by Waldrop says, "Now in science, we can never even attempt to make a frontal assault on questions like [the purpose of life]. But by addressing a different question—like, 'Why is there an inexorable growth in complexity?'—we may be able to learn something fundamental about life that suggests its purpose . . .") Momentaneity recognizes that each moment stands on the edge of time and that our response in each moment extends back in time and creates the future. Openness is about listening—from the other's perspective. It is about the quality of connections that we build. Humor is about self-acceptance, the wry, knowing smile that recognizes "the silly little half-made creatures that we are." This self-acceptance is the source of change. As Carl Rogers noted, we can change that which we accept about ourselves. Change is growth. Growth is learning. Learning is adaptation to the fierce and real world in which we find ourselves. Tolerance is about bearing suffering with serenity, using our suffering as the source of learning.

With these qualities, we serve our own growth and growth by our organizations. Greenleaf's ideas and the properties of complex adaptive systems seem consonant.

To Greenleaf, responsible servants, ". . . cultivate, as a conscious discipline, a lifestyle that favors their optimal performance as an antibureaucratic influence, over a lifespan of mature living. They bring their own unique meliorative influence to bear on the pervasive bureaucracy."

At the time of the Redlands address, Greenleaf felt that bureaucracy was an inevitable phenomenon of organizational development. Perhaps he would have been heartened by the "new" sciences of chaos and complexity. His beliefs in the essay seem aligned with the lessons coming from those sciences. Operate in harmony with nature. Live in the moment recognizing that our actions in this moment influence the future as we bound along the border between chaos and order. Engage the real life issues. Recognize the humor in our own insignificance. Be open to what nature and others are trying to tell us about the future from the perspective of their own genius. His message seems particularly attuned to the organizations that will emerge from the new sciences.

These organizations—particularly the social ones—require leadership. They require *servant-leadership* as opposed to the top-down, control-oriented leadership that emerged during the heyday of the machine bureaucracy. They require hierarchy. They require autonomous action from the leader and the members. And they require a certain wisdom—character, and intellectual development—from the leader.

Primus inter pares may be a matter of the moment. By being open to the unique genius of each organizational member, by listening to others' perspective, by being willing to change ourselves, by operating in harmony with the universe, by being informed by nature, and by encouraging those around us to grow, we may just create thriving organizations of spiritually thriving people. And the concept of servant-leadership takes on a timeless quality.

According to Waldrop, there is a "Tao of complexity" which suggests a new set of roles for leaders—roles that evoke servant-leadership. Recognize that successful, adaptive systems exercise control from the bottom up through the development of autonomous members. "Observe. Observe. Observe. Where you can make a move, you make a move." Openness and action from the heart. Hallmarks of servant-leadership.

22

Pyramids, Circles, and Gardens: Stories of Implementing Servant-Leadership

Don M. Frick

Pyramids

In 1897, a backwoods Indiana representative introduced a piece of legislation that would assure the Hoosier state of continuing royalties by recognizing the mathematical accomplishments of a constituent who had claimed to discover a new value for pi (he said Pythagoras had got it wrong), and had also learned how to mathematically square the circle. The idea was to patent the new formula (much like claiming a patent on gravity) and charge a fee every time someone used it in an equation. The state of Indiana would share in the goodies, *if* it would simply recognize this achievement through legislation.

It seemed like a good idea at the time. After a "Do Pass" recommendation from the committee on Swamps and Wastelands and support from the state's Superintendent of Education (who was in for a piece of the action), the state's House passed the measure. It made it to the third reading in the Senate, too, before the *Chicago Tribune* published a scathing story on the whole affair and forced embarrassed Hoosiers to recognize that some realities were written into nature and would never change, regardless of the greed and official laws of mere mortals.

Since the industrial revolution, pyramidal organizational structures seemed, like pi, an obvious, natural way of visualizing power. Pyramids are predictable, stable in storms, and have represented eternal verities in cultures through time. They make us feel comfortable, and heaven help the person who challenges a comfortable truth.

Circles and Gardens

In our time, a few leading-edge visionaries have had the audacity to challenge the pyramid as a metaphor for organizational structure. Robert K. Greenleaf was one of the first. He preferred circles and gardens over pyramids, for while a pyramid is based on an attractive intellectual notion of order and clear power, a circle is based on shared power. The view across a circle is much clearer than that up through a pyramid.

Gardens (Greenleaf and his wife were avid gardeners) are environments for growth. "Tending the garden" means enriching the soil (preferably without nasty chemicals), encouraging the growth of desirable plants which will bear fruit, and rooting out the weeds. Gardens are more like the inner geography of human beings. They hold unlimited potential within the constraints of the prevailing climate. They teach us through our failures, encourage us to live with and within nature, and are sources of beauty, sustenance, and learning. Gardening can be a left-brain scientific endeavor or a right-brain experiential journey. Furthermore, any experienced gardener knows that each year in the garden is different, with unpredictable, surprising harvests.

So, in our time, courageous people in varied institutions have read the Greenleaf essays and the writings of other prophets and responded to the intuitive rightness of a new direction. They have joined with their co-workers in redefining the workplace to make it an integrated expression of the human spirit. In the process, they have dismantled pyramids, turned squares and triangles into circles, invented new metaphors to explain the process, and have continued planting and nurturing their new gardens. A few are "kept revolutionaries" like Greenleaf, working quiet alchemy to turn organizational lead into gold. Others are more open and systematic about the process. None of the resulting new structures is alike because each is a product of human creativity and openness unleashed in a specific situation. There is no neat name for this phenomenon. But, there are several recurring themes:

- New organizational charts that eerily resemble mandalas, with interconnected circles forming a complex weave.
- A core group which buys into new values and initiates the process.
- Patience and maturity.
- Flexibility and openness to change.
- An attempt to make the intellectual underpinning of servant-leadership accessible to all.
- An appreciation for the value of diversity in the organization.
- Resistance from some in the organization.
- A leader who "goes ahead and shows the way."
- Shared vision and values which are *developed by the group.*
- Involvement in community issues and local needs.
- More patience.

Following are their abbreviated stories. If you call one of them tomorrow, expect the story to be different than it is told here. Gardens grow, and servant-leadership evolves as current actions inform future evolution. Moreover, the new sciences have daily offered new insights about pyramids since 1897.

Schneider Engineering Corporation: Grounding Greenleaf

Today, Schneider Engineering Corporation is a 120-employee firm in Indianapolis with four divisions: an architectural company (Bohlen, Meyer, Gibson and Associates), a Surveying and Mapping Division, an Engineering Division (which engages in civil and site engineering and includes the areas of environmental, transportation, geotechnical, mechanical, and electrical engineering), and a Support Division, which does what its name implies—provides support services to the other divisions. In 1989, the firm looked very different. There were fewer engineering services, there was no architectural division, and the organization was arranged as a traditional pyramid with layers of beauracracy. John Schneider, the president, was a benevolent Moses-type leader. Principals in the firm sensed that change was needed. For one thing, the company needed to diversify to make it more recession-proof. Beyond that business concern was a felt need for an organizational structure that somehow grew out of people in a different way, rather than a traditional one which was imposed upon employees.

Schneider remembers, "We were searching for a structure that was different, something that was more in tune with who we were and who we wanted to be. At times, we as an organization and I as an individual would feel very eyeballish and insecure. I'd ask myself, 'What am I doing here?' because if I or many others here took an entrepreneurial test, the results would say that we didn't belong in business, that we'd be eaten alive." He had read various management gurus and tried out a few ideas. As a result, some people in the organization were criticizing him for bringing in "the management theory of the week."

Then, Richard Smith, a consultant who now works with the Robert K. Greenleaf Center, introduced him to Robert Greenleaf's ideas. Something clicked. He notes that, "We already had a caring and people orientation, so servant-leadership gave some validity to who and what we were, which was not readily accepted in the traditional business world." Beyond the intuitive resonance, John Schneider and other company directors felt that servant-leadership might help them address the issues surrounding diversification, including the need for better communications within the organization.

Schneider and Smith took the ideas to a core group, which decided there was something important here to pursue. They committed the whole organization to a one-year exploration of servant-leadership, a timeline which later proved to be unrealistically optimistic.

The core group, called the Council, began meeting two to three hours each Wednesday to explore "trustee and conceptual issues arising from servant-leadership" and an equal amount of time each Thursday to look at "operational issues," the nitty gritty minutae of running a business. Smith facilitated these sessions.

In the Wednesday sessions, the group read excerpts from various Greenleaf writings, but focused on the book, *Servant Leadership: a Journey into Legitimate Power and Greatness.* Discussions centered on questions like, "What is Greenleaf saying? What does it mean to us? What are our own values and beliefs? How do we actually use power within our organization?"

It was during this process that Schneider realized the importance of "grounding Greenleaf" to help people understand that servant-leadership is a *practical* philosophy. "Our organization covers a spectrum of people, both in education and background," said Schneider, "and we're trying to bring everyone to the table. Sometimes Greenleaf has a religious overtone. We had to ground him and quantify him. We don't force Greenleaf and his writings on people. We pull out various pieces that everyone can relate to. We talk about it as something that is tangible, not abstract. We interpret his writings in our own way, try to convert it into reality and demonstrate how that reality can happen."

Eventually, Schneider wrote a philosophical statement summarizing insights from the group, which was used as a basis for further reflection. According to Smith, many in the group felt admiration for Schneider, and wanted to express their loyalty by complying with whatever he suggested. To encourage them to speak their minds, the issues of trust, loyalty, and individual differences were openly discussed.

Meanwhile, in the Thursday sessions, people who had heretofore operated in relative isolation were taught how to work collaboratively. Some of the smallest operational issues turned into hour-long discussions about nitpicky distinctions. The individual issues discussed were often a foil for a more important single issue—developing trust.

Within four months, the Council went on a day-long retreat and developed a mission statement, a document that survives to this day with a few very minor changes. The Council decided to live with the mission statement for at least two years, then turned its attention to strategic matters.

After another four months, the Council left for another retreat. This time, it was an intense three-day session with 10- to 12-hour workdays. It was a pivotal event, resulting in a 12-month operational plan and a two-to-four-year developmental plan. Each plan outlined significant critical issues, with goals, objectives, and tasks in area. The last night of the last day, the exhausted group sat back, surveyed the fruits of its work, and said a collective, "Wow!" Smith says he was honored to be there when the spirit broke its old bounds.

Members of the Council then went back and began sharing the excitement with people in their own divisions. The circle widened as more and more people were exposed to servant-leadership in various sessions.

In 1991, Jack Lowe from TDIndustries in Dallas shared in a conversation with Schneider during an evening with employees and spouses at the prestigious Indianapolis Athletic Club. This event cemented the validity and efficacy of servant-leadership as a grounding philosophy.

Results

Over the next several years, important changes occurred. Schneider Engineering Corporation began to diversify, with improved trust and communication making the process more comfortable. The former "beauracracy," which supported the organizational triangle, was turned into a separate division with the mission of supporting the strategic business units.

The original Council is now two groups. The nine-person Primus Council is composed of representatives from each of the four divisions. It meets at least once each week for at least two hours to discuss issues within each division as well as issues that affect the whole organization. During Primus Council meetings you often hear the question, "What can I do for you?" The four-person Trustee Council, per Greenleaf's suggestion, is charged with an oversight role. In the end, everyone is responsible to someone.

One happy result of conversion to servant-leadership as a philosophy is the blossoming of various people in the organization who had been held back in the old structure because they didn't have "pure" management skills. The original Council members gradually realized that the new path required more leadership rather than more management, and a whole new group of leaders was unleashed on Schneider Engineering. As a result, Schneider says the business has grown by leaps and bounds, doubling in employees since 1989 during a period that was not an economic bull in Indianapolis.

Now there are two major, three-day retreats each year, combining Primus Council and Trustees. The agenda for December is 80 percent organizational/operational issues and 20 percent team-building, with the Spring agenda reversed: 80 percent team-building and 20 percent organizational/operational issues.

The organization has created a new vision for itself, including goals for serving professional organizations, schools, and community. Each year, finances permitting, the whole company goes away for a golf-playing, horse-riding, picnic-relaxing weekend. There are frequent recognitions honoring achievements of employees. Even though the corporation gives to various nonprofit groups like United Way, the Indianapolis Foundation, and others, hands-on activities are emphasized more often. Employees volunteer for Meals on Wheels. Programs are organized to help needy children in the nearby inner city neighborhood. After asking various school superintendents what the company could do to help with curriculae, Schneider Engineering developed a program introducing students in middle schools to the professions and technology represented in the company. Experiential contributions are valued over passive donations.

A Development Center occupies a large, comfortable room at the company. The concept was borrowed from Mike Vance's idea of a Kitchen of the Mind, a place of stimulation and creativity. Employees can check out books, videos, and audio cassette programs. They can suggest new purchases, and are encouraged to implement any other ideas which will help the Center better meet their needs. The Development Center is a good example of the patience necessary while waiting for new ideas to take hold. "It sat here for 12 months, and now it's finally getting used," says Schneider. "You can't force it to happen. If it's not happening, you can ask, 'What's preventing it from happening?' then fall back on what Senge talks about in removing the barriers to let it take place naturally."

All the while, Schneider and his group have drawn on Senge, Block, DePree, Covey, and others to inspire new ideas on the journey. Schneider believes that, "If Robert Greenleaf were alive today, he'd be sitting around with a big smile on his face and saying, 'Finally, after all these years, we're seeing a significant movement.' The significance of all these ideas is empowering your people to be conscious of their need to care and their need to be concerned with customers and the community."

All has not been honey and wine since Schneider Engineering Corporation began implementing servant-leadership. While dealing with the everyday problems of individual jobs and divisions, it still takes a conscious effort to keep the picture of the whole organization in mind—to live out Senge's Fifth Discipline. Even though all employees have heard about servant-leadership, there is not 100 percent buy-in. Nevertheless, everyone stays posted on the journey. The dual Council structures are still inventing their roles, with occasional missteps along the way. Yet, it's a happy place to visit, with a spontanaeity unusual for most engineering firms.

"Excellence is what we're seeking," John Schneider. "Not just in the work environment, but to bring the impact of excellence to our community, to our planet, to our professions. That takes time. People have to see the positive things happening before they truly buy into the process. Five years is not an unreasonable period to get 90 percent to 95 percent buy-in. We're on a journey that will last several lifetimes. We're not rushing it."

Schmidt Associates Architects, Inc.: Spirit in Business and Community Profit Boards

Wayne Schmidt is the principal of Schmidt Associates, Inc., an Indianapolis architectural/engineering firm numbering about 40 employees. The office walls are decorated with pictures of the firm's designs—buildings that engage the eye and the heart, church structures that soar to the wind. Schmidt says the company prefers owners (clients) who demand and expect mutual respect. The firm has implemented servant-leadership ideas in a way that pays less attention to formal organizational restructuring (pyramids to circles) and more to restructuring of processes: teams taking responsibility for follow-through, open communications, an atmosphere of dignity, respect, creativity and flexibility.

The Early Years

Schmidt is an articulate man, a person of complexity and passion. He relates the story of his company's journey into servant-leadership better than any other could. "We started the firm on July 4, 1976. I think from the very beginning, through intuition, we practiced servant-leadership. It wasn't something I read about when I went through training and said, 'Oh, there's something I want to do!' The culture over the last 18 years was really a culture of serving. Robert Greenleaf provided one way of naming that culture."

Exposure to Greenleaf's Essays

"Fifteen years ago, I went through the Stanley K. Lacy Leadership Series. A handout was Robert Greenleaf's book, *Servant Leadership.* What aroused my interest was an academic approach to my Christian beliefs. Coincidentally, what Greenleaf was emphasizing was exactly what I was attempting to weave into our office values. As I thought about servant-leadership, however, I thought the part Greenleaf left out was the Christian aspect of servant-leadership. I see Christ as being the ultimate servant.

"Biblically, servant-leadership means being the ultimate servant, or the self as servant, with serving others as the mission. So, the *Bible's* notion fits the leadership concept. Even though the academic world doesn't really respond to the Christian belief, I think that is the strongest basis—you simply serve other people.

"I have to separate the words. It's easy to misconstrue servant and leadership. If I simply think about servanthood, that's a simpler concept for me, even if it's not a particularly popular concept in today's world because it sounds like being acted upon—servitude. And yet, if you think about being a servant as simply meeting the needs of other people, that's what we're all here for—to serve other people's needs.

"As a selfish business person on occasion, the better I serve my clients' needs, the more work we're going to have to do. I'm no longer meeting just our criteria—what it takes for me to be successful; we become the facilitator for the owner's success. We design a facility that's totally responsive to their need, not necessarily ours. So the first, most important thing we can do is serve the owner. That's servanthood. We allow their criteria to become our criteria.

"The other part is leadership. I believe that you are awarded leadership. I don't think you can ask for it. I think that someone simply says, 'Because you have met my needs, I'd like for you to lead me towards accomplishing something.' You've got to be ready to do that.

"I think a basic ingredient of servant-leadership is simply respect for other people. It's an attitude. It's not something you come in with and infiltrate the organization. It starts with an attitude of respect. You treat the receptionist—who by the way I think is the most important marketing person in the organization—with the same respect as you treat a vice-president. It doesn't matter because they are all there to serve other people's needs.

"Anyone within the organization can be called to leadership. And, likewise, I need to know when to be a follower, which is not synonymous, because I think the follower simply asks others, 'What role do I play this time?'"

Implementing Servant-Leadership

"To me, implementing servant-leadership is very simple, and sometimes I think Greenleaf makes it more difficult than it needs to be. It's simply respecting each other's opinion—truly listening and gathering from that person what's important—and then through synergy coming to conclusions, as opposed to compromise. Compromise is not leadership. Make resolutions through synergy. We've been doing that since the start of the organization.

"We've only really called it servant-leadership the last five years or so. In the last five years, the book *Servant Leadership* is required reading for every new staff member.

"When we interview potential staff, we go through three interviews. The first is simply to find out if they're competent to do the job. It's more technical in nature. The second interview is for attitude. Do they have an attitude of serving others, or are they there because of some vendetta or to become the architectural monument king or queen of the world? We think it's important to have the attitude of serving others. So, we hire people who have that attitude. We also make sure two partners interview any potential employee.

"About six years ago, we made the key decision to become an intergenerational firm. It was an incredibly significant decision. Once you decide that the firm will have its own life beyond your own lifetime, you ask yourself about each new hire, 'Would I want this person as a future partner?' Then, once you bring that person on, they're no longer an employee. They're now a future partner. So, of course, you want to bring them along, teach them, mentor them, develop them.

"We send them to seminars outside the office, and we develop career pathing within the office. Twice a year we sit down with each employee and discuss their professional goals, because I and the partners see our jobs as facilitating their success. Lo and behold, they're successful, and we're successful.

"When new people come into the firm, they are given a mentor who helps nurture that attitude. They're also given a sherpa. A sherpa is a guide over the Himalayan mountains. It is someone who has about two more years' experience than the person we're hiring. That allows the new hire someone at peer level to help them understand what our office is about and how things really work.

"I was speaking with a project architect last night. He's been with the firm five years. He went through all the kinds of things new graduates go through—rebellion, thinking that the owner doesn't respect him because the owner 'tells him what to do,' and all that. I asked him some of the questions I knew you were going to ask me today. He knew exactly what servant-leadership was about. Paraphrasing, he said, 'We're here to serve the owner's needs, to meet the budget, meet the schedule, get it in without any fuss, and make sure the building responds to what they need to have done in the building.' To me, that was proof positive. But, if I went down and asked our receptionist 'What's important about what we do?' I think she would say, 'Serving others' needs.'

"Another of the required reading items is Steven Covey's *The Seven Habits of Highly Effective People.* A lot of the concepts of servant-leadership come through in that, and I think his religious background is the source of a lot of that. I don't know if it's Greenleaf, *per se,* but Greenleaf is also grounded in other writings.

"Very quickly in our organization, a person needs to understand several main points. One is that communications is paramount. In some organizations, withholding information is a base for power. Not here. Everybody needs to know what's going on. Another point is that we do open critiques of projects, so an idea doesn't just develop with one person. It's an opportunity for synergy when you respect another person's opinion enough to bring an idea to it. When we critique anything, the first three comments are to be positive, reaffirming. What do I like about it? Then, you can find something that isn't working very well. But first let's reaffirm. There's always something good, but too often we look at something and say, 'I don't like this, this & this,' when you actually *do* like 99 percent of it. That's a reaffirming of a servant-leadership attitude."

Looking at Things Whole

"One of our corporate values is an environment of ideas, so that ideas can flourish and not be stomped on immediately. 'What will work about this idea? From this idea can we then go another level?' So when you add other ingredients to it, something else is happening.

That environment of ideas is one of our strong values supporting servant-leadership.

"I'm a firm believer that you answer questions right 99 percent of the time. It's the question you don't ask yourself that gets you in trouble. That's why we have this environment of ideas. Also, it encourages an attitude that you can ask anything you want to ask. So, when you're developing a detail, a floor plan, or whatever, there's lots of open communication, and then openness to be responsive to more questions. An often-asked question here is, "What are we not thinking of?' That's a question that's not always asked."

Building a Caring Society

"We're involved with many nonprofit boards. I'd like to change that name to 'community-profit boards.' There's no such thing as nonprofit. If it's a 'community-profit board,' you realize it exists for the benefit of the community.

"Our employees serve on a lot of community-profit boards in ways that strengthen the community. From the Ballet Theater board to the Chamber of Commerce, a lot of things. One of our other values is commitment to community. So, we do give money back through financial support to organizations. We give a lot of time to them, too."

Servant-Leadership and Other Management Concepts

"I think what Steven Covey wrote about created a compatibility for everything. Of all the books I've ever read, Covey is able to bring it all together in one book, in *Seven Habits.* So quality assurance, as an example, comes out of good communications, proactive thinking, beginning with the results in mind. If you do those things, the quality will be there."

Developing Trust

"A person is trusted here until we find out they can't be. We'll even work with them in conversation. That's one reason for the six-month orientation period. We want to make sure they get off to the right start. We value other people's judgment, and we've tried over the years to diversify the office to make sure we're including other people's background and experience before we come to a decision.

"Trust is related to hiring practices. We're very careful in our hiring. Other people in the firm know we're darned good at who we hire, because we hired them. If a person isn't beginning to work out, we'll work with them to try and bring them around, especially during the orientation period.

"I cannot outgive other people. So, the more I facilitate their success, the more successful the firm is. That's the attitude everyone here needs to have for everyone else here. They need to facilitate my success, too."

Vision

"Our vision statement would suggest that we want to be known as the premier architectural firm in the state. The way we are seeking it, our path, is to allow people to be the best they can absolutely be, to facilitate their success. I personally get the greatest pleasure out of seeing people grow in the organization and doing it better than I could've ever done it."

Advice on Implementing Servant-Leadership

"A lot depends on the starting point. Consider the stereotypical business person who looks at the bottom line and says, 'Are we making a profit or not?' and then concentrates on profit. That person can only gain by developing an attitude of servant-leadership. The bottom line is there *if* people are working effectively with an attitude of serving others. That's the reward.

"Our profit line is better than most architectural firms. But if you talk about servant-leadership, it sounds like a soft management style. It's the strongest philosophical business approach I could ever imagine. But don't distract people with what the bottom line needs to be. Let them concentrate on serving others, doing their job well, being the best they can be, and allowing them to be successful. The bottom line's there."

Demanding Distinction

"The firm has taken on its own distinction through peer support. A person who comes into our firm knows we expect the best from them. Not just me, but everybody else as well. Andria, our receptionist, expects people to be friendly in the morning. She expects them to return phone calls, and to be a civil human being who respects other people.

"During the first six months in the firm, a person is assigned telephone duty for several hours and works with Andria on how to answer the phone. We want that person to appreciate our receptionist and what she goes through, like juggling six calls at one time.

"Everybody in our firm knows we are a firm of distinction and that they are a vital part of it. It isn't Wayne Schmidt's distinction. It's that everybody here knows we only stand for excellence and the best quality we can produce."

The Townsend & Bottum Family of Companies: Servant-Leadership During Tough Downsizing

The Robert K. Greenleaf Center for Servant-Leadership publishes a booklet detailing the remarkable odyssey of an Ann Arbor, Michigan construction company that historically specialized in power plants. Titled *The Trusteed Corporation: A Case Study of the Townsend & Bottum Family of Companies,* the piece was written in 1987 by Carl Rieser. Here, we will summarize and update the events described in that publication. However, we recommend a full reading of Carl Rieser's publication available through the Greenleaf Center, to understand the complex legal moves that created this trusteed corporation and the false starts and successes of the two-council system.

The Days of Successful Experiments

Curtis E. Bottum, Jr. (Bill) was a management experimenter. In 1974, he began implementing some then-radical ideas of organizational development, notions like team-building. In the late 1970s, the Townsend & Bottum (T&B) companies were saving millions by delivering projects under budget and before deadline. Those were the heady days of 350 to 800-megawatt power stations. Before the electric construction boom went bust, T&B had 750 employees and more than 5,000 craftspeople scattered across the country and around the globe. The company grew by diversifying into 19 separate business units.

In the late 1970s, Mr. Bottum read Greenleaf and discovered that "it reinforced, focused, and gave us something to hang on to."

The desire to serve made imminent sense to the T&B management team, who began making changes ranging from the elimination of executive parking spaces to conscious application of consensus decision-making, a move that fit right in with the firm's team-building history. Meanwhile, the T&B team was pondering how to make their company takeover-proof and allow employees to share in the rewards of their efforts. In 1981, Bottum asked his secretary to "find Greenleaf, so he's not like so many of my other heroes who die before I can meet them." Luckily, this hero was still around, and Bottum began a fruitful friendship with Greenleaf, starting with a five-hour nonstop discussion.

In 1982, the T&B companies went through a major transformation that fascinated Greenleaf. Bottum called it the company's "Continuity Plan." Carl Rieser describes it best:

> In its new mode, T&B offers one of the few known instances in the world of a privately owned business enterprise that has no proprietor, stockholders, or partners. The "owner" is a self-perpetuating board of trustees; it controls the Townsend & Bottum Capital Fund, which in turns owns the various T&B operating companies. The Capital Fund itself is a Michigan nonstock corporation, a corporate form designed for nonprofit organizations and customarily used only for that purpose. Applied to the business world, the idea appears to many people to be a very radical one.

T&B's key people, with advice from Greenleaf, help from several friendly lawyers, and profound trust from a bank and bonding company, had created a "trusteed corporation" owned by the Townsend & Bottum Capital Fund, later to be renamed the T&B Family of Companies. The operations of the family of companies were supervised by the Administrative Council, members of which were mentored by the Capital Fund's Board of Trustees. This arrangement mirrors Greenleaf's notion of two councils.

The T&B companies in the late 1970s to mid 1980s were faced with a frightening downturn in the construction of megaproject power plants and the uncertainty of a concentration of high-risk, lump-sum projects. Revenues shrank from $324 million in 1978 to $109 million in 1986. Consultant Julian Moody had tried to prepare the company for this situation. In 1986 and 1987, T&B's management team was forced to make radical moves. The upheaval caused great trauma and grief. Yet, this team—which was more of a true community—felt it might make a contribution to the human race (a sentiment expressed without any grandiosity) and they couldn't let it die.

Update

The company almost did die; by 1988, three years of losses totaled over $12 million. In spring of that year, Tom Monaghan, of Domino's Pizza, purchased Townsend & Bottum's computer company, but did not purchase the whole family of companies. Monaghan's purchase was crucial, but it was not enough to forestall additional setbacks.

In June, 1988, T&B called the bank and bonding companies for an emergency meeting. The company, which could not make its payments, did not want to go into bankruptcy because of the ethical and moral obligations felt to all the company's stakeholders. T&B proposed the ultimate team effort—a three-way contract between T&B, the bank, and the bonding company. It was a risky venture for the financial people. Each had to loan an additional $600,000 to a company that could not make current payments. If the deal worked, the bank and bonding company would each save $2 to $3 million. If it did not, it could cost them each an additional $10 million. The strategy did work, and the company was saved. To solidify its position, T&B sold off the other business subsidiaries during the rest of 1988, usually to the people who ran them.

In 1989, Black and Veatch approached Townsend & Bottum about taking over the firm. Black and Veatch specialize in designing the kinds of facilities built by T&B. Furthermore, their values fit the servant-leadership culture of Townsend & Bottum, so the match seemed a good one. The constitution that still guided the Board of Trustees and the Administrative Council protected the firm against any takeover, but a loophole did allow for the trustees to approve an acquisition if the survival of the company was at stake. By the end of the year, it was clear that T&B would not survive without the takeover.

The lawyers and the banks got into the picture again, expressing nervousness that the servant-leadership phrases describing employee rights in the company's constitution might form the basis for future lawsuits. The lawyers also insisted on a traditional company with standard bylaws. An innovative trusteed corporation simply held too many unknowns for a legal system that operated by precedent. Bottum was willing to give on some of these issues but was determined to protect the original goals of the trusteed corporation.

The deal was eventually done. Gone was the trusteed corporation, the special relationship between the Board of Trustees and the Administrative Council. The deal called for Black and Veatch to exercise an option for final purchase when the net operating loss (NOL) reached zero. In the sometimes arcane world of business, a NOL is good because no income tax is paid on a loss.

Several good years followed, but in 1991, again on the edge of abyss, T&B's bank balked at forwarding any more money, saying, "We have no plan for your survival. We thought you would be out of business and out of our hair by now. Find another bank." Black and Veatch again came to the rescue, loaning money to T&B at the prevailing interest rate. In the meantime, an old bad debt was miraculously repaid, further strengthening the company's position.

By 1994, the company was recovering again, getting some of the old employees back, forging ahead with a renewable resource power plant in Michigan and other contracts in Utah, Kentucky, Massachusetts, Thailand, Egypt, and Florida. The net worth is still negative, but all the outside creditors have been paid.

The Effect of Servant-Leadership on Downsizing

Bottum says one of the intangible benefits of a servant-leader culture is that there is less bitterness and fewer lawsuits when tough times come. He credits the basic trust level that had been built by attempting to follow Greenleaf's servant-leadership principles.

"We found using an outplacement specialist to be in the spirit of servant-leadership. During own downsizing, we established two ground rules. One was that each supervisor was responsible for finding anther job for each of her or his people who had to be outplaced. The other was that if there was a choice of who should originally tell the employee the bad news, the one who finds it the most traumatic and heart-rending should do it. You can't fake compassion."

Some of the laid-off workers have as good or better jobs than they had before. Almost all have jobs. Many stay in touch. According to Bottum, "The bond between us is permanent and lasting and transcends the name on the paycheck. They want to come back when it's possible, and some already have."

Years ago, Bottum spent a decade studying the Beatitudes and translating them into modern language. One summary of his work is now used as the *Guiding Principles of Townsend & Bottum.* Bottum wrote a "separation of church and business" clause appropriated from Jefferson's Virginia Religious Statutes, into the company's constitution. People of all faiths have found resonance with these values:

- Self-transcendence: Be open, teachable, flexible, able to change and so able to grow; have humility; be unselfish, self-actualizing; be a servant-leader.
- Service: Have sensitivity to needs of others, including customers, practice compassionate understanding of co-workers, empathetic listening.
- Commitment to Values: Have commitment to ideals beyond self—toward making the world better; the business entity must stand for something—have a corporate culture that gives meaning and purpose to its endeavors.
- Achievement, Productivity: Practice achievement orientation, productivity; have enthusiasm, goals, objectives, focused will.
- Nurture the Positive in People: Overcome prejudice and antipathy; be nonvengeful, nonjudgmental; control anger; practice forgiveness, don't harbor grudges, see the positive in people, recognize talents and capacities of people.
- Integrity: Be genuine, sincere, open, authentic, trusting and trustworthy; give quality of products and services, integrity.
- Team Building/Peacemaking: Individual—equanimity, overcome anxiety, be calm, sure and serene, yet enthusiastic; organizational—conflict resolution with team building.
- Growth Through Adversity, Endurance: Learn, teach, train; have courage, be steadfast; have dedication, perseverance, and endure to the end.

With this core value structure in place, the principles of servant-leadership have endured at Townsend & Bottum. According to Bottum, "Some of the marks of servant-leadership are symbolic, such as eliminating status symbols like reserved parking places and using round conference tables. But the deeper levels are reached in the tough times. Then we know that the leaders of the future will be servant-leaders, motivated by a desire to serve and make the world better, rather than a desire for power and greed."

From Acorns to Forests: The Sisters of St. Joseph Health System and Leadership in a Christian Organization

The Sisters of St. Joseph Health System in Michigan (SSJ) is the largest organization practicing a form of servant-leadership. The SSJ System is divided into four regions plus a corporate office, employs over 15,000 people, and includes hospitals ranging from 67 to 702 beds, nursing homes, adult day care centers, home health care services outpatient facilities, clinics and other agencies, many of them products of local partnerships. Four years after its inception, an experiential program which came to be known as Leadership In a Christian Organization (as opposed to "Christian leadership," which would exclude non-Christian employees) had worked its way through the system, resulting in comments from employees like these: "It seems as if we are yearning for a more spiritual connection between our values, upbringing, and the way we lead our day-to-day lives. The experiential workshop introducing Leadership in a Christian Organization provided that in a nondidactic, nonevangelical way." "It was exciting to find that my values and the values of the system are the same."

The Beginning

The Congregation of the Sisters of St. Joseph of Nazareth began its work in Michigan in 1889, where it started a hospital in Kalamazoo. Through the years, the Sisters expanded their health care facilities, adding mental care, drug abuse, and other wellness and healing services to their ministry.

In the 1960s the Sisters began to broaden their governance by adding lay trustees. This was a radical move at the time, not initially supported by every sister. By the 1970s, the change had borne fruit, with greater community support and thriving operations. The next move was to add lay administrators. Again, there was understandable opposition, mostly based on a concern about keeping the Congregation's values of Christian compassion and service to others intact. This change eventually took root and resulted in the infusion of some wonderfully visionary people who enriched the organization while maintaining its Christian values. In 1982, governance was moved from the SSJ Congregation into a system.

The third evolution was hiring lay leaders. Today, layman John S. Lore, President and CEO of the SSJ Health System, and lay CEOs in the four Regional Health Corporations provide leadership within the organization. Through the years, as these changes took place, local operations and facilities in all four regions developed histories of fulfilling missions based on serving local needs and fostering strong community ties, resulting in what the Sisters call "the principle of local autonomy."

Now the group is in its fourth stage of development. Joyce DeShano, SSJ, Senior Vice-President of the SSJ Health System, and an interregional team have initiated a process which will ensure that the enduring values that gave life to this marvelous history are incorporated into the very fiber of each institution and employee. That brings us to the current LICO program.

Reflection on the broad sweep of this unique history reveals that there were practical as well as philosophical reasons for evolution. The Sisters of St. Joseph, like other congregations, have not been able to replenish its own leadership at a rate that could keep up with the tremendous growth of its missions; it needed lay leadership involvement. While giving up control and power was not easier for the sisters than for any other human being, they "realized that the health care mission did not belong to the sisters, but to all people of good will. Even if there were thousands of sisters, we would still need to implement this program, because we have a new understanding of the meaning of partnership," said DeShano.

Values, Not Programs

In 1990, the SSJ Health System Board discussed the idea of a process that would implement the fourth developmental stage—the migration of enduring values into organizational structures, managers, and employees. The program—Leadership in a Christian Organization—was conceived as an experiential extension of the Board's work to executive management so that "spiritual foundation and Christian values can be personally owned and integrated into the leadership of SSJ-sponsored health care institutions." It was a vehicle to partner the future, and the board preferred to allow its current leaders to create that vehicle rather than buying an off-the-shelf package for leadership training. DeShano says, "We resisted becoming a program. That's why we go very slowly and try to reach each group significantly." The pace may have been slow, but it did have direction.

Phase I

A steering committee task force, consisting of the four regional CEOs and executive councils, plus three executives from the corporate office, began meeting. They spent the first year simply talking, understanding who they were and who they wanted to become, what values drove them, what luminous visions sustained them during those frustrating days in the healthcare vineyard. They concluded that a better definition of values-centered leadership in a Christian organization was needed, something that management could use to articulate the difference with convincing logic to leadership, employees, and the general public.

The group, joined by others from around the system, spent a year reflecting on readings and holding discussions. After months of struggling, they came up with the following five "system values," which were Gospel-based but universally applicable:

- Service to the neighbor: Unhesitating outreach to those in need, respecting the dignity of each person. Which of these three, in your opinion, was neighbor to the one who fell in with robbers? The answer came, "The one who treated him with compassion." Jesus said, "Then go and do the same." (Gospel of Mark)
- Servant Leadership: The use of gifts and talents on behalf of all in a way that models what we can be and empowers us to try. "You know that among the Gentiles those who exercise authority lord it over them; it cannot be like that with you. Anyone among you who aspires to greatness must serve the rest." (Gospel of Mark)
- Compassion: The ability to enter into the deepest experiences of life and be present with one another in our need. Jesus said, "Go home to your people and tell them all that the Lord in compassion has done for you." (Gospel of Mark)
- Wisdom: The ability to appreciate the complexity of life and make sound judgments for the common good. Because you have asked

for yourself understanding to discern what is right . . . behold I give you a wise and discerning mind. (Book of Kings)

- Stewardship: Responsible, innovative use of human and material resources. "Then the one who had received the five talents came forward, bringing five more talents, saying, 'Master, you handed over to me five talents; see I have made five more talents.' The master said, 'Well done, good and trustworthy servant; you have been trustworthy in a few things; I will put you in charge of many things; enter into the joy of the master.'" (Gospel of Matthew)

These five system values have induced deep resonance in many of the employees who have been exposed to them. Like Greenleaf's servant-leadership essay, they articulate ideas people already sensed. Many have said, "Yes! These values are the reasons I work here. They are a source of real meaning."

It is interesting to note that the servant-leadership value did not come from DeShano, who was familiar with Greenleaf. Instead, group members hit upon it after discussions about leadership and what kind of leadership they believed in. It was not an ideological term, merely a descriptive one.

Phase II

With time, the core leadership group was ready to present its ideas to the next level of key managers. Design teams worked on the agenda for an executive retreat that was held in 1992. This and later retreats were remarkably successful in communicating LICO as well as in allowing people to experience the system's values.

Phase III

The Leadership Integration Series involved a period during which more top managers continued to experience retreats and reflect on the implications of consciously integrating values into their organizations.

Phase IV

Beginning in 1993, a system-wide implementation team made plans for extending the presentations to middle managers. System-wide teams also were organized to support regional initiatives.

Acorns and Stories

One of the highlights of each retreat is the showing of "The Man Who Planted Trees," an animated film by Jean Giono which won the 1987 Academy Award for Best Animated Film. In this moving parable, a shepherd, Elzeard Bouffier, began early in this century to transform a drought-ravaged land into a thriving oasis by planting acorns, which eventually became forests and changed an arid landscape into a place "where people want to live." The film, narrated by Christopher Plummer, shows the power of one patient, dedicated human spirit.

Each participant in the retreats is given his or her own wooden acorn to keep. This visible reminder of the power of planting values, one at a time, is now part of the corporate culture. DeShano says, "We are all moving through a cycle of change, and this film is symbolic of the process. In the film, the man transformed his environment. We're trying to transform our corporate culture. As he planted acorns, we plant value-based actions."

Visitors often are invited to give one or more presentations at these retreats, which also feature small group sessions, spaces for reflection, and material that helps integrate the system values into other ongoing programs like total quality management and continuous quality improvement. Ideas are shared from Deming, Senge, DePree, Block, and other management visionaries. The material explaining dimensions of transformations shows how real transformation begins with each person, then radiates out to team development, focused initiatives, and finally organizational structure, rather than vice versa. People are given an opportunity to think about their own values and behaviors, and reflect on those "moments of truth" when values and behaviors come together.

Trustees in the Know

It would have been more efficient to begin this entire process with the board trustees and working down, but that would not necessarily have been more resonant with the system values. While the trustees have been kept informed of the progress of LICO and are excited about what they hear, they did not personally go through the experience until more than four years after it began. In fact, the regional CEOs actually presented the initiative to the trustees. According to Lore, this was the only way to allow the system values and all its related implications to mature in each system. If the trustees had experienced it first, one of them might have contacted his or her favorite CEO, enthusiastically talked up the experience, and suggested that the CEO implement it as soon as possible. This would have bypassed the natural buy-in process. The evolution process might not have happened the same way in the presence of pressure (however benign and unintentional) from trustees.

Outcomes

Although the entire LICO process had some expected outcomes, specific outcomes are entrusted to each local organization. Some of those have ranged from expanded business with minority-owned suppliers to increased letters from appreciative patients and their families.

Accountability and deadlines are built into the evolution, but the accountability relates to the process, and the deadlines are flexible. This can be frustrating. Lore, a person of action, has learned from the experience. "There I was with my timetable, ready to go, and the regions came in and slowed me down. They said, 'We have to own it or it isn't going to go anywhere.' It's a wonderful general reminder." Perhaps there is now more patience system-wide, more openness to a process of consensus.

The system values ground and stabilize the organization and its parts. Employees now often refer to the system values when discussing issues ranging from patient care to disputes with supervisors. When President Clinton's administration proposed health care reforms in 1993, most major health care systems had difficulty responding with a unified voice, given their diversity. By contrast, the four regions of the SSJ Health System were able to reflect on health care reform from the perspective of their values and agree on a 20-point position statement, which was quickly adopted by the Board of Trustees and circulated to key stakeholders, including legislators, media, and community organizations.

The process of creating a conscious level of awareness of those values is not necessarily the easiest way to run a railroad—or a health system. Lore consults with four CEOs before making any major decisions that affect the whole system. He, DeShano, and others must give up the coercive power that comes naturally to traditional pyramid-based management structures. If they slip, employees remind them that their organization is based on five system values. Accountability works both ways. Lore paraphrased Max DePree as follows: "Leadership is a way of thinking about institutions. It's a way of thinking about stewardship as contrasted with ownership."

Showing the Way

Robert Greenleaf believed that servant-leadership is a territory and that various people can occupy the role of leader when chosen by followers to do so. Still, he spent considerable time discussing the qualities of a leader, one of the most important of which was the ability to "go ahead and show the way." The key people involved in the four situations reviewed in this chapter have taken the risk to get in the arena, to articulate and live their ideals, to persuade through patience and example. Without exception, all eschew personal credit for the massive changes wrought, instead praising their teams for the courage to reflect on deep values and innovative organizational structures. Each is genuinely modest in a mature way. Each regularly praises members of his or her team with cards, letters, and comments. They are astonishing people who have, as a result of creating an atmosphere of openness and trust, been forced to face their own shadows.

If courage is a quality most required in situations where the final outcome is not fully within personal control, these people have courage in abundance. Some have been called dreamers and idealists by hard-nosed detractors, but each believes the principles of servant-leadership, no matter what the local name or adaptations, are a practical, workable, even profitable foundation for running a successful business or organization. We are reminded of a line from The Man Who Planted Trees: "I never saw him lose heart . . . nor was he ever deterred and often, God knows, it must have seemed that heaven itself was against him. I never tried to imagine his frustrations, but to achieve such an end he must have had to overcome many obstacles; for such passion to succeed he must have surely fought and conquered despair."

23

Creating a Culture of Servant-Leadership: A Real Life Story

Tina Rasmussen

Since the record-breaking introduction of the first books on culture—*In Search of Excellence* and *Theory Z*—a debate has been raging about whether corporate culture can actually be influenced. Like beauty or quality, most people find culture difficult to define but easy to recognize. Some speculate that the concepts of culture and vision have become popular because our society is so hungry for inspiration. Even former U.S. President George Bush spoke of "the vision thing" before he was voted out of office.

At the same time, a unique and humanistic philosophy of leadership has been evolving and slowly emerging into the mainstream. As noted in the June 1993 issue of *Training* magazine, "In an environment racked with stress, insecurity, tough decisions and 60-hour weeks, you might expect a resurgence of a management model based on Machiavelli's Prince, Leona Helmsley, or some other Theory-X icon. Instead, there's a stirring in the opposite direction: A flood of management books, articles, and musings try to make sense of the current chaos by proposing a management model filled with heart—and soul." A 1990 issue of *Fortune* magazine also noted that one of "the most powerful, encouraging, and sometimes disturbing ideas that will influence our lives and our livelihood" is a new altruism and a spirituality of work.

More than 20 years ago, the seed for this trend was planted with the concept of servant-leadership, originated by Robert K. Greenleaf. Like the concept of culture, servant-leadership can be hard to define, even elusive. Still, a number of organizations have broken new ground in implementing innovative approaches to influence their culture based on Greenleaf's ideas.

Recent Harvard University research shows that only a small percentage of organizations that try to consciously influence their culture have succeeded while most have failed, leaving a trail of meaningless vision statements hanging dusty on office walls. How have some been able to influence their cultures? And what tools has one organization that aspires to servant-leadership used to nurture a culture that brings those values to life?

By the end of this chapter, you will have answers to these questions. You will be able to determine for yourself the degree to which it is possible for organizations to actualize the values of servant-leadership. You will see how to use practical tools to evolve a culture, as demonstrated in a real-life case study organization which has attempted to weave the values of servant-leadership into its day-to-day actions. And you will find the two key steps leaders must take in making servant-leadership a reality.

The Mystery of Corporate Culture

Many of the following ideas were stimulated by the work of Edgar Schein in his book *Organizational Culture and Leadership.* A variation on his definition of culture which has the most meaning to me is: "A pattern of shared basic assumptions and values that a group has adopted as it has solved its problems, which have worked well enough to be considered valid." In this definition, we can see that culture is a stabilizing force which creates social reality for its participants. Because culture is based on shared assumptions and values about "what works," it creates a common framework of thinking and acting which is reflected in that group's way of life.

Schein points out that we often try to create or analyze culture at a superficial level, which does not address the organization's more important underlying assumptions. The three stages of culture he identifies are represented below.

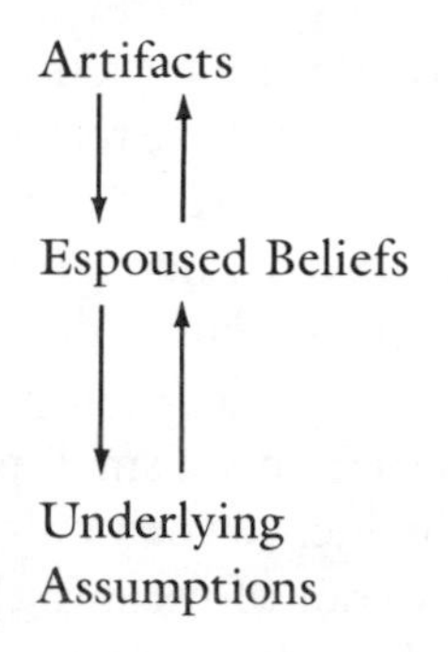

Visible organizational behaviors and processes (hard to decipher as values, easier to change)

Stated strategies, goals, philosophies (justifications and explanations of artifacts, may or may not be aligned with underlying assumptions)

Unconscious, taken-for-granted values and perceptions which drive behavior (difficult to uncover, difficult to change)

At the artifact level, we see culture exhibited by phenomena such as commonly used language, rules for social acceptance, organizational documents, and buildings and office layouts. Artifacts can provide clues to the espoused beliefs and eventually the underlying assumptions or root beliefs that drive the organization. Underlying assumptions are so ingrained that they are taken for granted as absolute truths. They unconsciously drive behavior and sometimes only become apparent if they are challenged, in which case people find it "out of the question" to even consider the alternatives because "that's not the way we do things around here."

Schein's model is useful in many ways. It can help us understand how to create a new culture, analyze a culture, or attempt to change an existing culture. It also demonstrates that to influence culture we must move beyond the superficial level of artifacts or even espoused beliefs and impact the underlying assumptions. Trying to influence culture at the level of artifacts is like rearranging the deck chairs on the Titanic. It might make us feel like we were doing something, but that it would not actually make much of a difference.

If underlying assumptions are so deeply ingrained, how do they originate? I believe culture is influenced most strongly by the behavior of an organization's leaders through the use of Schein's framework of "embedders" and "reinforcers." Embedders are the original mechanisms that implant values into the organization and establish them at a deep and lasting level. Once values are embedded, reinforcers maintain the culture and give it life and stability in people's actions. We will review these specific examples of embedders and reinforcers, and how they have been used in our case study organization:

Embedders that establish values:

- larger context
- leadership
  - what leaders pay attention to and measure
  - how leaders allocate resources
  - how leaders give rewards and status
  - how leaders hire, promote, and excommunicate people
  - how leaders react to critical incidents and crises

Reinforcers that bring the values to life:

- infrastructures
  - rites and rituals
  - stories and myths
  - formal philosophy statements
  - systems and procedures

To the conceptual framework for understanding culture, we will bring the theory to life through our case study organization. We will then look at how embedders and reinforcers contributed to the formation of this organization's culture.

Santa Barbara Bank & Trust

My role at Santa Barbara Bank & Trust (SBB&T) was to lead teams in designing and implementing training and organizational development efforts which would move the company toward fulfillment of its vision and goals. In this role, I searched for an understanding of the history and culture of Santa Barbara Bank & Trust. I interviewed people from all levels and areas of the company. I began discovering things that seemed incredible. Initially, these facts did not seem extraordinary because they were so ingrained that long-time employees didn't pay much attention to them. However, one of the first things new employees often commented on was "how strong a corporate culture" the bank had.

Santa Barbara Bank & Trust was founded in 1960 by three well-established local businessmen. They wanted to create a financial institution that would foster economic growth and stability for community residents and businesses. They made the bank a publicly owned institution so it would become "the bank that belonged to Santa Barbara," a community of about 300,000 people. They established this modest institution with one small office. The bank gradually added branches and expanded to offer commercial loan, trust, real estate, and escrow services. Now, more than 30 years later, it is a billion dollar institution with about 500 employees and 11 branches spanning about 40 miles of California's central coast.

In 1992, SBB&T was identified by *Money Magazine* as one of the two strongest banks in California, and one of the 97 strongest in the United States. Sheshunoff, the leading national bank rating service, has consistently given the bank the highest ratings of A or A+ for being well-managed. Although bank stocks generally haven't done well recently, SBB&T has increased earnings to their stockholders for the last 27 years in a row. The bank is the market leader in its area, even with prominent competitors such as Bank of America and Wells Fargo. More people choose SBB&T as their primary institution than the next two competitors combined, while at the same time many institutions in the area have either been acquired or seized by the federal government. The people of Santa Barbara consistently vote SBB&T the best in the community. In 1993, after five years as "best bank," the newspaper that conducted the poll had to retire SBB&T as a "living legend" because no other institution was getting a chance. When the bank hired a market research firm to conduct customer focus groups, the researchers presented one word to describe customers' perceptions of the bank: noble.

People respect and admire senior management, especially President and CEO David Spainhour. He isn't a "motivational speaker" in the Lou Holt or Robert Schuller tradition. Instead, he is consistent, even-tempered, and caring. People are struck by the fact that, if you meet him in the hallway, he'll ask you questions and then just listen. Sometimes people are even uncomfortable and don't know what to say; its so rare that *anyone* listens these days, let alone the president.

One year, Chairman of the Board Don Anderson was voted Santa Barbara'a Man of the Year. The same award was given to one of the founders of the bank, Rubin Irvin, who greeted customers from his desk in the main lobby until he died in 1989 at the age of 90. "Rube" Irvin also worked with more than 30 civic organizations in his lifetime. To this day, nearly all of the 150 officers volunteer with at least one nonprofit organization.

As employees, we often pondered why the bank was so successful. We didn't consider ourselves to be at the leading edge of every new business trend. Some of us came to the conclusion that we were successful because we did what we did thoroughly instead of just talking about it. We had minimized the gap between "*talking* the talk" and "*walking* the talk." Our espoused values were fairly consistent with our actions.

Despite all this, the bank isn't perfect. Because people value their relationships with each other, they sometimes fall into a "groupthink" mentality. Because collaboration is valued and everyone's perspective is considered, decisions often take a long time to make. Sometimes there is a sense of things getting "bogged down," and an aversion to risk-taking. Some pockets of the organization don't embody the vision as well as others. People get frustrated because they want to stay with the bank, but can't always find opportunities for advancement.

It was hard for me to leave the bank. But the perspective I have now that I'm outside it is just as valuable as what I learned when I was there, because I can better analyze what makes it so exceptional. One element that stands out is its underlying values of servant-leadership.

The philosophy of servant leadership created by Robert K. Greenleaf in his book of the same title is defined as:

- Emphasizing service to others.
- Using a holistic approach to work.
- Promoting a sense of community.
- Sharing power in decision-making.
- Having an effect on the least privileged in society of benefit, or at least causing no further deprivation.
- Developing a relationship in which those being served grow as persons by becoming healthier, wiser, freer, more autonomous, and more likely to become servant-leaders themselves.

A striking element of this description is that the criteria are values-based, in contrast to other descriptions of leadership which are behaviorally based. We will refer to these values as they apply in our analysis of the bank's attempts to weave them into its culture.

Embedders That Establish Values

What are the practical tools organizations can use to establish values in an organization? Schein's work with hundreds of organizations indicates that underlying values initially become ingrained in the organization through the actions of the founding leaders. But before we delve into the embedding mechanisms, we will review how the larger context in which the organization is set can influence the leaders themselves.

Larger Context

Stepping beyond Schein's framework to take a larger system view, I have found it helpful to consider an organization's culture within the context of the broader culture in which it exists. For example, the practices of Japanese management work superbly in Japan—a society that values collaboration, interdependence, and loyalty. But does that mean Japanese management always works well in the United States? We have seen that it does not. Therefore, the influence of the larger society's values and norms needs to be considered.

SBB&T is strongly linked to its larger context, the Santa Barbara community. Nearly everyone I knew who worked there volunteered time to a local nonprofit. Customers in focus groups often stated that "I've seen the bank or bank employees involved in just about every charitable event I've been to in Santa Barbara." The fact that the Santa Barbara community wants to retain its small-town feel—and fend off the influences from nearby Los Angeles—is an important factor which has contributed directly to the bank's values and vision. One advertising campaign was based on the theme: "The expertise of a big bank with the heart of a local bank." SBB&T know that the people of Santa Barbara want to be treated in a friendly, personal manner unlike that found in the "big banks," and goes to great lengths to provide that individualized service. The bank still has in-branch loan officers who actually make the loan decisions, while the large banks send their loans to a remote location to be approved by someone the customer will never meet. Being "the bank for Santa Barbara" creates a context in which large, strong competitors find it difficult to compete.

This community link is also a source of pride, satisfaction, and ultimately culture formation for employees. People often report that when they tell acquaintances "I work at Santa Barbara Bank & Trust," the response is nearly always one of impressed appreciation. Employees are pleased to consistently receive positive affirmations from the larger culture about their association with the bank.

Leadership

The impact of leadership on culture is found not only in the influence leaders have, but also in leaders' roles as figure heads. Whether intentionally or by default, senior managers are symbols of the behavior that is most valued by the organization. This can have a positive reinforcing effect when their actions match the espoused values. However, when they do not "walk the talk," they become representations of the fact that the espoused beliefs and vision are "just words." Because of this, role modeling is not listed here as a specific action, but rather is regarded as an all-encompassing activity that impacts all the leaders' actions. We will examine five specific categories of leaders' behavior in depth:

- what leaders pay attention to and measure
- how leaders allocate resources
- how leaders give rewards and status
- how leaders hire, promote, and excommunicate people
- how leaders react to critical incidents and crises

What Leaders Pay Attention to and Measure. Leaders pay attention to what they care about. This is demonstrated by how they spend their time, what they exhibit an ongoing interest in, and what they actually measure. For example, in a management meeting the company president says, "It's important that managers take time to develop their people." But, if in his or her individual meetings with managers, all he or she ever asks about is whether financial goals are being met, managers will focus their energies on making the numbers rather than on developing people.

At SBB&T, senior management's attention is focused squarely on customer satisfaction and on employees as the vehicle for making it happen. An example of this is the way in which Spainhour takes a significant amount of time to read customer letters aloud at quarterly officers meetings. The bank also measures retail offices regularly on customer satisfaction via surveys.

How Leaders Allocate Resources. Budget allocations provide another indication of what is important. Often, companies claim that "our employees are our most valuable asset," and then neglect to invest money in them the way they would in an advertising campaign. People realize the true values when leaders fail to "put their money where their mouth is." For example, SBB&T has made a significant investment in its Human Resources area. They employ six people in the Educational Resources Department, with a total of 12 in Human Resources. This is an employee-to-Human Resources ratio of 41:1, compared to the national average of 100:1—a statement not just in word but in action that people are an important asset.

How Leaders Give Rewards and Status. We have all heard the saying, "What gets rewarded get done." Although modern motivational theory shows us that people are motivated by a variety of things, rewards and status are still among them. Decisions that leaders make about giving rewards tell people what is most valued. For example, companies sometimes espouse that they want employees to "strive for a balance of work and personal life." But if people who work late and on weekends are rewarded while those who don't are looked down upon, the underlying assumption becomes clear.

SBB&T has had a long struggle over that particular issue. The true test came when a vice-president wanted to go to a three-day work week after she had a child. The bank had an espoused belief that people who are happy in their personal lives make better employees. When it came time to "walk the talk," senior management decided that as long as the vice-president was flexible in making it work, they would give it a try—and it worked. Other employees took this as a clear signal that striving for personal balance in one's life is okay, and even valued.

How Leaders Hire, Promote, and Excommunicate People. The impact of decisions about selecting, promoting, and deselecting members is similar to that of giving rewards. In many companies, the "good old boys-girls club" is the primary vehicle for hiring and promotion; "fast trackers" turn out to be friends or relatives of key leaders. Sometimes, these people are given opportunities that exceed their capabilities, embedding a value that being "in" with leaders is more important than a person's skills. Similarly, leaders who refuse to take corrective action with people who contradict the values send a message that avoiding conflict is more important than the espoused values.

In the hiring process at SBB&T, many job candidates are found via employee referrals, for which a bonus is paid. This recruitment method is accompanied by a sophisticated screening process consisting of a clear definition of job requirements before recruiting begins, a battery of tests for all applicants, and multiple interviews with several people. This simultaneously embeds two values: "collaborative relationships are important," and "we hire the candidate who best fits the position."

How Leaders React to Critical Incidents and Crises. It is easiest to live by our espoused values when things are going well. When the going gets tough, though, we sometimes revert to behaviors that reflect our less evolved but more deeply ingrained beliefs. Therefore, times of stress can serve as shortcuts in revealing underlying assumptions. For example, the financial industry has been in distress since the 1980s. In search of higher returns, many banks and savings institutions chose to make risky foreign investments. The leaders of SBB&T also faced this decision and opted not to contradict their value of being "the bank for Santa Barbara." If they were supposed to serve the community by investing in it, how could they justify investing overseas? As it turned out, they were rewarded financially for their stance. The decision also showed customers, stockholders, and employees the commitment to the values.

Another critical incident occurred when the newspaper published the Bank's Living Legend award. The published photo of Chairman Don Anderson included his handwritten quote: "We think our staff is what sets us apart." To employees and customers, this reinforced that service is the bank's top priority, and only quality employees can provide that service.

Reinforcers that Bring the Values to Life

Once the values have begun to be embedded in the organization, reinforcers can be used to support those values and translate them into actions. Reinforcers are the infrastructures that give the values substance, like sturdy beams that support a well-built house. They include:

- Stories and myths
- Rites and rituals
- Formal philosophy statements
- Systems and procedures

Stories and Myths

The stories and myths passed down through history are relevant in defining an organization's culture, just as they are in defining a nation's culture. The books and movies of America's pioneer days of settling uncharted territories have undoubtedly had a significant impact on our deep-seated value for rugged individualism. An organization's stories support its values in a subliminal yet powerful manner.

The bank has a rich legacy of stories of the three founders, their dream, and their history with the Santa Barbara community. These are known by every employee via the new employee orientation. The director of Public Relations, a 30-year employee, shows historical slides and passes around memorabilia for all participants to touch and examine. Photos of the founders and historical mementos are framed at various locations to keep the history alive. People still tell tales of founder Rube Irvin with a wistful look and an appreciative smile.

Rites and Rituals

Large group events can evoke strong emotions and generate a sense of continuity and stability. When rituals are repeated on a regular basis, they become woven into the fabric of people's experience of the culture. They also serve as rites of passage in marking people's tenure or experience with the group.

Ritual and ceremony are used frequently at the bank to develop norms that support the vision. In 1992, when Spainhour was asked to address the Pacific Coast Banking School for executives on what made SBB&T so successful, he said:

> There are three important areas I have focused on: quality customer service, development of our people, and maintaining our financial

> strength. I may have a personal vision of what quality customer service should be. But until it becomes shared and others are committed to expanding on it, the vision won't go very far. So we looked for ways to incorporate reinforcement into our culture to move from personal vision of a few to shared vision by many. This included:
>
> - New Employee Orientation
>   Either I or a senior vice-president speak to each class regarding reasons for the bank's success, giving examples of excellent customer service, and communicating our expectations regarding their joining our team and continuing the approach that has created this success.
> - Quarterly Officers' Meetings
>   We use this as a vehicle to challenge the officers to become part of the vision, and to recognize instances of excellent customer service.
> - Annual Awards Banquet
>   We rent the ballroom at the Red Lion resort and have a dinner for all employees to recognize accomplishments for the past year. It's a fun evening with a serious purpose.

These are just some of the approaches the bank has used to communicate and reinforce the values.

Formal Philosophy Statements

Formal philosophy statements clarify the values and create a vision that provides a common foundation from which people can make decisions. Unfortunately, many philosophy statements are reflections of espoused beliefs which do not truly represent underlying assumptions. But when the two are in alignment, philosophy statements can be valuable reinforcers in providing common direction for all organizational members.

The bank's values come together most solidly through its planning process, the first part of which is defining the vision. Other bank's visions often read something like this: "To increase our market share to 25 percent in five years, taking 7 percent away from competitors." In contrast, SBB&T's is: "To be a strong community-oriented organization where every employee is motivated, prepared, and enabled to fulfill their commitment to customer satisfaction." The four values described in the expanded version are satisfaction of employees, customers, shareholders, and the community. The way the vision is commonly perceived by employees is as follows:

> We want to help our customers feel like they made a good decision to bank here. We want them to feel their money is safe with us, that we'll take good care of it and them. We want to do everything possible to make their banking experience easy, hassle-free, and comfortable. We want them to feel at home when they come into a banking office or call us. We want to enjoy working with each other, and to grow as individuals. We want to make smart business decisions, which will produce a profit. Santa Barbara Bank & Trust's purpose in being is to serve this community and the people in it by providing high-quality, high-value financial services which people can depend on.

Banking is often viewed as a cold, heartless industry. We are barraged with images of crooked bankers being taken to jail during the era of failed savings and loans. Those people may have believed the only way to "make it" in banking was to be cut-throat business people. They might have laughed if someone suggested that a caring approach would produce superior results. But through the bank's values of servant-leadership, its vision has meaning which powerfully influences its culture and inspires people to act.

Systems and Procedures

Systems and procedures link the values to employees' day-to-day activities. They are the concrete outcomes of a philosophical ideal. It is easy for organizations to overlook systems and procedures because they seem somewhat mundane, but in reality they are a constant reminder of "how things really work around here." For example, a company that says employees are empowered to serve customers, but has procedures that require several approvals for decisions, is actively preventing employees from enacting the vision.

The second part of the bank's planning process is to link the values and vision to each team's and individual's performance plan. In the speech previously mentioned, Spainhour said:

> The planning process is designed to include participation from the bottom up by responding to the mission, competitive strategy, and key areas of attention, and soliciting input from all levels. All employees are expected to respond to the bank plan by revising their job descriptions to incorporate appropriate goals.

Although the actual steps of the bank's planning process are similar to those at many organizations, I believe the bank's process is unique in that it is highly integrated and holistically developed. Hundreds of people have input before goals are finalized, through an up and down, back and forth, and sideways communication process which spans a period of months. In addition, the plan documents are extended to a level of detail in which each team and individual can graphically see how their specific duties and annual goals directly link to the values and strategy. This is then incorporated directly into each person's job description.

I remember people leaving bank plan meetings expressing immense pride in contributing to something they thought was worthwhile. Many felt almost overwhelmed at the effort the company had invested to make sure everyone had a voice and understood the importance of their specific role. The company had a genuine interest in finding out what people thought was important, and pieces of their ideas could be seen in the final plan. This translated an intangible, philosophical vision of servant-leadership into concrete actions which would later be taken by each team and individual to make it a reality.

The Role of Leaders in Creating a Culture of Servant-Leadership

In reviewing the previous ideas, what specifically can leaders do to influence their organization's culture? We have examined the embedders and reinforcers leaders can use. Of everything discussed, I believe that leaders' commitment to and follow-through in consistently role modeling the desired values is the single most important lever for influencing or changing an organization's culture. At SBB&T, we can see the previously defined values of servant-leadership embedded and role modeled by leaders in the following ways.

Service to others is emphasized by the focus and commitment to the organization's stakeholders. For customers, it is demonstrated in the constant verbal reinforcement and measurement of behaviors that result in customer satisfaction. Spainhour still calls on customers himself so he doesn't lose touch with their needs and concerns. For employees, it is demonstrated by the leaders' decisions to invest in Human and Educational Resources services which benefit employees on both the professional and personal levels. Service to stockholders is demonstrated by 27 consecutive years of increased earnings. Community service is reinforced by the decision to reinvest in the community even when other investments might be more lucrative.

Using a holistic approach to work is exhibited not only in such decisions as agreeing to the vice-president's reduced schedule, but in leaders' openness to the importance of their own personal lives and the benefits of balance, as well as encouragement of others to be open about their need for time or flexibility in family and personal issues.

Promoting a sense of community is exhibited by the importance of stories, myths, rites, and rituals. Group events are a regular, ongoing way of life in which all employees participate. Stories evolve around these events, building legends of what has happened over the years. The officers keep a photo album of major events on the coffee table in their lobby, so people can review the organization's history just as a family would at a reunion.

Sharing power in decision-making is exemplified in the planning process, which is done in a reciprocal, iterative process between senior management, middle management, and front-line employees. An opportunity for communication up and down the organization takes place before the bank plan is finalized.

Having an effect on the least privileged in society of benefit is exhibited in the bank's leaders' dedication to community service. Employees are often given work time to participate in community events at the bank's expense.

The final value is that *leadership is a relationship in which those being served grow as persons by becoming healthier, wiser, freer, more autonomous and more likely to become servant-leaders themselves.* This is exhibited in less tangible ways, embodied by the concept of continuous role modeling of servant-leadership values by the senior managers who inspire others to the same values. A good example is the personal excellence class led by a senior vice-president in which he or she communicates his or her personal belief that only by elevating others can we achieve excellence ourselves. It is one of the most popular classes the bank offers.

Where do leaders find the strength and inspiration to live these values in a world where people can provide so many reasons to falter from them? In answering this question, we come to the second key step of servant-leadership, which is the willingness to take a leap of faith.

Leaders must trust their people, their business plans, their intuition, and their customers enough to say, "I know what we're doing is right. It provides value to our customers at a fair price. If we focus on doing the right thing, as effectively and efficiently as we can, we will achieve excellence." Leaders who don't trust their company's products and their people's ideas are not willing to take the necessary leap of faith, even though it would lead to long-term profitability by unleashing the organization's human potential.

This trust in the good emerging is reminiscent of a story about the great artist Michaelangelo. When asked how he was able to create a magnificent sculpture out of a lump of marble, he responded that the statue was already contained within the marble. All he did was chip away the excess rock. For servant-leaders, the leap of faith is a natural outgrowth of their innermost, deepest beliefs. They believe their companies are on this earth to provide a service, not just to make a profit, and the way to do this depends on trust in the people and the vision as much as it depends on cold, hard, rational business practices.

If a leader uses the embedders and reinforcers, and has the internal fortitude to take the leap of faith, to what degree is it reasonable to expect that an organization's culture can even be influenced—and is it worth the trouble? This question has been heavily debated in the past decade. The 1992 book *Corporate Culture and Performance* documents the Harvard University study of more than 40 large U.S. corporations which revealed that "although it is tough to change, corporate cultures *can* be made more performance enhancing." The key element of positive culture was found to be an unwavering emphasis on all the organization's stakeholders—also the first defining value of servant-leadership.

Although fully conclusive findings are still being argued, engaging in the debate allows us to question the myth of Western society: that the rational alone guides our behavior. Viewing organizations in light of their culture is a welcome contrast to regarding them as machines designed to "crank out" deliverables through a process of planning and predicting, commanding, and controlling. It helps us recognize the power of symbols, history, and common yet intangible shared meanings which may influence us even more strongly than numbers and graphs.

Corporate Culture and Performance summed it up with this statement: "If our organizations are going to live up to their potential, we must find, develop, and encourage more people to lead in the service of others. Without leadership, firms cannot adapt to a fast-moving world. But if leaders do not have the hearts of servants, there is only the potential for tyranny."

24

Servant-Leadership and the Future

Robert A. Vanourek

I was first exposed to Robert Greenleaf's ideas of servant-leadership in 1974. I had the good fortune to work for a short year for Jan Erteszek, the president of Olga, a ladies apparel company in California. Erteszek was a man of vision, a student of creativity, and a very successful entrepreneur. He built his wonderful company on Judeo-Christian values. He believed deeply in people and created a special environment for them. Years later, his pioneering small company, along with Pitney Bowes, my current company, were both selected as two of the 100 best companies in America.

It was more than just a coincidence, I think, that Erteszek gave me some of Greenleaf's pamphlets shortly after they were published. It was 10 years, though, before I was able to weave them together with other ideas in a fashion that clicked for me.

For those who may not know, Robert Greenleaf spent 39 years in management with AT&T. Then he became a trustee to several universities, an author, and a philosopher. His focus was on leadership. Having lived in institutions of all kinds throughout his life, Greenleaf knew how they dominate our lives through business, government, schools, and church. He also knew that large institutions are the sum of many small institutions or departments.

Robert Greenleaf was a deep believer in human potential. One of the great philosophical questions of the ages deals with human potential—"Is the nature of man good or evil?" And it's one of the mysteries of life that man can be either. We can be incredibly capable or unbelievably evil. I believe we can spiral upward into noble deeds on an infinite continuum. Or, we can spiral down into war and exploitation. As Greenleaf said, we are "capable of great dedication and heroism if wisely led." Much depends on our leaders.

Like most students of leadership, Greenleaf didn't subscribe to the "great man" theory which holds that leaders are "born." He defines leadership as "going out ahead to show the way" and "venturing creatively." But how? Leadership is certainly complex. And we'll define here the very *best* of leadership, the kind of leadership only rarely seen. Unfortunately, all too often, we see cheap imitations of leadership which is really something else—management that attempts to lead but really doesn't.

The true leader has a sense of history. The true leader sees the whole and also has vision to foresee what might happen. The true leader is action-oriented, realistic, and has superb communication skills. Most authors and students of leadership would agree on all those points, as Greenleaf did, but here is where he stepped away from the others so significantly. He repeated that the true leader, most paradoxically, *serves.*

Yes, good leaders excite our imagination. They have a gift for articulating a dream. But the best leaders are symbols who point to a reality greater than themselves. The leader is servant to the vision. The leader does not usurp the vision.

Too often we have special people with some of these leadership traits who are confused as leaders. The visionary may excite our imagination, but may only be a dreamer with no will to initiate. The charismatic articulator may be a persuasive spokesperson with no depth. The best leaders go beyond all this to serve; they synthesize all the elements of leadership for the group to be served.

And we measure service by looking at the individuals in the group. They grow. They become healthier, wiser, freer, more autonomous, more likely themselves to be servant-leaders, even the very least of them.

Simply said, leaders have followers. They have followers in good times and in bad, followers for the long-term. And how does a leader gain followers? By *serving them,* not just the vision. Leadership is bestowed by the followers. Another paradox. It is not wrested away. It is not mandated from above. True leadership flows from those willing to be led, the followers. And who will the followers follow? Someone who serves them. A paradox. The power to lead comes from giving up the personal need for power in order to serve the group.

This idea was inspired in Greenleaf by a German writer, Hermann Hesse. But the idea is thousands of years old. The *Bible* is replete with servant-leader stories, as are most religions—Islam, Zen, Taoism. "The leader follows though a step ahead," according to the *Tao.* The leader is not above the others. No one person is better than the rest. True leaders take up their group's burden, just as servants take up the burden of the baggage. When they lead, they really stand behind. When they take their place of leadership, they do not obstruct the peoples progress.

The true leader cares about the people. Without caring about people you cannot be a leader. The leader places the well-being of the followers ahead of himself or herself. So, enlightened leadership is service, not selfishness.

And why does the leader care? Because he or she knows the potential that is there in each of us. He or she respects those untapped powers. And he or she wants to see the individual soar to new heights. He or she wants to see the group reach new plateaus, to see them move toward their shared visions. The leader wants to empower the people, to unlock those hidden potentials.

People intuitively sense that. They aren't foolish or dumb. They can't be tricked for long. They know in their hearts that a true leader is worthy of their trust. So they commit. Voluntarily. With their whole mind and their whole body and their whole heart. Great victories are won in the hearts of people. The best leadership comes from committed followers. Volunteers who intuitively sense the leader will serve them. Sustained loyalty is volunteered.

The true leader listens first. He or she doesn't push. "People can't be led where they don't want to go." But if they want to go, then get out of their way! You can't stop them.

What keeps these true leaders from emerging? Frequently, it is their need for power. Arrogance. Impatience. Or superiority. Negativism. Lack of belief in the people. Fear. Lack of trust. Why does this happen? What causes it? Often, we have not clearly seen the dangers inherent in the pursuit of power. So we romanticize the tough guys, the lonely commanders. We assume they have some answers better than ours. We seek benevolent leaders, but then we often watch them fall victim to the drug effect of power in office. The power too often becomes coercive or manipulative.

But coercive power only strengthens resistance. It's a sign the group wants a different direction or is not ready yet. Manipulative power doesn't really care about the people. Instead, the leader's skills at "facilitating" the group should be used. The ideas should evolve from the group. Then the leader can simplify them in a persuasive fashion. Then commitment to the vision can be gained. First to serve. Then to lead by persuasion.

Leadership Skills

Power corrupts, as Lord Acton said. So servant-leaders share power with the group and with their trustees. The trustees protect the leader from becoming too egotistical. The servant-leader guides. The true leader uses the least force required. The true leader, unlike most of us, doesn't try to fulfill his or her own desires. He or she knows the danger in the superstar's own brilliance outshining the vision. It's the ego that gets away from the complacent leader, an ego born in our deepest insecurities.

Leaders should not be lonely and out of touch with their people. As Peters and Waterman said, "Manage by wandering around." Leaders should be deeply in touch with their people, connected in the most basic way. They should shun the glory that feeds our insecure egos. A Tao verse tells us, "The best leader is one whose existence is barely known by the people. Next comes one they love and praise. Next comes one they fear. Next comes one they defy." The poem concludes with, "when their task is completed, the people will say, 'It happened to us naturally.'"

So the very best leader has many skills. Action-orientation. Communication skills. Foresight and vision. But the most important ingredient of all is the primary need to serve. Can this be true? Is this Greenleaf's theory? Or just religious philosophy? Can this apply in the rough competition of the free market or in the nuclear age of super powers?

The Circle of Values

Let me try to answer these questions by sharing some of my own experiences from a variety of different circumstances. For me, my own reflections, reading, discussion with wonderful colleagues, and many hard lessons have crystallized into the picture of a circle that forms a value system in which I can find answers. This value system anchors and guides my actions. Why are we here? What purpose do we serve? What purpose does an organization or institution serve? A Pitney Bowes' chairman, George Harvey, said "Business is a set of relationships." Isn't that interesting? Remember, we are all connected, so any organization or institution is a set of these relationships.

I suggest that the purpose of an organization or institution is to "create value for people." An organization should identify the people connected to the organization and "create value for them," fill their needs, help them grow and prosper. In other words, to serve them. The purpose of an organization is simply to serve the people connected to it. Who are those people, and how do we serve them, or create value for them? Let's use the example of a business organization. Picture a large circle divided into five wedges or segments. Each segment represents one group of people connected to the business. Like a clock, let's start at the top and trace the interrelationship of those segments.

Customers

First come the customers, the starting point of any business. Frequently, the "vision" of the business is defined around the markets and customers. We must "seek and serve" customers. And how do we create value for them and fill their needs? First, we must listen to them. We must seek them out and talk with them. We must discover their problems through market research. Then we must design and deliver products or services that fill their needs. We can't foist off junk on them. People are smart, so we must build world-class quality products for them. In too many cases, American industries have stopped doing this, and customers felt cheated. But Americans are reawakening—fast. World-class quality is being inculcated into our vanguard companies, and we are serving our customers better as a result. I've seen it happening in office products, autos, steel, and many basic industries.

Employees

The second group of people we must serve in our organizations is the employees, and their families. We can do this in many ways. Naturally, we pay them fair wages and benefits. Beyond that, leading companies care about their job security practices. Indiscriminate firings and layoffs without concern about their impact have no place in a leading company. Instead, retraining is emphasized to balance employee skills with changing company needs. People are shifted to where work does exist, and care is taken to provide for their security.

When a reduction is absolutely necessary because the business is threatened, people know that every other realistic option has been carefully explored first. So trust is built, and a sense of common purpose. Shared values are linked to bind the group to the organization and to the series of smaller groups within the larger group. For institutions to effectively change, trust must exist, and trust flows from knowing their institution will serve them.

Finally, in truly leading-edge companies, the employees are served because a special environment is created for them—an environment where people can grow closer to their full potential as human beings. These are organizations where work is not drudgery, but a meaningful part of one's life. Not where smart bosses tell dumb people what to do, but a place where people collaborate on how to achieve their shared vision, each playing a role and each knowing their role is necessary and valuable to the overall vision. People in the organization might not love all their fellow employees, but they will respect and rely on one another. Within the company, their roles will be balanced with their family lives, their spiritual lives, even their personal lives. In this fashion the whole person is healthy and strong.

I have been privileged to see this kind of special environment created several times. In California, in Ohio, in Connecticut. In large organizations and small. Growth businesses and turnaround situations. I have seen blacks and whites, male and female, college educated and grade school drop-outs all do it. New products brought to market in half the normal time. Quality problems fixed in record time. New ventures started. I have seen recessions weathered easily because the people had an infinite reservoir of ideas to draw upon.

Most businesses, like people, operate far below their full potential. When the right environment is created for the people, the results can be, truly, almost magical.

Vendors

The third group for whom we create value in our circle is our vendor group, our suppliers. We don't do this by whipsawing them into submission, but by involving them early in our plans, building long-term mutually profitable relations, and asking them for quality products delivered on time at competitive costs. At Pitney Bowes, for example, our vendors are taught manufacturing process control techniques at no charge to them. These programs can be used throughout their business. But we know the efforts will benefit us too. So, in serving our vendors we serve ourselves. We know we can count on them for help in an emergency.

Local Communities

The fourth group in our circle is our local communities. We must give not only our money, but more important, our time, to help the local schools, and neighborhoods, to keep our streets safe, our bridges repaired, our communities healthy. By serving this way we create good living places for our employees and visitors.

Shareholders

Who is the fifth group we serve in this continuous wheel? The shareholders, of course, because they have given us the financial means to run our business, and we must give them an excellent return on their investment. We must also generate the capital to keep renewing our business. Without profit to renew, our organization would die and no one would be served, so we must survive independently and flourish. Then we can have a continuous flow around the wheel.

Balance Is Essential

Sometimes we depict this circle more simply as a triangle with customers, employees, and shareholders as the three sides. Balance among all three sides is essential. Too much focus on profit, and the other groups are threatened. Too much focus on job security, and corporate survival may be threatened. Balance is the key.

The management that says, "It's really only the bottom line that counts" makes the dollar its value system. This "bottom line only" value system doesn't guide typical daily decisions. If we say it's only the bottom line that counts, what might the shipping clerk do at the end of the quarter when a defective product is noticed? He ships it. Without this value system what might a vice-president do at the first sign of a business slowdown? He lays off the factory workers without exploring other options first.

The circle or triangle can be easily remembered and used by everyone in the organization. It can help answer those daily questions that come up about what to do. No more asking the boss what to do on every issue. No more making only the short-term dollar driven decision. When the tough decision to guard the short-term is necessary, it is a shared commitment from everyone in the group based on their trust and open dialogue.

Money becomes only a measurement vehicle for one element, profit. Other measures can be used for the other people connected to the business, measures like market share, defect rates, employee attitudes, attrition, and so on.

Similarly, in government aren't we seeking servant-leaders who can be trusted to lead us toward our collective visions in ways that benefit us, not their place in history, or their own need for power and influence?

There is no doubt in my mind that this value system is enormously helpful in guiding people in their daily decisions. And the guiding principles are based on creating value for people, serving them in a balanced way, seeing their relationships to each other.

A Special Synergy

But where do we go from here? What about the servant-leader and the future? We can lead by serving. We can help people move closer to achieving their potential. Does it stop there? No. The most exciting phase of all comes once we have this recognition. Why? Because the future focus won't be on the leader. It won't even be on the vision. The future focus can be on the group, the team, the small institutions inside the large institutions. And it's here that a literal transcendence can occur.

Why does the leader serve the group? We said to "create value" for them. The leader doesn't serve himself or herself because the group, including the leader, is better than the leader alone or the leader without committed followers. The group has essence greater than the sum of its parts. I hesitate to use an overworked word, but "synergy" is the only way to describe it. Life is not a zero-sum game. It is not, "I win, so you must lose," not plus one here, minus one there, and the total equals zero. In this kind of committed group led by a servant-leader, we have more than a zero-sum game, even more than 2 + 2 equals 4. It's here we can spiral up to 2 + 2 equals 5, 10, or 100.

Creativity, as Erteszek showed me, is stimulated by the group. It's the collective thought processes which then stimulate new impulses in those brains of ours to "innovations." There is so much untapped in our minds, but we'll only get a small part unlocked in isolation from each other. Yes, we need quiet time to reflect and understand. But we'll evolve to new plateaus when we spark each other in our interactions. Our dialogues will challenge each other to new heights.

The human potential movement has long focused on helping us achieve our individual potential. But the capability of the group or the team to soar to new heights is even more exciting.

Why should the leader serve? To create value for the group of which he or she is a member. Then all are better off. Our world is a set of relationships. The servant-leader can build institutions by welding teams of teams together and helping them lift themselves to new plateaus. The true leader will facilitate this process, like the midwife assisting at birth. That can only be done inside the institutions, where leadership can exist in every department, class, or section. One can't serve the followers by criticizing from the outside of the institution. One must patiently, caringly, carefully facilitate the process from within by serving. Each of us can do that. Leaders can exist throughout the organization, with each of us being a personal role model. For the servant-leader who has the capacity to be a builder, one of the greatest joys to be experienced is in building.

This process can be very difficult. We are used to power, toughness, and decisiveness. Servant-leaders must endure a great deal of abuse. Flexibility is needed to bend and flow. Paradoxically, the soft touch will be the strongest. It will not be easy, but the strength will come from the united, committed, voluntary action of those who are led. There is absolutely no tough decision that can't be implemented by such a group of united, committed, volunteers under a servant-leader. Trustees will be needed to watch out for the drug effect of power in the leader, but the servant-leader is the key.

The more I learn, the more I realize that serving is the highest form of leadership and achievement. Through serving others completely and caring enough to facilitate their journey toward their true potential, we enable them, and we ennoble ourselves.

I see our institutions changing, from hierarchical chain of command groups with rigid rules led by superior, elitist bosses who direct the activities of subordinates seen as inferior to a whole new approach. I see an open, participative, entrepreneurial environment with loose flexible teams. I see a core set of values being well understood by everyone. I see a common venture with clear linkages to a shared vision, where value is created for people, where people see how they are connected, where they can grow and realize more of their innate potential. I see organizations with trust and caring, where work is a meaningful part of your life experience. And, most of all, I see servant-leaders guiding these institutions, servant-leaders at all levels throughout them.

And maybe if we begin doing that on a small scale with our departments, our classrooms, our parishes, the results will be so good that soon our towns, our states, and even our countries are guided by servant-leaders. Then our circle approach will really take the form of a globe, like the earth, to symbolize what humankind is truly capable of.

25

Meditations on Servant-Leadership

James B. Tatum

The words "servant leadership" bring a vision of softness to the minds of some of the uninitiated. Some see it as touchy-feely. Some see it as weak and ineffective. The fear of spiritual things makes it suspect for certain people. Life-long patterns of practicing leadership in an authoritative manner are ingrained for many. It is assumed that the way to lead is from a position of power; using that power seems to cause people to believe in their superiority. Until that assumption is challenged, little happens to change it. Oddly, the fact that tragic results occur from such leadership does not seem to change many people. They look for an explanation of failure in all the wrong places. Quite often, the solution comes through that special insight which says, "I didn't try hard enough." Renewed energy and commitment in pursuit of controlling power is the answer. Never mind that the effort is fatally flawed; hard work will overcome anything.

A healthy sign for the future is that more and more people have decided to take a look at something quite different. That look has resulted in a vision of leading through serving. The broadening vision of service sees leadership as demanding the skills of listening, consensus-making, ethical decision-making and conflict resolution. Such a vision sees the whole with the organization being an entity existing for all individuals to become more deeply people of quality. Such a view also would liken life to the ascent of a mountain with no peak. The climb is eternal and real elevation cannot occur for the group until all are immersed in the skills demanded of those who would lead, appropriately creating a base for the movement upward. The rarified atmosphere at higher levels in such an ascent can be a factor in shaping the organization into one which accepts changed ways of operating as the norm. Losing oneself in the beauty of togetherness for the worthy work of service to others seems to be the highest value to me.

The journey is not easy. The pathway is not level or smooth. The signs posted along the way become seductive as they suggest we revisit our former habitats of behavior. It is possible for the mind to move to embrace the memory of past behavioral patterns, blocking out all of the reasons we thought we had for starting a new journey.

These temptations can lead to a return to a commitment of coercive power. They can also lead to a modified approach to leadership which results from a person thinking, "I will give lip service to the words servant-leadership and I will let people be practioners up to a point." Such a decision comes from a person who is either practicing self-delusionment or chicanery. The former displays ignorance; the latter, premediated wrong-headedness. Both are destined for trouble.

Obviously, I am not trying to paint a picture of easy accomplishment, or to ignore the problems of the servant journey. I am attempting to be a realist who believes strongly that the commitment to (and practice of) servant-leadership is the way to go. Affirmation for the conviction comes to me when I identify the people I most admire, and the results of their work.

Near the end of a recent Servant-Leadership Conference, a new friend posed the question, "What have you learned as a result of this conference?" Inasmuch as I usually spend some time musing about an event like this, it was a premature question for me. However, the question elicited this response, "The fact that people are at different points in their journeys seems always to bring renewed affirmation of that reality in group processes like this one." My answer certainly was not profound. However, it helped me begin to identify some issues that demonstrated differences. It also gave me a chance to honor and celebrate diversity.

There was a special spirit present which was sensed by most of those in attendance. The very fact that this was the case, and the fact that people see and feel things quite differently (people are at different points in their journeys) heightened my awareness, once again, of our differences in understanding the issue of spirit and spirituality. Most of us can identify that something exists other than the material and the intellectual. We know that a special piece of connective tissue exists between people as they work together with common purposes. Perhaps the acknowledgment that something truly mystical is present allows us to acknowledge spirit and spirituality. People of diversity will, however, assess this phenomenon through the special filters created by their own experiences. It is observable that with some frequency one person's sense of the spirit is anathema to another. Rhetorically one could ask, "Does this mean that we are to be angry with each other forever because the noncorporeal side of ourselves is held to be absolute in our view? Is there nothing to learn in the spiritual realm from each other? Is there a definition of spirituality that allows the full spectrum of society to unite in service institutionally and individually?" Robert Greenleaf had this to say on the subject, in his essay titled, "Spirituality as Leadership":

> I take the first [definition] listed, in the dictionary I consulted, in defining spirit: that which is traditionally believed to be the vital principle or animating force within living beings. But that definition does not help establish spirituality as leadership unless one adds a value dimension to it. I would prefer to say that spirit is the animating force that disposes one to be a servant of others. The test is that those being served grow as persons; while being served they become healthier, wiser, freer, more autonomous, more likely themselves to become servants. And what is the effect on the least privileged in society? Will she or he benefit, or, at least, be not further deprived? No one will knowingly be hurt by the action, directly or indirectly.

Servant-leadership is not the special domain of any one religious group or any one profit or nonprofit group. It is the domain of those who are caught up in the spirit of service. The bond that ties us together is beautifully overarching as we heighten our awareness of the substantive and the mystical. To deny the spirit is to deny the fullness of our growth and that of others.

The R. K. Greenleaf Center was once called The Center for Applied Ethics. It is understandable why this title was chosen, because one cannot be in the role of legitimate leadership without the solid underpinning of ethical rightness. It would naturally follow that the leader would seek always to move to a higher level of ethical practice. As in all of life, ethical growth requires that we see things as wholly as possible and bring understanding that will result in a more ideal environment in which to help prepare people to live in an increasingly complex world.

Stimulated by the words of Gus Tyler, Assistant President and Political Director of the International Ladies' Garment Workers' Union, I have attempted a thought process that responds to the challenge and attempts to create a vision of ethical rightness. I do not claim exclusivity to this vision. It has wisely been said that there is nothing new in this world. For a surety, others have made this conceptual journey before I undertook it. It is true, however, that when we have that "aha!" moment—when the thought becomes our own—it is as fresh as the morning dew. Tyler, in addressing the issues of our day, concluded with these remarks:

> Finally, how can we overcome our tendency to focus narrowly and learn to widen our vision to absorb the myriad influences on people and societies coming from all parts of the universe? The answer may lie in our ability to conceptualize—to condense detailed data into abstractions, inventing a word or a formula that transforms into a simple, understandable unit a plethora of items.

Tyler's remarks touched me with resonance at the deepest level, and I committed to attempt to deal with the issue of ethics using such a process. Because I value so highly the work that Michael Josephson of the Josephson Institute for the Advancement of Ethics has done, I felt it was important to begin with his list of ethical values and principles. This is a list that people who are believers from all of the world's great religions can come to oneness about. For that matter, most people I have known who embrace no religious belief would also agree with these values. They are:

1. Honesty
2. Integrity
3. Promise-keeping
4. Fidelity
5. Fairness

6. Caring
7. Respect
8. Citizenship
9. Excellence
10. Accountability
11. Protection of the public trust

Contemplating these ethical values and principles with a view toward choosing those that seem more meaningful brings about deeper understanding of each of the values and how they are intertwined. It reveals that it is possible to include some values as part and parcel of another, and to determine which is transcendental. The exercise of identifying the most important one is bound to cause the chooser to have a more encompassing vision of what that singular choice means.

It is possible that such thinking will lead to another word or phrase that has a broader, deeper meaning than those listed above. I choose the word "trust" because it connects us all in a common but important way. It is a word that describes the results of actions conforming to all of the listed values. It brings both an experiential meaning and an intuitive one. Intuition in this case could be defined as a memory of the truth, carrying the ring of authenticity.

If trust is all that this writer believes that it is, it could well be viewed as an icon. To make an icon out of a word rather than an image—such as the Cross or the Star of David, among others—is a bit different, but appropriate nonetheless. The word as an image is representative of deeper, more complex understandings. The use of the word trust as an icon—with the ability to pull into the brain the full spectrum of ethical values with the mere thought of the word—seems altogether fitting, proper, and possible.

Think of it this way. Suppose every decision is prefaced with deliberate questions: "Will this build trust?" "Will it build long-term trust?" "How might it destroy trust?" Such a simple approach is not so simple. It really means that we have the obligation to train our minds to encompass all of the values with one vision and have an ability to apply the issue of building trust with wholeness.

The person who truly serves earns justifiable trust. Trust given and received creates the climate for service at the deepest level.

Afterword

Reflections on Robert K. Greenleaf

Newcomb Greenleaf

My father wrote his own epitaph:

Potentially a good plumber,
ruined by a sophisticated education.

We don't know how seriously he intended this, but after mulling it over we decided to go ahead and use it on his headstone.

Now, when I think back on his life, on my memories of growing up with him, of the many stories that he told, of the wisdom that he tried, with little success, to pass on to me, the epitaph seems to sum the life up in many ways. It's a nice expression of Bob's quirky and humorous modesty, turning the usual notions of achievement upside down. It says a lot about his intense and ambivalent attitude toward his own schooling and our modern educational system. And it speaks to the split between his practical, Midwestern upbringing and the life of ideas that he came to lead after leaving Terre Haute, Indiana.

In point of fact, Bob remained a reasonably good plumber, good enough to do all but the most difficult jobs around our house. And he enjoyed it. Until late in life he did not at all shrink from unclogging a drain, installing a new faucet, or just changing the washer in a leaky one.

He was also a fine carpenter. Many pieces of furniture in our house were his creations, hardwood tables beautifully assembled and meticulously finished. One of them remained in his last room at the Crosslands retirement community, in Kennett Square, Pennsylvania, and now sits in my study.

And he was very comfortable working with electricity. He had begun his telephone career as a lineman and used to tell of his last day on the poles. He was part of a crew which had been moving a telephone line back from a road to allow its expansion into a highway. That last day was cold and wet, and Bob spent much of it on top of a pole which had been moved, taking in slack that the move had created in the lines. The job had to be finished to avoid interrupting telephone service, so the crew worked well past dark. The continual small shocks that he received from the lines, which were still in operation, added to the overall discomfort. When finally done, he broke all the rules and slid down the pole. It was a memorable last day.

Perhaps it was his experiences on the poles which led to a fairly casual attitude about electric shock. I remember several occasions when jolts of 120 volts knocked him to the floor, blows which he regarded with apparent equanimity. Only later did I discover that such an attitude towards electricity was not at all universal.

My grandfather, George Washington Greenleaf, had been a master machinist who, for many years, ran the shops at Rose Polytechnic Institute (now Rose-Hulman Institute of Technology) in Terre Haute. While Bob was by day a thinker and leader, in the evenings and on week-ends he returned to his roots and worked with his hands. This transition was vividly and abruptly manifest in his dress. When he came back to our suburban home in Short Hills, New Jersey from a day at AT&T headquarters at 195 Broadway in New York City, he was the impeccably dressed executive, wearing a conservative suit. Invariably, his first act was to race upstairs and change into his old work clothes. Then, in the summer, he would go out to the large vegetable garden, which provided much of our cuisine during that season. In the winter he would head for his shop in the basement.

I was not so keen on weeding the garden, but I loved being with him in the shop. It was a magical center of my boyhood, both because of what it contained, and because of the extraordinary mastery which Bob displayed over the many crafts he practiced there. Whatever need arose, he had the right tool (from Bunsen burner to jigsaw to oscilloscope), the right part (stowed systematically away in an immense warren of drawers and boxes), and the skill to do the job well.

During the years after 1945 the surplus shops of lower Manhattan were full of marvelous electrical, optical, and mechanical devices from the second world war, elegantly finished with burnished brass, now being sold for a song. Week after week Bob would come home with a new treasure. Together we would disassemble these beauties, with the goal either of reassembling them in working order or salvaging prize parts from their innards.

Bob also made a great effort to bring me into his other world, to pass on some of the skills and wisdom that he had acquired at 195 Broadway. Often I accompanied him to the seventeenth floor of the AT&T building, and occasionally I went with him on trips to outposts like Chicago or Montreal. He passed numerous stories and aphorisms about the working life on to me. He had in mind the model of his father, who had involved Bob both in his mechanical work and his political career.

Many of Bob's stories involved accompanying his father to various work locations. These included meetings of the City Council and School Board of Terre Haute, on which his father served, and various factories where his father would repair heavy machinery, often with a single magical tap of a mallet or an immediate observation that something was incorrectly installed.

But Bob's effort to share his world of work with me was not particularly successful. His field of activity was far removed from our home, and what he was doing was rather abstract. To me at the time it seemed totally obscure and uninteresting. And I was defining myself in opposition to him, particularly over the issue of education. I embraced education for its own sake and went on to a career in mathematics, taking pride for many years in the "purity" and lack of application of my research. Only much later did I begin to take a serious interest in his work. From his papers I now know that he felt very keenly his failure to pass down his heritage to me.

He was particularly distrustful of education "for its own sake," and felt that he had learned little of use during his own college years. After two years at Rose Poly, where he discovered that he did not want to be an engineer, he went on to finish his studies at Carleton College. He was very disappointed in Carleton, which he found, in the 1920's, to be a rather frivolous place. Shortly after his graduation he had an opportunity to meet with Carleton's president and expressed this opinion in fairly strong language. "Surely, Mr. Greenleaf," responded the president, "you must have learned something useful during your years at Carleton." "Yes, I did," my father responded. "I learned how to make a little bit of work look like the result of a large effort."

But Bob did receive one priceless nugget from his years at Carleton which set the course of his life. He often told the story of the advice given by Professor Oscar Helming in a Sociology course taken during his last semester. During an otherwise dull lecture, Helming laid out a challenging suggestion: those who wanted to change the world for the better should work from the inside of large institutions. He pointed out that we were becoming a society dominated by such institutions, which were not serving us well, and which could only be fundamentally changed from the inside.

That advice set the course of Bob's life. After graduation he told the father of a classmate that he wanted to work for a large organization.

The response was that he should try to work for the largest company there was: AT&T. It was 1926 and Bob had never heard of AT&T, having always lived in areas served by independent telephone companies. But the classmate's father had a contact in Ohio Bell, and soon Bob was learning the telephone business from the ground up on a line crew in Youngstown.

He used to say, in some seriousness, that an essential element of his career with AT&T was that he couldn't type and hated drafting. Several times when he was newly-hired he was asked to do some typing, but his two-finger hunt-and-peck technique quickly got him reassigned to more interesting work.

Soon Bob was dealing with the management training issues that were to occupy him through his AT&T career. He led training groups for foremen, teaching them how to train their craftsmen. At one point he even developed a technique for teaching algebra to workers who were dealing with more sophisticated equipment which required some mathematical skills. While his methods were very successful, they depended on the high motivation of the workers, so he concluded that they would not work in a typical school setting.

Except for a few early years at AT&T Bob held only jobs which did not exist before he had them. His role within the company was open and he clearly came to like it that way. He loved to tell how the president of AT&T, when asked what was Bob's role, replied that he was AT&T's "kept revolutionary." Bob was both highly appreciated and viewed with some alarm.

I recall my excitement at hearing one day that Bob had been offered a title of "Vice-President" of AT&T. At last I would have something definite to tell my friends about what my father did! But my excitement was short lived, for Bob added that he had convinced his superiors that his work would be more effective if he did not have that title. He tried to explain that a title could circumscribe and limit as much or more than it gave power and authority. This was many years before he read *Journey to the East,* but it eerily foreshadows the figure of Leo, who had no title but servant.

There was another, darker side to his rejection of titles. This was that he did not feel himself to be a part of the group of AT&T executives in a whole-hearted way. He often contrasted his feelings at AT&T with those he had in high school, and at Ohio Bell.

His high school years stood out for him as a golden time when he felt totally in harmony with his group, and comfortably at the center of the "in crowd." He was treasurer of his junior class and president of the senior class of 300 at Wiley High School. He was also very active in the HiY club, and HiY was the source of a remarkable transformation which took place at the school during Bob's senior year.

The principal of Wiley was a very unpopular figure, stiff and remote, with a bad limp, and the constant butt of student jokes. At the end of their junior year the members of HiY decided that negative feelings about the principal were casting a pall on their school experience and decided to try and change it. They resolved to go out of their way to express positive feelings toward the old principal, even to dedicate their yearbook to him. Since this group included most of the key student leaders, they quickly effected a great change in attitude in the school, which led to an even greater change in the old principal himself, who seemed to mellow and was often seen with a cheerful smile. It was an inspiring example of changing an institution from within.

After graduating from Wiley and leaving Terre Haute, Bob never again found a true community immediately around him. Ohio Bell perhaps came close, but the sympathetic culture which he found there had died out at AT&T when he arrived in New York in 1929. This feeling of alienation was particularly reflected in where our family lived. My parents met in the city and lived there for seven years, with one year spent in Mt. Kisco in Westchester County. But then they moved to New Jersey, where they lived from 1941 until after Bob retired from AT&T in 1964.

My sisters and I were not very fond of New Jersey, and we used to ask our parents why they had chosen to move there. The reason was simple. Most AT&T executives lived in Westchester. If we had lived there Bob would have been drawn into a social life with them which he scorned. It would have been awkward to fail to show up at the cocktail parties and club events. But, living in New Jersey, he could be totally removed from it all.

So my parents created, over the years, their own community of close friends. A few were telephone people, but most were from other arenas: writers, artists, theologians, business philosophers. My mother, Esther Hargrave Greenleaf, provided a balance to Bob in their social life. Where he was temperamentally rather shy and quiet, she was warm and gregarious. It is time for me to say something of her role in Bob's work.

My parents were unusually tightly bound together. Both played major roles in the others' work. To support Esther's painting and pottery Bob stretched and framed canvases, built and maintained kilns and other equipment, and, as his aesthetic sensibilities deepened, became an involved appreciator and critic. I should add that this was not always true. When they met in 1931, Esther, fresh from a year in Paris, was full of enthusiasm for abstract art. Bob, fresh from the Midwest, had no doubt that modern art was a bad joke, an outlook which he eventually outgrew.

My mother's role in Bob's work was not quite so evident. Primarily, she was his intellectual scout. She was a voracious and energetic reader, who always had several books going, ranging from biography and religion to thrillers. Bob read only what was clearly useful to him. On many occasions he felt the need to broaden his understanding in a new area. Esther would set out and read her way through it, recommending the essential books to Bob. While I don't know this, it is likely that it was she who first read *Journey to the East* and recommended it on to Bob as a book not to be missed.

Over the years I am sure that my father tried many times to pass on to me some of what he had learned. While I generally paid little attention, one lesson was so surprising that it did stick in my mind. "Suppose that you had a really good idea for your organization. How would you go about trying to get it accepted?" It must have seemed a strange question to me, and I don't recall how I responded. "This is how I have learned to do it," said Bob. "First, decide who are the key people in getting the idea adopted. Then begin to tell them the idea, but only suggestively and a bit at a time. Let them come to the idea themselves, so that they think that it is their own idea." "But how will they know that it really was your idea?" I asked. "They will never know," he answered, as if that were the core of the beauty of the stratagem. Again, one thinks immediately of Leo.

Bob always brought a historical perspective to his analyses. The name of Theodore N. Vail, the president of AT&T from 1907 to 1920 was familiar to me in my childhood. Bob regarded Vail as a great statesman and lamented that subsequent management had lacked the breadth of vision that Vail provided. He was particularly appalled that the managers of AT&T, including the president, had little sense of the history of the company and barely knew who Vail was. When John Brooks wrote a popular official history of AT&T, *The Telephone*, for the 100th anniversary in 1976, he was directed to Bob, then living in Peterborough, New Hampshire, for a historical perspective which no one in the company could provide.

By the time Bob retired from AT&T and launched his second career of teaching, consulting, and writing, I was long gone from the nest, with a family of my own, often living across the continent. So I have fewer personal memories of that part of his life. But his involvement with the Ford Foundation in India was so exotic that I did hear a lot about it.

At first, Bob was very enthusiastic about his work in India. From the viewpoint of a Western businessman the inefficiencies and disorganization of Indian commerce were painfully evident. What better way to help than to show how things should be done? One aspect of the project involved creating a Western-style business school, sort of a Harvard Business School on the Ganges.

But this turned out to be not such a great idea. Bob became increasingly disillusioned with the project, and, in the end, he felt that he had learned a painful but useful lesson about arrogance. He and the Ford Foundation had gone to India with the idea that they had a great deal to teach and nothing much to learn. They encountered a culture that was much older than ours and which, in many ways, was wiser and subtler than he and his colleagues could appreciate. The project was doomed from the start.

It his later years my father became increasingly disillusioned with the direction that AT&T had taken. When asked how he felt about

AT&T he would often growl "When I worked for them, there were 1,000 people on the staff at central headquarters. Now they have 1,000 lawyers there." He felt that the company had lost its unique and great vision and instead was trying, in the modern corporate manner, to maximize profit by taking advantage of every legal loophole and technicality.

My parents had always been completely clear about funeral arrangements. They would be cremated. There would be no public funeral, only a small memorial service for friends and family. Several months after my mother's death, my father told me that he had had a change of heart. He wanted to be buried in Terre Haute, in the same cemetery as his father. This was such an unexpected announcement that I queried him repeatedly for several weeks. Was this really what he wanted? And indeed he was firmly resolved. So the epitaph that he wrote can be found on a simple headstone in the Highland Cemetery in Terre Haute, marking the return of a simple Hoosier who, though never totally comfortable in the wider world had, in his quiet way, served.

Notes

Chapter 3

1. "A View of Managerial Ethics," p. 1, 1959.
2. "Ethics in Business," p. 1, undated.
3. Untitled, undated book manuscript, p. 6.
4. "Suggested Introductory Notes on Ethical Implications of Business Action," p. 3, undated.
5. Letters from George Greenleaf to his son, Robert Greenleaf, 3 December 1926 and 13 November 1928.
6. "The Search and the Seeker," p. 3, 4 April 1966.
7. Untitled, undated book manuscript, p. 2.
8. "Servant, Retrospect and Prospect," p. 2, 1980, 1988.
9. Untitled, undated book manuscript, pp. 3–4.
10. "The Institution as Servant," p. 1, 1972, 1976.
11. "The Search and the Seeker," p. 1, 4 April 1966.
12. *Ibid,* p. 2.
13. "A View of Managerial Ethics," p. 3, 1959.
14. *Ibid,* p. 1.
15. "A View of Managerial Ethics," p. 1, 1959; untitled, undated book manuscript, p. 7.
16. *Ibid,* p. 12.
17. *Ibid,* p. 13.
18. *Ibid,* p. 16.

19. "The Servant as Leader," p. 16, 1991.
20. Untitled, undated book manuscript, p. 46.
21. *Ibid,* p. 45.
22. "A View of Managerial Ethics," pp. 17–18.
23. Untitled, undated book manuscript, p. 47.
24. *Ibid,* p. 47.
25. *Ibid.*
26. *Ibid.*
27. *Ibid,* p. 54.
28. "The Ethic of Strength," p. 5.
29. *Ibid,* p. 12.
30. "Ethics in Business," p. 1, undated.
31. "Suggested Introductory Notes on Ethical Implications of Business Action," pp. 1, 4, undated.
32. *Ibid,* p. 3.
33. *Ibid,* p. 5.
34. "An Observer's View of the Chief Executive Officer's Role," p. 10, 1978.
35. "Servant, Retrospect, and Prospect, p. 31, 1980, 1988.
36. "An Observer's View of the Chief Executive Officer's Role," pp. 10, 12, 25, 1978.
37. *Ibid,* pp. 16, 19, 20, 24.
38. "Servant, Retrospect and Prospect," pp. 30-31, 1980, 1988.

Published Greenleaf Works Cited

"Advices to Servants," Robert K. Greenleaf Center, 1975, 1991.

"The Institution as Servant," Robert K. Greenleaf Center, 1972, 1976.

"The Servant as Leader," Robert K. Greenleaf Center, 1991.

"Servant: Retrospect and Prospect," Robert K. Greenleaf Center, 1980, 1988.

Unpublished Greenleaf Manuscripts Cited

"A View of Managerial Ethics," 1959.

"An Observer's View of the Chief Executive Officer's Role: Some Aspects of What It Might Be." for Business Roundtable, December 1978.

Correspondence from George Greenleaf to Robert K. Greenleaf - 3 December 1926 and 13 November 1928.

"The Ethic of Strength," no date.

"Ethics in Business," no date.

"The Search and the Seeker," 4 April 1966.

"Suggested Introductory Notes on Ethical Implications of Business Action," no date.

Untitled, undated book manuscript.

Chapter 5

1. This address is a revision of a paper entitled "The Evolution of the Servant Leadership Idea and Some Implications" given as part of the Spring Research Colloquia on February 11, 1988 at the School of Business Administration, The University of Western Ontario, London, Canada. The author wishes to thank his colleagues (particularly, Professor Al Mikalachki) for their constructive comments and suggestions. He also wishes to acknowledge with thanks the useful suggestions of Mr. Paul M. Olson, president of the Blandin Foundation.
2. These remarkable sessions were funded by the generosity of John Musser, who maintained a long interest in the work of Robert K. Greenleaf.
3. As much as I understood the variety of his interactions, it was still highly revealing to go through 10 years of his calendar/diaries to examine the range of people with whom he had met *after* the servant essays had been widely distributed. Even with his winnowing out the merely curious, the variety of people he engaged was staggering. The pattern of increasing attention to people connected to religious organizations also emerged and is, of course, consistent with the writing he did about seminaries and the increasing importance he has placed on spirit and its nurturance.
4. This is one of the ways Bob managed to stay young throughout his life. When I first met him, he was more in tune with the major influences on the current generation's thinking than were many of that generation; 25 years later it was equally true. Only in the past three or four years when he has deliberately withdrawn from activity in favor of meditation has he started to be out of touch with thinking among the young. He has clearly demonstrated the seeking and prophetic behavior which he himself advocated in *The Servant as Leader*.
5. The Niagara Institute is a non-profit organization in Niagara-on-the-Lake, Ontario, Canada, which sponsors a wide variety of leadership development programs. One of the distinctive features of the Institute is its practice of bringing executives of various sectors (private, government, labor and non-governmental organizations) together in their programs.
6. The Liberal Party in Canada is one of three main political parties.
7. It is not by chance, I think, that the organizations Bob cites as inspiring these ideas are European, where group orientations are more dominant in the various cultures. Similarly, when I introduce the ideas from his second essay in Asian countries which also have more group-oriented values, they are received

with much more openness and approval. The huge Indian conglomerate, the Birla Company, for example, is organized and run at the top on *primus inter pares* principles.

8. Bob sees a business statesman as a person able to see ahead, to recognize the major forces affecting the business and to manage to accommodate to these realities before adaptation becomes impossible, either because the forces have become too strong or the organization has become too rigid.
9. In this regard many readers of the essays have noted that their internal structure follows a similarly intuitive pattern, which some have difficulty in following. Rev. Raymond Baumhart, a devotee of Greenleaf's writing, reported his initial frustration in reading the essays in an interesting way. He said that as a Jesuit, he had been trained to think, and write, in a logical, linear, deductive way. But reading Bob was a different experience which he described as being like "jumping from the edge of a lake and discovering a rock just under the surface, which you land on. You repeat the process and discover another safe landing after the next jump!" He said that after several "jumps," he realized that Bob often ended up in a place similar to that reached by deductive reasoning. Once he realized that, he felt more comfortable with Bob's approach and could take the first jump in reading a new essay with the faith that he would end up in a valuable place.
10. He has written an unpublished essay entitled "Inner-City Churches" about what is possible, using these two churches as examples.

Chapter 6

References

Benner, S. (1984, August). Three companies in search of an author. *INC. Magazine,* pp. 49–55.

Camus, A. (1961). *Resistance, Rebellion and Death.* New York: Alfred A. Knopf.

Greenleaf, R. K. (1977). *Servant Leadership: A Journey into the Nature of Legitimate Power and Greatness.* New York: Paulist Press.

Hesse, H. (1956). *Journey to the East.* New York: The Noonday Press.

Peters, T. J. & Waterman, R. H. Jr. (1982). *In Search of Excellence, Lessons From America's Best-Run Companies.* New York: Harper and Row.

Stogdill, R. M. (1974). *Handbook of Leadership: A Survey of Theory and Research.* New York: Free Press.

Chapter 7

For further information on FCE's services contact: The Foundation For Community Encouragement, P.O. Box 449, Ridgefield, CT 06877, Phone: 203/431-9484.

Chapter 9

References

Dossey, Larry. *Space, Time & Medicine.* Boston: New Science Library, 1984.

Greenleaf, Robert K. *The Servant as Leader.* Indianapolis, Indiana: Robert K. Greenleaf Center, 1991

McGee-Cooper, Ann and Trammell, Duane. *Time Management for Unmanageable People.* New York: Bantam Books, 1994.

This article was taken from a work-in-progress *Time Management and Becoming a High-Performing Team* by Ann McGee-Cooper, Ed. D. with Duane Trammell.

Chapter 16

1. Chris Argyris and Donald A. Schon well addressed this experienced condition in their book *Theory in Practice: Increasing Professional Effectiveness* (1974), where they proclaimed "theories are vehicles for explanation, prediction, or control."

References

Chris Argyris and Donald A. Schon, *Theory in Practice: Increasing Professional Effectiveness;* Jossey-Bass, 1974.

James L. Hayes, *Memos For Management: People, The Reason And The Key,* AMACOM, 1983.

John Naisbitt, *Megatrends,* New York; Warner, 1982.

Chapter 17

References

Italics based on passages from Robert K. Greenleaf, *The Servant as Leader,* Indianapolis: Robert K. Greenleaf Center, 1991.

Bennis, Warren and Burt Nanus, *Leaders: Strategies for Taking Charge,* New York: Harper & Row, 1986.

Block, Peter, *Stewardship,* San Francisco: Berrett-Koehler Publishers, 1993.

Castaneda, Carlos, *Tales of Power,* New York: Washington Square Press, 1986.

Covey, Steven, *The Seven Habits of Highly Effective People,* New York: Simon & Schuster, 1992.

DePree, Max, *Leadership Jazz,* New York: Dell Publishing, 1992.

Foster, Steven and Meredith Little, *The Book of the Vision Quest,* New York: Simon and Schuster, 1992.

Kouzes, James and Barry Posner, *The Leadership Challenge: How To Get Extraordinary Things Done in Organizations,* San Francisco: Jossey-Bass Publishers, 1990.

Nanus, Burt, *Visionary Leadership,* San Francisco: Jossey-Bass Publishers, 1992.

Stern, Jesse, Editor-in-chief, *The Random House Collegiate Dictionary,* New York: Random House, 1968.

Chapter 21

References

Block, Peter. *The Empowered Manager.* San Francisco: Jossey-Bass Publishers, 1987.

Block, Peter. *Stewardship: Putting Service Ahead of Self Interest.* San Francisco: Berrett-Koehler Publishers, 1993.

Campbell, Joseph with Bill Moyers. *The Power of Myth.* New York: Mystic Fire Video, Inc., 1988.

Crichton, Michael. *Jurassic Park.* New York: Ballantine Books, 1990.

Davis, Stanley. *Future Perfect.* Reading, MA.: Addison-Wesley Publishers, 1987.

Gleick, James. *Chaos: Making a New Science.* New York: Viking, 1987.

Pfeffer, Jeffrey. *Power in Organizations.* New York: Harper Business, 1981.

Senge, Peter. *The Fifth Discipline: The Art and Practice of the Learning Organization.* New York: Doubleday/Currency, 1990.

Thompson, Gregg and Sue Dutton. "Mythological Inquiry: Finding the Music that Organizations Dance To," *OD Practitioner,* Fall 1993.

Greenleaf, Robert. *Servant Leadership: A Journey into the Nature of Legitimate Power and Greatness.* New York: Paulist Press, 1977.

Mintzberg, Henry. "Organizational Design: Fashion or Fit?", *Harvard Business Review,* volume 59, 1981.

Waldrop, M. Mitchell. *Complexity: The Emerging Science at the Edge of Order and Chaos.* New York: Touchstone, 1992.

Wheatley, Margaret. *Leadership and the New Science: Learning About Organization from an Orderly Universe.* San Francisco: Berrett-Koehler Publishers, 1992.

Zukav, Gary. *The Dancing Wu Li Masters.* New York: William Morrow, 1979.

Permissions and Copyrights

The Foreword is an original essay created for this collection by Max DePree. Copyright © 1995 Max DePree. Printed with permission of the author.

The Introduction, "Servant-Leadership and The Greenleaf Legacy," is an original essay created for this collection by Larry Spears. Copyright © 1995 Larry Spears. Printed with permission of the author.

Chapter 1 is an edited version of "Life's Choices and Markers," by Robert K. Greenleaf, copyright © 1986 by The Greenleaf Center. Reprinted by permission of The Greenleaf Center.

Chapter 2, "Reflections from Experience," is edited from an unpublished manuscript by Robert K. Greenleaf, as contained in the Greenleaf Archives. Copyright © 1995 by The Greenleaf Center. It is used with the permission of the Franklin Trask Library, Andover Newton Theological Seminary and The Greenleaf Center.

Chapter 3, "Robert K. Greenleaf and Business Ethics: There is No Code," is an original essay created for this collection by Anne Fraker. Copyright © 1995 Anne Fraker. Printed with permission of the author. Quotes from materials contained in the Greenleaf Archives appear with the permission of the Franklin Trask Library, Andover Newton Theological Seminary and The Greenleaf Center.

Chapter 4 is an edited version of "Claiming Servant-Leadership as Your Heritage," by Carl Rieser, copyright © 1988 by The Greenleaf Center. Reprinted with permission of the author and The Greenleaf Center.

Chapter 5 is an edited version of "Tracing the Vision and Impact of Robert K. Greenleaf," by Joseph DiStefano, copyright © 1988 by The

Greenleaf Center. Reprinted by permission of the author and The Greenleaf Center.

Chapter 6 is an edited version of "The Strategic Toughness of Servant-Leadership," by Dennis Tarr. It first appeared in the Autumn, 1985 issue of *Continuum*, the Journal of the National University Continuing Education Association. Reprinted by permission of the author and The Greenleaf Center.

Chapter 7, "Servant-Leadership Training and Discipline in Authentic Community," is adapted from a keynote address by M. Scott Peck, M.D., P.C. at the Greenleaf Center's 1993 Servant-Leadership Conference. Copyright © 1995 M. Scott Peck. Printed by permission of the author.

Chapter 8, "The Search for Spirit in the Workplace," by Ron Zemke and Chris Lee is reprinted with permission from the June 1993 issue of *Training* magazine. Copyright © 1993. Lakewood Publications, Minneapolis, MN. All rights reserved.

Chapter 9, "Servant-Leadership: Is There Really Time for It?," is taken from a work-in-progress, *Time Management and Becoming a High-Performing Team* by Ann McGee-Cooper, Ed.D. with Duane Trammell. Copyright © 1994. Printed by permission of Ann McGee-Cooper and Duane Trammell.

Chapter 10, "The Leader as Servant," by Walter Kiechel III first appeared in the May 4, 1992 issue of *Fortune* magazine. Copyright © 1992 Time Inc. All rights reserved. Reprinted by permission of *Fortune* magazine.

Chapter 11, "Some Executives Are Trying to Make Companies Heed a Higher Authority," by Edward Iwata is reprinted with permission of *The Orange County Register*, copyright © 1993.

Chapter 12, "First Among Equals," by Deborah Brody first appeared in the September/October 1992 issue of *Foundation News*. Copyright © 1992. Reprinted with permission of *Foundation News* and the Council on Foundations.

Chapter 13, "Servant-Leadership and Corporate Risk Taking: When Risk Taking Makes a Difference," is an original essay created for this collection by Sheila Murray Bethel. Copyright © 1995 Sheila Murray Bethel. Printed by permission of the author.

Chapter 14, "Becoming a Servant-Leader: The Personal Development Path," is an original essay created for this collection by Isabel Lopez. Copyright © 1995 Isabel Lopez. Printed by permission of the author.

Chapter 15, "Managing Toward the Millenium," by James Hennessy, John Killian and Suki Robins is adapted from a talk given at the 1989 World Management Congress. An earlier version first appeared in *Managing Toward The Millenium,* edited by James E. Hennessy and Suki Robins. Copyright © 1991 NYNEX. Reprinted by permission of NYNEX and the authors.

Chapter 16, "Team-Building and Servant-Leadership," is an original essay created for this collection by Phil Chamberlain. Copyright © 1995 Phil Chamberlain. Printed by permission of the author.

Chapter 17, "Power and Passion: Finding Personal Purpose," is an original essay created for this collection by Juana Bordas. Copyright © 1995 Juana Bordas. Printed by permission of the author.

Chapter 18, "The New Leadership," by Michael Kelley appeared in the January 26, 1993 issue of *The Commercial Appeal.* Copyright © 1994, *The Commercial Appeal,* Memphis, Tenn. Used with permission.

Chapter 19, "Servant-Leadership: A Pathway to the Emerging Territory," is an original essay created for this collection by Richard W. Smith. Copyright © 1995 Richard W. Smith. Printed by permission of the author.

Chapter 20, "Robert Greenleaf's Legacy: A New Foundation for Twenty-First Century Institutions," is adapted from a keynote address by Peter M. Senge at the Greenleaf Center's 1992 Servant-Leadership Conference. Copyright © 1995 Peter M. Senge. Printed by permission of the author.

Chapter 21, "Chaos, Complexity and Servant-Leadership," is an original essay created for this collection by Jeff McCollum. Copyright © 1995 Jeff McCollum. Printed by permission of the author.

Chapter 22, "Pyramids, Circles, and Gardens: Stories of Implementing Servant-Leadership," is an original essay created for this collection by Don Frick. Copyright © 1995 Don Frick. Printed by permission of the author.

Chapter 23, "Creating a Culture of Servant-Leadership: A Real Life Story," is an original essay created for this collection by Tina Rasmussen. Copyright © 1995 Tina Rasmussen. Printed by permission of the author.

Chapter 24, "Servant Leadership and the Future," by Robert Vanourek. Copyright © 1988 The Greenleaf Center. Reprinted by permission of the author and The Greenleaf Center.

Chapter 25, "Meditations on Servant-Leadership," by James B. Tatum, is adapted from several columns which originally appeared in *The Servant-Leader*—the newsletter of The Greenleaf Center. Reprinted by permission of the author and The Greenleaf Center.

The Afterword, "Reflections on Robert K. Greenleaf," is an original essay created for this collection by Newcomb Greenleaf. Copyright © 1995 Newcomb Greenleaf. Printed by permission of the author.

Recommended Reading

Block, Peter. *Stewardship.* San Francisco: Berrett-Koehler, 1993.

Cheshire, Ashley. *A Partnership of the Spirit.* Dallas: TDIndustries, 1987.

DePree, Max. *Leadership is an Art.* New York: Doubleday, 1989.

DePree, Max. *Leadership Jazz.* New York: Dell Publishing, 1992.

Greenleaf, Robert K. *Advices to Servants.* Indianapolis: The Robert K. Greenleaf Center, 1991.

Greenleaf, Robert K. *Education and Maturity.* Indianapolis: The Robert K. Greenleaf Center, 1988.

Greenleaf, Robert K. *Have You a Dream Deferred.* Indianapolis: The Robert K. Greenleaf Center, 1988.

Greenleaf, Robert K. *The Institution as Servant.* Indianapolis: The Robert K. Greenleaf Center, 1976.

Greenleaf, Robert K. *The Leadership Crisis.* Indianapolis: The Robert K. Greenleaf Center, 1978.

Greenleaf, Robert K. *Life's Choices and Markers.* Indianapolis: The Robert K. Greenleaf Center, 1986.

Greenleaf, Robert K. *My Debt to E.B. White.* Indianapolis: The Robert K. Greenleaf Center, 1987.

Greenleaf, Robert K. *Old Age: The Ultimate Test of Spirit.* Indianapolis: The Robert K. Greenleaf Center, 1987.

Greenleaf, Robert K. *Seminary as Servant.* Indianapolis: The Robert K. Greenleaf Center, 1983.

Greenleaf, Robert K. *Servant Leadership.* New York: Paulist Press, 1977.

Greenleaf, Robert K. *The Servant as Leader.* Indianapolis: The Robert K. Greenleaf Center, 1991.

Greenleaf, Robert K. *The Servant as Religious Leader.* Indianapolis: The Robert K. Greenleaf Center, 1982.

Greenleaf, Robert K. *Servant: Retrospect and Prospect.* Indianapolis: The Robert K. Greenleaf Center, 1980.

Greenleaf, Robert K. *Spirituality as Leadership.* Indianapolis: The Robert K. Greenleaf Center, 1988.

Greenleaf, Robert K. *Teacher as Servant: A Parable.* Indianapolis: The Robert K. Greenleaf Center, 1987.

Greenleaf, Robert K. *Trustees as Servants.* Indianapolis: The Robert K. Greenleaf Center, 1990.

Hennessy, James E. and Suki Robins, editors. *Managing Toward the* Millenium. New York: Fordham University Press, 1991.

Hesse, Hermann. *The Journey to the East.* New York: The Noonday Press, 1992.

Kelley, Robert. *The Power of Followership: How to Create Leaders People Want to Follow . . . And Followers Who Lead Themselves.* New York: Doubleday/Currency, 1992.

Kouzes, James M. and Barry Z. Posner. *Credibility: How Leaders Gain and Lose It, Why People Demand It.* San Francisco: Jossey-Bass Publishers, 1993.

Liebig, James E. *Business Ethics: Profiles in Civic Virtue.* Golden, Co.: Fulcrum Publishing, 1991.

McGee-Cooper, Ann, Duane Trammell and Barbara Lau. *You Don't Have To Go Home From Work Exhausted!* New York: Bantam Books, 1992.

Peck, M. Scott. *The Road Less Traveled.* New York: Simon & Schuster, 1978.

Peck, M. Scott. *A World Waiting To Be Born: Civility Rediscovered.* New York: Bantam, 1993.

Renesch, John, editor. *Leadership in a New Era*. San Francisco: New Leaders Press, 1994.

Renesch, John, editor. *New Traditions in Business: Spirit and Leadership in the 21st Century*. San Francisco: Berrett-Koehler Publishers, 1992.

Rieser, Carl. *The Trusteed Corporation: A Case Study of the Townsend & Bottum Family of Companies*. Indianapolis: The Robert K. Greenleaf Center, 1988.

Senge, Peter M. *The Fifth Discipline: The Art and Practice of the Learning Organization*. New York: Doubleday/Currency, 1990.

Contributors

Sheila Murray Bethel, CPAE, is a business consultant, the best-selling author of *Making a Difference, 12 Qualities That Make You a Leader* and an internationally acclaimed lecturer. She is the founder and co-chair of the Bethel Leadership Institute based in the San Francisco Bay Area. She has served on the adjunct faculty of Indiana-Purdue University and San Francisco State University. Ms. Murray Bethel is the recipient of the CPAE award, the highest honor for excellence in speaking given by the National Speakers Association.

Juana Bordas is a Senior Program Associate with the Center for Creative Leadership in Colorado Springs. She has 15 years' experience managing nonprofit corporations and building partnerships with the private sector to support innovative social programs. This includes being the founding president and CEO of the National Hispana Leadership Institute (NHLI), and a founder and executive director of Mi Casa Women's Center in Denver, Colorado. Juana has written several publications that foster diversity and pluralism in America, most recently *Follow the Leader: Women's Ways of Mentoring*. She has been honored as a Wise Woman by the National Center for Women and Policy Studies. She also was chosen a "Wonderwoman" by the Wonderwoman Foundation in 1984 because of her contributions to women and because "her vision weaves ancient wisdom with new hope."

Deborah Brody is the Director of Private Foundation Services at the Council on Foundations. As the Council on Foundation's Director of Research from 1986 to 1990, she managed several studies on foundation management, including topics such as investments, compensation and benefits, and grant and program evaluation. In 1990, Ms. Brody started the Council's private foundation services division, which includes services such as board development and training, management assistance, and publications and other resources for family and private foundations. She is currently directing the Council's Family Philanthropy Initiative as well. Prior to joining the Council's staff, Ms. Brody worked for a U.S. Senator and for a public policy research firm. She is the author of numerous articles and publications on foundations and family philanthropy.

Dr. Philip C. Chamberlain, Ph.D., is a professor at Indiana University, Department of Leadership and Policies Study, School of Education; and adjunct professor of Philanthropic Studies, I.U. Center on Philanthropy. He has assisted many institutions as a development advisor, and as a board trustee. Chamberlain also serves as Provost for the Institute for Professional Studies, located in St. Louis, Missouri, an external degree program dedicated to leadership development.

Joseph J. DiStefano is a Professor of Business Administration, School of Business Administration at the University of Western Ontario, where he has also served as Associate Dean, Human Resources. He is also an Adjunct Professor at IMEDE International Management Development Institute in Lausanne, Switzerland. Professor DiStefano's special field of interest is international business with particular attention to management problems rooted in cultural differences. He and a colleague, Harry Lane, coauthored a book in this field, *International Management Behavior: From Policy to Practice,* published by PWS-Kent. His other interests include managing diversity, the development of interpersonal skills for managers and executive team effectiveness. His most recent book in the latter area is *Effective Managerial Action,* coauthored with three U.W.O. colleagues and published by Prentice-Hall Canada in June 1988. He is also active as a consultant engaging in assignments for multinational companies, universities, and governments in 17 countries in various parts of the world.

Anne Fraker is a member of the Greenleaf Center's staff since September 1992. She works with the archival materials from the Greenleaf Archives. She has undergraduate and graduate degrees from Indiana University, and is the author of several book reviews and articles on religion and American history. She is also the editor of *Religion and American Life: Resources* (University of Illinois Press, 1989).

Don Frick joined the Greenleaf Center staff in September 1992 and holds B.S. and Master of Divinity degrees. He has worked in radio as a deejay and creator of the radio series, "The Nineteenth State," a syndicated program about Indiana history. Don has also worked in television as a member of floor crews, director, producer, and on-air talent. He has also served as Director of Electronic Media for the Indianapolis Museum of Art, Director of Public Relations for Indiana Central University (now University of Indianapolis), a consultant on numerous national media projects, owner of his own production business, and a speaker and consultant. In 1993, The Pentera Group of Indianapolis published *Target Ethics,* a book authored by Don exploring ethical issues for insurance professionals. In addition to his work with the Greenleaf Center, Don writes and produces documentary, training, and promotional materials for national and local clients. Don was first introduced to Robert Greenleaf's writings by his mentor, Dr. Ann McGee-Cooper.

Newcomb Greenleaf has spent most of his life as a teacher. He began by teaching mathematics at Harvard, Rochester, and Texas. For a period he taught Buddhism at The Naropa Institute. More recently he has been teaching computer science, and is a former Professor of Computer Science at Columbia University, where he concentrated on teaching introductory courses for computer science majors and for the liberal arts. He serves on the Board of Trustees of The Robert K. Greenleaf Center, and on the staff of Dharmadhatu, a Buddhist meditation center in New York City.

Robert K. Greenleaf spent most of his organizational life in the field of management research, development, and education at AT&T. Just before his retirement as Director of Management Research there, he held a joint appointment as visiting lecturer at MIT's Sloan School of Management and at the Harvard Business School. In addition, he held teaching positions at both Dartmouth College and the University of Virginia. His consultancies included Ohio University, MIT, Ford Foundation, R.K. Mellon Foundation, Lilly Endowment, and the American Foundation for Management Research. As consultant to universities, businesses, foundations, and churches during the tumultuous 1960s and 1970s, his eclectic and wide-ranging curiosity, reading, and contemplation provided an unusual background for observing these institutions. As a lifelong student of organization, that is, how things get done, he distilled these observations in a series of essays on the theme of "Servant As Leader"—the objective of which was to stimulate thought and action for building a better, more caring society.

James E. Hennessy serves as Chairperson of the Board of Trustees, Adjunct Faculty Member and Executive Director of the Palisades Institute at Dominican College of Blauvelt (New York). In 1990, he retired early from NYNEX after 32 years and two dozen jobs, the last of which was Executive Vice-President. In that capacity, he had oversight of several NYNEX companies, had responsibility for having quality permeate the NYNEX family of companies, and served on the CEO's seven-person Management Committee. **John F. Killian** is Vice-President—Massachusetts for NYNEX New England. Mr. Killian has served on the boards of a number of civic, cultural, and charitable organizations, and chaired the Governor's Blue Ribbon Commission on Day Care and the 1990 Annual Campaign of the United Way of Southeastern New England. He is also a member of the President's Council of Providence College. **Suki Robins** is a staff manager at NYNEX Science & Technology, Inc. At various times in her career she has been a methods and procedures analyst on Wall Street, a full-time homemaker, and a college writing instructor.

Edward Iwata has been a general-assignment reporter and business writer for the *San Francisco Chronicle* and the *Orange County Register* (Los Angeles, California). He has worked on diversity issues in the news media for the Asian American Journalists Association in San Francisco, the Maynard Institute for Journalism Education in Oakland, and UNITY '94 (trademarked), a coalition of four minority journalism associations that is based in Reston, Virginia.

Michael Kelley is a native of Joplin, Missouri and a graduate of The University of Memphis. He is a feature writer for *The Commercial Appeal* in Memphis. Kelley has previously worked as a reporter for *The Springfield News-Leader, The Tulsa World,* and *The Kansas City Star.*

Walter Kiechel III is Managing Editor of FORTUNE. He joined FORTUNE in September, 1977 as a reporter-researcher. In 1978, he was made an Associate Editor and full-time writer. In December 1982, he was elected to FORTUNE's Board of Editors. In April 1988, he was promoted to Assistant Managing Editor, and in December, 1992, to Executive Editor. Mr. Kiechel became Managing Editor in May 1994. For much of the 1980's, Mr. Kiechel edited the magazine's coverage of managerial issues. Since 1981, he has also written a column called "Office Hours" that deals with issues of managerial psychology, sociology, and technique. A collection of the columns was published as a book entitled *Office Hours: A Guide to the Managerial Life.*

Chris Lee came to TRAINING magazine as associate editor in 1981, and has held the position of managing editor since 1984. As managing editor, Lee's responsibilities include reporting, writing and editing, and working with freelance writers. She also works closely with TRAINING's production department in planning, scheduling, and laying out each issue of the magazine. **Ron Zemke,** Senior Editor, has been a regular with TRAINING magazine since 1976. He also contributes to *The Service Edge* and *Training Directors' Forum* newsletters. He has written and edited several books, including *Figuring Things Out: A Trainer's Guide to Needs and Task Analysis, Service America! Doing Business in the New Economy, The Service Edge: 101 Companies that Profit from Customer Care, Delivering Knock Your Socks Off Service, Managing Knock Your Socks Off Service,* and *Sustaining Knock Your Socks Off Service.* Zemke is president of a Minneapolis-based research and consulting firm he founded in 1972.

Isabel Lopez heads Lopez Leadership Services. A former corporate executive with 20 years' experience, Isabel has supervised hundreds of people and managed multimillion-dollar budgets. Her experience includes marketing, strategic planning, operations, employee assessment, quality measurements, labor relations, supervision, management training, and development. An active member of the community, Isabel is a board member of the Institute for International Education, the Regis University Alumni Association, and the Board of Higher Education and Ministry of the United Methodist Church. She chairs the selection committee for the annual Colorado Corporate Social Responsibility Awards, and is the executive producer of "Leading Voices," a daily commentary show on KUVO Public Radio's "Morning Edition." Isabel is the recipient of numerous awards and has been listed in the "Who's Who of Hispanic Americans" since 1992.

Jeff McCollum is Director of Organization Development for Warner-Wellcome, a consumer health products manufacturer and is principal and owner of Star* Thrower Associates, an organizational consulting practice based in Belle Mead, New Jersey. He is also a member of the Board of Trustees of the Robert K. Greenleaf Center.

Before establishing his own firm, he spent 25 years with AT&T, where he held executive positions in human resources, marketing, and sales. He consults with senior executive teams, boards, and line managers to develop high-performing organizations through alignment of organizational purpose, strategy, and practices. His work is built on the beliefs that organizations can become places where individual creativity and the human spirit can flourish and that leadership must be exercised at all levels for organizations to satisfy customers and succeed in today's demanding environment. He holds an undergraduate degree in History from Princeton University and a Master's degree in Organizational Development from Pepperdine University.

Ann McGee-Cooper, Ed.D., is an author, lecturer, business consultant, creativity expert, and principal of Ann McGee-Cooper and Associates, Inc., of Dallas, Texas. **Duane Trammel** is managing partner of Ann McGee-Cooper and Associates. Ann and Duane are coauthors of *Time Management for Unmanageable People* and (with Barbara Lau) *You Don't Have To Go Home From Work Exhausted!*

M. Scott Peck, M.D., is the author of *The Road Less Traveled,* the extraordinary work that has remained on *The New York Times* best-seller list for more than nine years. His other best-sellers include *People of the Lie, The Different Drum, A World Waiting To Be Born,* and the novel *A Bed by the Window*. He has also written a fable, *The Friendly Snowflake* (illustrated by Christopher Scott Peck), and is the coauthor of *What Return Can I Make? Dimensions of the Christian Experience.* He lives with his wife, Lily, in Connecticut.

Tina Rasmussen serves as group facilitator, internal consultant, and coach in her role as corporate Management Development Manager at Nestlé Beverage Company, a division of the world's largest food company. Her background includes more than 10 years of experience helping executives and managers develop humanistic methods of leading organizations within the high tech, retail trade, financial services, and consumer products industries. She also has been a newspaper reporter and editor of a daily column. Her specialty is in working with senior executives to understand their vision and goals, and helping people to translate them into tangible plans, programs, and processes resulting in lasting, large-scale change. Ms. Rasmussen is also a Ph.D. candidate completing her doctoral dissertation on leadership at the Fielding Institute, and she is a contributing author to *Leadership In A New Era.*

Carl Rieser is a writer and editor who was formerly on the editorial staffs of *Business Week, Fortune,* and the Committee for Economic Development. He is coauthor with Daniel I. Kaplan of *Service Success! Lessons from a Leader on How to Turn Around a Service Business,* published in April 1994 by John Wiley & Sons, Inc. He has also edited and written for various business and financial newsletters. Among his writings on servant-leadership is "The Trusteed Corporation: A Case Study of the Townsend & Bottum Family of Companies," distributed by the Greenleaf Center. He is currently writing a book on servant-leadership from a Jungian perspective. He is a member of the executive committee of the Analytical Psychology Club of New York City, an associate of the Order of the Holy Cross (Episcopal), and a lay chaplain with hospitals.

Dr. Peter M. Senge is a faculty member of the Massachusetts Institute of Technology and Director of the Center for Organizational Learning at MIT's Sloan School of Management, a consortium of corporations that work together to advance methods and knowledge for building learning organizations. He is author of the widely acclaimed book, *The Fifth Discipline: The Art and Practice of the Learning Organization,* published by Doubleday/Currency (circulation 300,000). He is also a founding partner of the management consulting and training firm, Innovation Associates. Dr. Senge has lectured extensively throughout the world, translating the abstract ideas of systems theory into tools for better understanding of economic and organizational change. His areas of special interest and expertise focus on decentralizing the role of leadership in an organization to enhance the capacity of all people to work productively toward common goals. He has worked with leaders in business, education, healthcare, and government.

Richard W. Smith is an organization development specialist; co-owner of Smith-Brandt Associates, Indianapolis, Indiana; and a program director for the Greenleaf Center. For the past 26 years, Richard has helped individuals and organizations process change, and understand the change process. Seventeen years ago he was introduced to servant-leadership by his mentor and for the past seven years has been helping organizations adapt servant-leadership concepts. As an organization development specialist Smith has worked with for-profit and not-for-profit organizations of all sizes. As an educator/trainer he has facilitated more than 600 seminars and workshops. As a student of adult learning, he has facilitated undergraduate, graduate, and continuing studies courses for colleges, universities, and technical schools.

Larry Spears was named Executive Director of the Greenleaf Center in February, 1990. He grew up in Michigan and Indiana, and later graduated from DePauw University with a degree in English. After college, Larry lived in the Philadelphia region for 14 years prior to returning to the Indianapolis area. Larry has previously served as either director or staff member with the Greater Philadelphia Philosophy Consortium, the Great Lakes College's Association's Philadelphia Center, and *Friends Journal,* a Quaker magazine. He is also a writer, editor, and publications designer who has published more than 200 articles, essays, and book reviews during the past 20 years; and, he has written numerous successful funding proposals. Larry is a contributing author to an anthology of essays on leadership, *Leadership in a New Era.*

Dennis L. Tarr is Minister at the First Presbyterian Church of Miami, Florida, and a former dean at the School of Continuing Studies, University of Miami, Coral Gables, Florida.

James B. Tatum is a graduate of the United States Military Academy at West Point, New York. He has been an owner and operator of Tatum Motor Company, in Anderson, Missouri, for more than 40 years. As one of the pioneers in the community college movement in Missouri, coauthor of initial creative legislation, and cofounder and trustee of Crowder College for more than 30 years, Jim has served as national President of the Association of Community College Trustees. He has been the recipient of several awards for trustee leadership. He also served on the Greenleaf Center's board of trustees for seven years—six of those as Chairman.

Bob Vanourek became President and Chief Executive Officer of Recognition in December, 1991. He joined the company in 1989 as co-chief executive officer. Prior to joining Recognition, Bob held positions with Pitney Bowes as Group Vice-President of the Mailing Systems Division and President of their Monarch Marking Systems, Inc. subsidiary. Previously he was a division Vice-President/General Manager at Avery International. Bob is a member of the Board of Directors of the Association for Imaging and Information Management (AIIM), the Association for Work Process Improvement, and the American Electronics Association.

Index

Accountability, 108–109, 212, 280–281, 312
Acknowledge, as risk-taking strategy, 141, 144–145
Acton, Lord, 29, 301
Adams, Robert, 128
Adaptive systems, 248–250, 255
Addiction, development of, 235–236
Adler, Mortimer, 167
Advanced maturity, 231
The Age of Paradox (Handy), 150, 160
Aggression, in the workplace, 108–109
Alcoholics Anonymous, 12, 89, 93
Alternative universe, 221
Altruism, 283
American Express, 99
American Foundation for Management Research, 2
American Leadership Forum (ALF), 56, 219
American management model, 241
American Society of Newspaper Editors, 104
American Teilhard de Chardin Society, 239
Anderson, Don, 286, 291
Andover Newton Theological School, 40
Antileadership vaccine, 51
Arrogance, 26–27
"Art of conceptualizing," 59
Arthur, Brian, 251–252
Artifacts, corporate culture element, 284
Ashland Oil, 168
Assessment process, 253
AT&T, 2, 11, 18–19, 32, 34, 230, 245
Authentic community, 88
Authoritarian leadership:
  institutional leadership as, 236
  pattern of, 308
  servant-leadership *vs.*, 5–6, 165–167
Autocratic leadership, 2
Autonomy:
  complexity and, 256
  personal, 248, 253
Awareness:
  evolution and, 240
  managerial ethics and, 42
  significance of, 5
  time management and, 115

Bacon, Francis, 225
Bakken, Earl, 110
Balance, 203, 305
Barber, Lloyd, 71–72, 77
Barnard, Chester I., 33–34
Bellman, Geoffrey M., 103, 112
Benchmarking, 140, 167
Benevolent caretakers, 253
Bennis, Warren, 188–189
Berry, Thomas, 239–240
Berry, Wendell, 157
Bible, servant-leader stories, 107, 127, 300
Black and Veach, 272–273
Blake, Robert, 101
Blanchard, Kenneth, 105, 111, 127
Blandin Foundation, 130–131
Blindness, *see* Job burnout, 142
Block, Peter, 8, 11, 13, 100, 103, 111, 189, 244, 248, 252, 263, 279
Boehm, Edward, 251
Bohm, David, 226, 232
Bordas, Juana, 12
Bottom line value system, 305
Bottum, Curtis E., Jr., 270, 272–274
Bouffier, Elzeard, 279
Bracey, Hyler, 106, 110, 124
Bracketing, 93
Brandeis, Louis, Justice, 168

Brooks, John, 319
Brown County Meeting, 77–78
Bruner, Jerome, 36
Business ethics, 38. *See also* Ethics
Business trends, impact of, 161

Campbell, David, 190
Campbell, Joseph, 251, 253
Camus, Albert, 80, 157, 182, 240
Cardozo, Benjamin, 36, 63
Caring concept:
  application of, 82, 312
  development of, 51–52
Castaneda, Carlos, 185–186, 192
Categorization, puzzle solution strategy, 204
Cause-and-effect, 246, 250
The Center for Applied Ethics, 2, 242, 252, 310–311
Center for Creative Leadership (CCL), 12, 105, 107
Centralized management, breakdown of, 231–232
Ceremonies, as reinforcement technique, 292–293
Change:
  incidence of, 212
  resistance to, 92, 108–110, 168
  types of, 222–224
Changing organization, strategies for, 243–244
Channeling, 180
Chaos, 91–92, 255
Chardin, 239
Chief executive officer(s) (CEOs):
  control and, 249
  creativity of, 32
  Greenleaf on, 45–47
  as power-wielder, 44
  role of, 46–47
  stewardship and, 6–7
Choice, aspirations and, 80
Christ Hospital and Medical Center, mission statement analysis, 176–177
Christian Monasticism, 89
The Church of the Savior, 74
Circles:
  balance in, 305
  organizational structure, 258–259
  service values:
    customers, 302–303
    employees, 303–304
    local communities, 304
    shareholders, 304
    vendors, 304
Ciscel, David, 194–195
Citizenship, 312
Classical economics, 251–252
Classification, puzzle solution strategy, 204
Coaching, by servant-leader, 120
Coercive power, 25, 280, 301, 309
Collaborative management, 81, 211
Combining Service and Learning (NSEE), 11
Command and control management, 249
Commitment, significance of, 7
Commitment-competence-confidence cycle, 146–147
Communication:
  conversation, 225–226
  dialogue, discussion *vs.*, 226, 228
  team-building component, 172–173
Community(ies):
  building, *see* Community-building
  defined, 87–88, 97–98, 169
  sense of, 296
  as servant-leadership component, 2
  service to, 304
  team-building and, 169–170
Community-building:
  change and, 56, 174
  four stages of, 91–94
  as leadership education model, 10–11
  metaphor, 228
  models of, 8
  personal development and, 157–158
  problem resolutions, 174–175
  resistance to, 92
  as servant-leadership, 94
Competence:
  in successful companies, 83–84
  team-building component, 173
Competition, ethic code and, 48
Complexity:
  in adaptive systems, 250–251
  new science of, 245–246, 255
  power and, 252–253
  Tao of, 256
Compromise, acceptance of, 42
Conceptualization, as servant-leadership component, 6
Conceptual leadership, 233–234
Conflict resolution, 250
Confucius, 56
Consensus, 123, 211
Continuity, significance of, 57
Continuous improvement, 9
Control, 207–208, 249
Conversation, function of, 225–226
Cooperation, 55, 68
Coordinated action, development of, 231
Co-ownership, risk-taking strategy, 140, 142
Core group, development of, 259–260
Core workers, function of, 241

Corporate culture:
analysis of, 284
defined, 283–284
embedders, 284–285
leadership roles, 295–297
reinforcers, 284–285
Santa Barbara Bank & Trust (SBB&T) model, 285–295
stages of, 284
Corporate Culture and Performance, 297
Corporate dislocation, 243
Corporate ladder climbing, 42
Corporate risk-taking, *see* Risk
Corruption, power and, 29, 30–31
Council of Equals, 210–211
Countervailing power, 252
Covey, Stephen, 104–105, 112, 127, 182, 191, 263, 267–268
Cowan, George, 251
Creativity:
defined, 306
in leaders, 31–35
mandated risk and, 137
significance of, 35
"Creativity in Business," 56
Crichton, Michael, 254
Crisis management, 223
Cultural attitude, influence of, 68
Customer:
focus on, 138, 167, 194, 248, 289–290
service to, 302–303
Cynicism, 202, 206, 210

Dances with Wolves, 227, 232–233
The Dancing Wu Li Masters (Zukav), 246
Davenport, David, 124–125
Davis, Elmer, 19, 21, 62
Davis, Stanley, 244, 249, 254
Day-to-day focus, 6, 113
DDB Needham, 159
Decision-making:
collaboration and, 287
consensual, 54, 208
employee involvement in, 2, 115–116, 140, 196
empowerment and, 232
group-oriented, 8
risk-taking and, 140
shared power in, 296
Delayering, 243, 245
De Mello, Anthony, 152, 154
Deming, W. Edwards, 279
DePree, Max, 9, 11, 13, 101, 109, 122–123, 183, 263, 279, 281
Descartes, 225, 254
DeShano, Joyce, 276, 278–280
Designated leader, 210
Developmental learning, emerging model and, 207
Dharmic management, 126
Dialogue:
change process, 233
conversation, function of, 225–226
discussion *vs.,* 226, 228
theory of, 232
Differentiation, 240
Digital Equipment Co., 99
Directors:
control and, 249
education of, 9–10
functions of, 6–7
liability of, 72
role development, 72–73
servant-leadership applications, 9–10
Distelhorst, Garis, 148
Doer behavior, expectation of, 71
Don Juan, 186, 192
Dosick, Wayne, Rabbi, 128
Dossey, Larry, Dr., 114
Downsizings, impact of, 106, 243, 245
Drucker, Peter, 101, 166

Eclecticism, 62–64
Economics, 222, 251–252
Education, 45, 237–240
Edwards, Gwen, 140, 148
Eliot, T. S., 96
Embedders, 284–285, 288–291
Emerging model of servant-leadership:
beliefs, 201, 208
defined, 199
details of, 201–202
follower styles, 202, 211–212
foundation, 201
leadership styles, 202, 209–210
puzzle solutions, 202, 208–209
values, 201, 207–208
Emerson, Ralph Waldo, 25, 225
Emotional support, risk-taking strategy, 142
Empathy, 5, 59, 81
Employees, service to, 303–304
Empowerment:
impact of, 123, 130, 138, 144, 167, 196, 232
vision and, 248
Emptiness, community-building stage, 92–93
Entheos, significance of, 43–44
Enthusiasm, power of, 43–44
Environmental deterioration, impact of, 162–164
Equilibrium, 203, 250
Era of integration, 161, 165, 167

Erteszek, Jan, 298, 306
Esalen Institute, 128
Espoused beliefs, corporate culture element, 284
"The Ethic of Strength" (Greenleaf), 44
Ethics:
of ghostwriting, 30–31
significance of, 2
values and principles, 311–312
Excellence, 312
Executive, emerging model role, 210
Experiential education, 11, 168, 196

Failure, 147–148, 188
Fairness, 311
Faith, 63–64
Farmer, Dyne, 255
Fidelity, 311
Flag pole imagery, mission statement analysis, 177
Floating seminars, 251–252
Follow-through, significance of, 57
Ford Foundation, 2, 319
Foresight:
development exercise, 155–156
as managerial trait, 42–43
as servant-leadership component, 6, 186
Formal community-based structure, 171–172
For-profit organizations, 9–10, 58
Fortune 500, 99
Foundation for Community Encouragement (FCE):
community-building stages, 90–94
leader selection and training, 95–98
mission statement, 98
peacemaking technology, 88–89
Foundations, trustee/director development, 75
Fragmentation, 207
Friendliness, superficial, 27
Frost, Robert, 63, 213, 220
Fuller, Buckminster, 224

Gaia Hypothesis, 239
Galvin, Bob, 229
Gandhi, Mahatma, 181
Gardens, 258–259
Gardner, John, 51, 55
Gender differences, lifestyle survey, 159–160
General Electric, 99, 168
General Motors Corp., 99, 195, 231
George, William W., 109
Ghostwriting, 30–31, 33, 45
Gibson, Walker, 36
Gifford, Walter S., 33
Gillette, Douglas, 12
Giono, Jean, 279
Glacier Hills Retirement Center, 58
Gleaton, William, 108
Globalization, impact of, 162, 164, 194–195, 222, 243–244
Goethe, 225
Goldberg, Arthur, 72
Graham, Gerald, Dr., 123, 195, 197
Great man leadership theory, 299
Greenleaf, Esther Hargrave, 318
Greenleaf, George Washington, 38–39, 314
Greenleaf, Robert K., *see specific components of servant-leadership*
archives, 40
AT&T:
career path, 22–27, 33, 40–45, 50–51, 129, 165, 221, 298, 316–318
retirement from, 19–20, 22–24, 51, 130, 165, 319–320
awards, 10
background of, 2, 37–39, 50–52, 122
on chief executive officers, 45–47
Code of Ethics, 40–45
community-building, 318
community leadership programs, 10
education, 315
father, influence of, 38–39, 62
following of, 53–54
as ghostwriter, 45
historical perspective, 319
influences on:
generally, 17–21, 38–39, 51–52, 122
Journey to the East (Hesse), 3, 20, 51–52, 55, 62, 65, 122, 180, 219–220
legacy of, 217–240
personal development path, 151, 154
power, reflection on, 24–36
profile of, 313–314
publications, 44, 46
relationships, 38–39, 62, 314–315
servant-leader defined by, 4–7
team-building concept, 169–170
themes of, 62–70
Greenleaf Archives Project, 13
Greenleaf Center for Servant-Leadership, 13
Gridlock, 228
Grundtvig, Nikolai Frederik Severin, 187
Guiding Principles of Townsend & Bottum, 274
Gulf Oil of Canada, 11

Hadamard, 36, 63
Hammerschmidt, Peter, 123
Handbook of Leadership: A Survey of Theory and Research (Stogdill), 80
Handy, Charles, 150, 160
Harvey, George, 302
Hayes, James L., 170
Healing, as servant-leadership component, 5, 124
Heard, Gerald, 75–76
Heisenberg, Werner, 226
Helming, Oscar, 18, 21, 316
Herman Miller Company, 8–9, 109, 130
Herzberg, Frederick, 101
Heschel, Abraham, 73
Hesse, Hermann, 3, 19–21, 51, 55, 62–63, 65, 122, 180, 219–220, 246, 248, 300
Hierarchical leadership:
  adaptive systems *vs.*, 249–250
  human relations and, 26–28
  power in, impact of, 28–29
  risk-taking and, 137
  "top down," 8, 245, 255–256
  traditional, 2, 137
High-participation management, 245
Hitler, Adolf, 30
Holistic leadership, 42, 47, 96, 126–127, 130
Holland, John, 248–250
Holographic inquiry, 209
Holt, Lou, 286
Honda, 167
Honesty, 311
Housing Facilities Dept., University of Michigan, 8
Human motivation theory, 101
Human potential, 299, 303–304
Human-potential movement, 101, 306
Human relations, power and, 26–27
Human spirit, nurturing, 75–78
Humility, 63–64
Humor, 44–45, 255
Hurry sickness, 114–11

Iacocca, Lee, 121
Iatrogenic pathology, 234
IBM, 99, 231
Imagination:
  power and, 30–31
  in power-wielders, 31–35
  significance of, 299
Inaction, 210
Indiana University School of Business, 196
Individualism, as barrier, 67–68
Industrial jungle, evolution and, 239
Industrial planning, 250
Informal community-based structure, 171–172
Information Age, industrial models and, 244–245
In Search of Excellence (Peters/Waterman), 82–83, 282
Institutes of Chairing, 74
Institute of Servant-Leadership, Emory University, 54, 59
Institution, 170, 225–228
Institutional-Building Model (IBM), 177–178
Institutional Distinctiveness Survey (IDS), 175–176
Institutional leadership, new view of, 228–237
"The Institution as Servant," (Greenleaf), 64, 66–70, 242
Integration, 5
Integrity, leadership based on, 167–168, 311
Intercommunication, 240
Interdependency, 211
Interiority, 240
International Conference on Servant-Leadership, 13
Intuition:
  development of, 189
  opportunities and, 189–190
  significance of, 181–182
  vision and, 155
Irvin, Rubin, 287
Islam, 300
I-STAR model, components of:
  acknowledge, 141, 144–145
  inspire, 141–142
  overview, 141
  reward, 141–145
  support, 141–143
  train, 141, 143–144

Japanese, influence of, 54–55 123, 195, 243
Jaworski, Joe, 56, 219
Jaworski, Leon, Judge, 56, 219
Jefferson, Thomas, 187, 236
Job burnout, 142
Johnson, Robert Wood, 168
Josephson, Michael, 311
Josephson Institute for the Advancement of Ethics, 311
Journaling, reflective, 191
Journey to the East (Hesse), influence on Greenleaf, 3, 20, 51–52, 55, 62, 65, 122, 180, 219–220, 246, 253, 317
Jungian archetypes, 12

Kennedy, John F., 143, 187
Kiefer, Charles F., 102
King Jr., Martin Luther, Dr., 181, 194
Kitchen of the Mind, 263
Kofman, Fred, 224
Koran, 107, 127
Kouzes, James, 181

Labor relations, 24–26, 243
Labor shortage, impact of, 163–164
Lao Tzu, 242
Lawler, Edward E., 112, 127
Leader-first, 80, 114
Leadership:
  influential forces, 162–164
  skills, *see* Leadership skills
  types of, *see specific types of leadership*
Leadership and the New Science (Wheatley), 247
Leadership in a Christian Organization (LICO), 275–276, 278–279
Leadership Is an Art (Depree), 101–102
Leadership education, 11
Leadership Jazz (DePree), 110, 183
Leadership skills, management skills *vs.*, 137
Leadership training, need for, 65
Learning, types of, 237–238
Learning organizations, 11
Levering, Robert, 8–9
Levinson, Harry, 108–109
Lewin, Kurt, 101
Lewis, John L., 24–25
Liabilities, 97, 136, 152–153
Lifestyle survey, results of, 159–160
Likert, Rensis, 101
Lilly Endowment Inc., 2, 10
Lincoln, Abraham, 30–31, 35
Listening:
  coordinated action and, 232–233
  institutional leadership component, 229
  personal purpose path and, 185
  as servant-leadership component, 4–5, 81, 123, 130–131
  unlimited liability exercise, 153
L. L. Bean, 167
Lombardi, Vince, 143
Lore, John S., 276, 280–281
Low, George, 71
Lowe, Jack, 9, 118, 124, 262

McCain, Jessie, 119
McCarthy, Joseph, Senator, 30
McCollum, Jeffrey, 128
McGee-Cooper, Ann, 12–13, 57, 59
McGregor, Douglas, 101
Machine bureaucracy, 244–245, 247, 249
MacLaine, Shirley, 104
Management, *see specific types of management*
  as messiah, 110–112
  traditional, 6
Management consulting, 89
Management by objectives, 111
Management skills, leadership skills *vs.*, 137
Manager, emerging model role, 210
Managerial ethics, elements of, 40–45
Managing from the Heart (Hyler), 106, 110, 124
"The Man Who Planted Trees," 279, 281
Maslow, Abraham, 101
The Master of the Game (Hesse), 248–249
Matusak, Larraine, 131
Maynard, Herman Bryant, Jr., 127
Mead Corporation, 2, 11
Meaningful work, 58, 123
Mechanical model, servant-leadership *vs.*, 199–206
  transition to emerging model, 212–213
Meditations, 308–311
Medtronic Inc., 109–110
Metaphors, 228
Middle-management:
  communication role, 241
  functions of, 102, 163
  risk-taking and, 137
Midwest Universities Consortium for International Activities (MUCIA), Institutional-Building Model (IBM), 177–178
Minorities, 12, 193
Mintzberg, Henry, 241, 244
Mission, value of, 59
Mission statement, *see* Vision statements
  one-way leadership and, 229
  survey analysis of, 176
MIT, 2, 58, 237
Momentaneity, 255
Monaghan, Tom, 272
Moody, Julian, 271
Moore, Robert, 12
Morgan, J. P., 32–33, 69, 72, 75
Morphogenic fields, 247
Moskowitz, Milton, 8–9
Motivation, 3, 238
Mouton, Jane, 101
Muckrakers, 39
Multiculturalism, 12, 194
Murphy, Gardner, 36
Mutuality, 54
Myers, Michelle, 56
Myths, as reinforcement technique, 292

Nairn, Ronald, 64–65
Naisbitt, John, 170

Nanus, Burt, 181, 188–189
National Association for Community Leadership (NACL), 10
National Community Leadership Award, 10
National Labor Relations Act, 26
National Society for Experiential Education (NSEE), 11
Native Americans:
  personal purpose and, 179, 183–184
  talk starts, 227
New Age philosophy, 108
New economics, 251–252
New leadership paradigm, 194–195
New science, lessons from, 245–251
Newton, Isaac, 199, 202, 225, 254
Newtonian science, 243–244, 246, 254
New Traditions in Business (Ray), 102
Nonmanager managers, 102–103
Not-for-profit organizations, 9–10, 58
"Nurturer of the human spirit," 50
Nurturing, reception of, 77
NYNEX, 168

Objectivism, 203
O'Brien, Bill, 231
Occupations, hazardous, 35
"Old Age: The Ultimate Test of Spirit" (Greenleaf), 150–151
Olson, Paul, 77, 130–131
One-way leadership, 229
On-the-job training, 168
Openness, 42, 124, 255
Order, control *vs.*, 207–208
Organizational changes, 138–139, 243, 245
Organizational chart, 28–29, 259
Organizational culture, 10, 109. *See also* Corporate culture
Organizational Culture and Leadership (Schein), 283
Organizational development (OD), 242
Organizational structure, 66, 98, 130, 165–167, 170
Organization development metaphor, 228
Organization pyramid, 165–167
Ouchi, William, 101
Overarching purpose, 185
Over-specialization, 164
Ownership, emerging model and, 208, 212

Page, Arthur, 33
Palmer, Parker, 12
Paradox, 150, 199, 212
Pareto, 34
Path of Relationship, 207
Patience, 63–64
Patriarchal contract, 252–253
Patriarchal management, 204, 244–245
Peacemaking technology, 89–90
Peale, Norman Vincent, 105
Peck, M. Scott, 10, 12–13, 87, 104
Pena, Federico, 191
People-building institutions, 57
People-using institutions, 57
Performance levels, raising, 159
Personal development:
  community-building, 157–158
  legacy, honoring, 191–192
  liberating vision, 155–156, 159
  life story, writing, 191
  passion, recognition of, 190–191
  persuasion element, 156
  power, ethical use of, 158–160
  Robert Greenleaf's steps, 150–151
  self-knowledge, 154–155
  unlimited liability, 152–153
Personal growth, 11–12
Personal purpose:
  defined, 179–180
  intuition and, 181–182
  Native American approach to, 183–184
  path to, cairns, 185–190
  power through, 182–183
  search strategies, 179–180
  of servant-leaders, 180–181
  vision and, 181
Persuasion, 5–6, 25, 156
Peters, Thomas J., 82–83, 101, 107–109, 127, 301
Pfeffer, Jeffrey, 252
Philips, 66
Philosopher-king, leader as, 199, 203, 236
Philosophy statement, formal, 293
Physical support, risk-taking strategy, 142–143
Pitney Bowes, 304
Pitt, William, 29
Plato, 199, 202
Pope John XXIII, 30–32, 35, 76–77
Posner, Barry, 181
Power:
  coercive, 25–26, 280, 301, 309
  complexity and, 252–253
  consequence of, 26–27
  corruption and, 29–30
  ethical use of, 158–160
  in hierarchy, 27–29
  imagination, impact on, 30–31
  interlocking circle model, 137–138
  nonviolent, 26
  personality distortion and, 30–31
  personal purpose and, 182–183
  shared, 132, 196, 211, 301
  understanding of, 83
Primus inter pares concept, 66–68, 130, 158, 244, 250, 256

Priorities, 117–119
Procter & Gamble, 168
Productivity, improvement strategies, 163
Professional growth plan (PGP), 173
Promise-keeping, 311
Pseudocommunity, community-building stage, 91
Public trust, protection of, 312
Purpose, sense of, 44–45
Pyramids, 257–258

Quakers, 6, 50, 52, 89
Quality, strategies for, 167
Quality assurance, 268
Quality circles, 54
Quality of life, 12

Ray, Michael L., 56, 102
Readiness, 62–63
Receptive listening, 5
Reductionism, 204, 234, 237, 239–240, 246
Reflection, listening and, 5
Regeneration, continuous, 208
Reinforcers, 284–285, 292–295
Religion, spirituality *vs.*, 109–110
The Religious Society of Friends, 6
Resistance, 92, 301
Resolution, team-building component, 174–175
Respect, 312
Responsibility, team-building, 172
Restructuring, 124
Reward, 141, 145, 290
Rieser, Carl, 270–271
Right-wrong value, 203, 207
Risk, *see* Risk-taking
Risk-taking:
- examples of, 148
- failure and, 148–149
- I-STAR model, 141–145
- lead by example, 147
- organizational changes, 138–139
- psyching up for, 139–140
- risk, defined, 135
- risk analysis, five-steps process, 136
- self-powering cycle, 145–147
- sharing risk, 137–138

Rites and rituals, as reinforcement techniques, 292–293
R. K. Mellon Foundation, 2
The Road Less Traveled (Peck), 93
Robert K. Greenleaf Center:
- community leadership programs, 10
- establishment of, 2
- ethics and, 311
- as floating seminar, 252
- logo, symbolism of, 13–14
- mission of, 130
- organizational development and, 242
- spiritual management, 127
- workshops, 131–132

Rockefeller Foundation, 33–34
Rogers, Carl, 255
Role models, selection of, 136
Rollins, Les, 77
Rosenblum, John, 125
Rouse, Ray, 67
Routine workers, 39
Royal Dutch Shell, 66

Sampson, Patsy, 12
Santa Barbara Bank & Trust (SBB&T) model, 285–291
- leadership roles, 295
- reinforcers, 292–295

Sante Fe Institute, 248, 251–252
SAS, 167
Saturn Corporation, 138
Schein, Edgar, 283–284
Schmidt, Wayne, 264, 270
Schmidt Associates Architects, Inc.:
- mission statement, 130
- servant-leadership implementation model:
  - background, early years, 8, 264–266
  - caring society, building, 268
  - downsizing effect, 273–275
  - experiments, successful, 270–272
  - firm of distinction, 269–270
  - implementation advice, 269–270
  - management concepts, 268–269
  - program implementation, 266–267
  - update, 272–273
  - wholism, 267–268

Schneider, John, 260–264
Schneider Engineering Corporation, servant-leadership implementation model, 8, 259–264
Schroeder, Patricia, Congresswoman, 181
Schuller, Robert, 286
Scientific management, 202–203, 243
Seekers, types of, 41
Segmentation, 204
Self-acceptance, 255
Self-awareness, 5, 12
Self-directed work teams, 210–211
Self-fulfillment movement, 56
Self-insight, 185
Self-knowledge, 154–155
Self-organization, 242, 248
Self-realization movement, 56
Self-righteousness, freedom from, 42
Seminaries, as pivotal institutions, 70–75
Senge, Peter, 9, 11, 13, 248, 251, 263, 279
Senior management, 244, 249
Sensitivity, 42, 57
Sensitivity group movement, 89

"Servant, Retrospect and Prospect" (Greenleaf), 48
Servant-first, 80–81, 150
Servant image, biblical, 55
Servant-leader(s):
attributes of, 58–60
benevolent caretakers *vs.*, 253
characteristics of, 4–7, 110–111, 123–125, 151–152, 196
employee requests for, 110
function of, 165, 255
personal development path, *see* Personal development
selection and training of, 95–98
time management by, 119–120
"The Servant as Leader" (Greenleaf), 2–3, 43, 64–67, 70, 113, 122, 130, 179, 217–219
Servant-leadership:
action-oriented, 82–83
application of, 4, 8–12, 82
as commitment, 83
defined, 2–4, 195–196
as growing movement, 13–14
history of, 1–2
multiculturalism and, 12
overview, 287
response to, 218–219
territories, 199–206, 281
test for, 118–119, 248–249, 254
Servant Leadership (Greenleaf), 9, 56–57, 80, 217, 219–220, 261, 265–266
Servant-Leadership Conference, 309–310
"Servant Responsibility in a Bureaucratic Society" (Greenleaf), 254
Servant within, 49–50, 55–56
Service-learning programs, 10–11
Servo-mechanism, leader as, 244
The Seven Habits Of Highly Successful People (Covey), 191–192, 267–268
Shakespeare, 26, 28
Shannon, James P., 132
Shared vision:
collaboration and, 303
core values and, 307
creation of, 111, 125
development of, 229–231
in institutional leadership, 229
for spirituality, 105–108
Shareholders, service to, 304
Shearer, Tony, 183–184
Sheldrake, Rupert, 247
Shifting the burden principle, 234–235
Simonides, Constantine, 77
Sims, Bennett, 59
Sisters of St. Joseph (SSJ) Health System, servant-leadership implementation model, 275–282
Skills, 177, 188, 301–302
Smith, Richard, 260–261
Social glue, loss of, 54–55
Social responsibility, corporate, 47
Sophisticated workers, 39
Spainhour, David, 286, 295
Speakers Bureau, 13
Spears, Larry, 127, 130, 132, 195, 229
Specialization, age of, 161, 163–165
"Spirituality as Leadership" (Greenleaf), 310
Spiritual journey, 221
Spiritual management:
need for, 99–104, 126–128
resistance to, 108–110
timing of, 104–105
vision of, 105–108
Spiritual support, risk-taking strategy, 143
Staff, emerging model role, 210
Stakeholders, multiple, 162, 164
Stanford Research Institute, 128
Stanley K. Lacy Leadership Series, 265
Status quo, overcoming, 74–75
Stempel, Robert, 195
Steward-managers, 110
Stewardship, as servant-leadership component, 6–7, 103, 126–127
Stogdill, Ralph M., 80
Stories, as reinforcement technique, 292
Strategic apex, 241, 244
Strength, 42, 44, 71–72, 83
Structure, team-building component, 171–172
Successful organization, defined, 46
Suffering Servant image, 55
Sunbeam-Oster, 99
Suppliers, *see* Vendors
Support, as risk-taking strategy, 142–144
Support staff, function of, 241
Surprise, machine bureaucracy element, 250
Synergy, 98, 305–307
Systems and procedures, as reinforcement techniques, 294–295
Systems thinking, 234, 236, 237–240

Taoism, 300–301
"The Task of Motivating" (Gardner), 55
Tavistock model, 89
Taylor, Frederick Winslow, 39, 199, 202–203
Taylor, Robert, 123
TDIndustries, 8–9, 59, 118–119, 124
Teacher as Servant, 77
Team-building:
community components, 171–175
function of, 54, 169
megatrends, 170–171
process outline, 178
Team spirit, encouragement of, 82
Teamwork, as servant-leadership component, 2
Technical staff, function of, 241

Technological growth, impact of, 222
T-groups, 57
Theology, 74, 75
Theology of institutions, 47
Theory X, 101, 282–283
Theory Y, 101
Theory Z, 282
Thompson, Fred, 195
Time management:
  hurry sickness, 114–116
  by servant-leader, 119–120
  servant-leadership as priority, 117–119
  teamwork, 114
Time Management for Unmanageable People (McGee-Cooper/Trammell), 113–114
Total Quality Management (TQM):
  community-building and, 157
  overview, 11, 196
Toughness, strategic, 79–83
Townsend & Bottum Family of Companies, 8
The Townsend & Bottum Family of Companies, servant-leadership implementation model, 270–274
Traditional leadership, 204, 206, 208
Training, 143–144, 168
Traits managers, ethics for, 41
Trammell, Duane, 113
Transformation, 4–5
Trickle-down theology, 75
True community, 7, 88, 93–94
True leader, 195, 299–301, 306
True leadership, characteristics of, 3
Trump, Donald, 121
Trust:
  basis of, 44–45
  communication and, 212
  development of, 268–269, 303, 312
  mutual, 174
  significance of, 52, 54
The Trusteed Corporation: A Case Study of the Townsend & Bottum Family of Companies, 270
Trustees:
  characteristics of, 71
  education, 9–10
  function of, 6–7
  questions for, 130–131
  role development, 6–7, 72–73
  servant-leadership applications, 9–10
"Trustees as Servants" (Greenleaf), 10, 64, 68–71, 130
12-step programs, 12, 89, 104–105
Tyler, Gus, 311

Underlying assumptions, corporate culture element, 284
Unilever, 66
United Parcel Service, 167
Universe, participative nature of, 248
University of Denver, 197
University of Tennessee, 196–197
Unlimited liability, 97, 152–153

Vail, Theodore N., 32–33, 69, 75, 319
Vance, Mike, 263
Van der Post, 63
Vanourek, Robert, 60
Vendors, service to, 304
Vision:
  institutional leadership and, 229
  intuition and, 155
  liberated, 155–156, 159
  Newtonian science and, 247–248
  philosophy statement and, 293–294
  properties of, 248
  service and, 308–309
  shared, *see* Shared vision
  superficial compliance with, 230
  value of, 59
Vision quest, 179, 183–184
Vision statements, 229, 269

Wahlig, Jack, 139–140
Wainwright House, 5
Waldrop, M. Mitchell, 245–246, 250–251, 255–256
Waterman, Robert H., Jr., 82–83, 101, 301
Welsh, Jack, 99
Westminster Presbyterian Church, 74
"What Are People For" (Berry), 157
Wheatley, Margaret, 245, 247–248
White, E. B., 19, 31, 62–64
White, Randall, 105–106
Whole learning, 82
Wiesel, Elie, 147
W. K. Kellogg Foundation, 10, 131
Women, 12, 193
Woolman, John, 187
Work ethic, 57–58
Workshops, servant-leadership, 131–132
Work teams, self-directed, 210–211
World Business Academy, 128
Worldview, changes in, 224–225

Xerox Corp., 128
Xerox Technology Ventures, 128

Zen, 300
Zukav, Gary, 246–247